Ann Barson (nee Portus) is the daughter of Carys Harding Browne. After graduating at the University of Adelaide, she acted professionally with Adelaide's Theatre 62 before training at the Drama Centre London. She then performed in England in children's theatre, and for the BBC Radio for thirteen years. From 1989 she worked as a teacher in London. She also ran a puppetry business for young children performing at parties, nurseries and schools. Since returning to Adelaide in 2000, she has performed widely in theatre productions at the Bakehouse Theatre, the Company of Muses, on the Adelaide Fringe and in puppetry projects.

Carys with Gavin, 1941

CARYS

Diary of a young girl, Adelaide 1940-42

EDITED BY ANN BARSON

ETT IMPRINT, SYDNEY

Exile Bay

This edition published by ETT Imprint, Exile Bay 2018. Reprinted 2018.

These are extracts from Carys Harding Browne's diaries 23rd February 1940 to 13th July 1942, edited and researched by Ann Barson.

ETT IMPRINT
PO Box R1906
Royal Exchange NSW 1225 Australia

Copyright © Ann Barson, 2018

ISBN   978-1-925706-29-1 (paper)
ISBN   978-1-925706-30-7 (ebook)

Design by Hanna Gotlieb
Cover: Portrait of Carys by Ernest Milston, 1941

To my husband Robin Barson (1950-89)
and my children Rosanna and Edward

Carys used smallish 1940 and 1942 diaries for her writing and for her 1941 diary used a larger notebook. Very occasionally, she made up some words which I have not changed. I have corrected the odd misspelling and I have sometimes added a word or two to make sense of the identity of a person or place or event.

CONTENTS

INTRODUCTION

It is February 1940 in Adelaide, South Australia. Carys ("loved one" in Welsh) Harding Browne, aged 17, lives in Molesworth Street, North Adelaide with her mother and two brothers. Her mother, Eirliw, works in the frock department of the Myer Emporium. Eirliw's husband, Clifford Harding Browne, an accountant, left the family in 1933; the couple were married at the end of World War I in Eirliw's birthplace of Harlech in North Wales. Carys's brother, Richard, is aged 19 but already is a well-known radio announcer on 5AD, while her younger brother, Bryan, aged 15, is studying at Pulteney Grammar School. Carys aspires to be a writer but is reluctantly learning typing and shorthand at Miss Ward's Training College for Young Business Girls. She would rather be at the University. The family have one maid called Lillian Hamilton, aged 28, who had lived in a children's home after the death of her mother.

Carys's best friend, Sibyl Brookman, lives nearby in Barton Terrace, North Adelaide. Aged 15, Sibyl is a student at Wilderness School, a private girls' school which Carys has just left. Sibyl has two older brothers, Michael aged 23, who is already at the Woodside Military Camp with the A.I.F., and Graham aged 17, who is at the University of Adelaide studying engineering. She also has an older sister called Phyllis (Phyl) who is married and living in India. Carys is close to all the Brookman family and calls Sibyl's parents Aunt Polly and Uncle George.

Of the young men who are to appear in Carys's life, Donald Beviss "Sam" Kerr, a poet aged 20, is living now at St Mark's College, North Adelaide. He is in his honours year, studying English at the University of Adelaide. He is also an editor of the University's literary magazine, "Phoenix", and one of the founders of the famous journal, "Angry Penguins", which will replace the "Phoenix" in May 1940. Sam's father died when he was eight, which may partly explain his attraction to Carys, whose father departed when she was ten.

Peter Anderson, aged 19, was educated at Geelong Grammar School in Victoria and is now working in his father's firm M. G. Anderson and Co Ltd, who are Adelaide agents for the Orient Line.

John Portus, aged 26, is Secretary of the Law Society of South Australia, after studying law at New College, Oxford. While overseas, he attended the opening of the 1936 Olympic Games in Berlin, and after climbing on a monument to see, watched Hitler, Goering and Goebbels enter the Olympic Stadium. '

CARYS'S DIARY

1940

Friday 23rd February 1940: Ward's Business College shot by at a tremendous rate and I dashed home, practised the piano, had tea and dashed back to have my hair done at Myers. It looked delightful, softly falling down to my shoulders and slightly waved and the curls on the top, rolled into one and slightly curved. "Bizz" Brookman, Sibyl's cousin and "Buffy" Hawker had been there too, poor souls, getting primped up for their dance tomorrow night. I am wearing my blue taffeta to their dance. The neck has been renovated into looking a different frock when two years ago Bizz Brookman gave her only other dance and I had bought it for that! Nevertheless, it looks quite attractive. There was a bit about me in this week's "News" - "What an attractive sub-deb Carys Harding Browne is! Glimpsed her in town with a softly coloured blue Liberty creation and she was hatless. Her flaxen locks were tied back by a powder blue velvet bow." The sub-deb who never blooms! All the same, I'd rather they gave me a job. The papers are full of the first Australian troops arriving in Palestine and cheating orange-sellers and being particularly ANZAC - like their fathers.

Saturday 24th February: I posed, looked halfway up ceilings, sat on grassy banks in front of Watteaus, grinning, looked thoughtful, limply drooped dahlias and Blodwen Thomas, the photographer, took everyone and finished each, saying "good as gold". The "News" had rung up asking me to have my photo taken at Blodwen Thomas's, being in the social set and at their expense. Very gratifying. The photo will be ready in a week, went to a dress-making lesson, didn't finish my frock, had lunch at home, did my nails after, had a sleep and felt <u>foul</u>, nasty taste, weak, tired. After tea, felt better, after bath better still, shared taxi to Hawker-Brookman debutante dance, chauffeur on the pavement let us out; maids showed us about the house, went into wonderful marquees, lights in the garden and lighting up trees and roses and water lilies in ponds, had delightful partners, Billy Foster, Mike Brookman, Mike Tipping, Sam and Willy Kerr, my brother Richard, David Walters, Peter Hopton - <u>and</u> Edward Godfrey. Three with him including the supper dance, flirted with him outrageously, I was the only girl on the floor who could make him laugh and talk - the only hope! Missed one dance; everyone years and years older. Terrifying lovely dance. Darling Edward.

Sunday 25ᵗʰ February: Last night got to bed at three. Edward drove me home. He's like Stonewall Jackson. Even when I fished for compliments, he didn't catch on and I had to supply the answers. That's what I like. If he gave in, I'd hate him. Every boy there seemed in the army. I had to buck up innumerable boys. All very young, very disillusioned, very "heroic", very afraid of dying. I had a terrifying argument with the family about the war. I said Australia didn't think of it enough and by the time I'd finished was in tears. It was one of those moments when the hideousness of war dawns on you and those decent boys! After teaching Sunday school at the North Adelaide Baptist Church, I went to dinner at the Brookman's with innumerable men in uniform.

Monday 26ᵗʰ February: The dance didn't look nearly attractive enough in the paper; but Edward's name looks nice in print. Donald Beviss "Sam" Kerr told me Mic Sandford, an old family friend of ours, was often talking about me, that he had often threatened to introduce us - so he introduced himself and was very sweet and grown-up - and so was I until he said, "It's no good. I know how old you are!"

Wednesday 28ᵗʰ February: At lunch Mother and I went to see the proofs for the Blodwen Thomas photos; they are disappointing. The smiling ones are lots of teeth, a Gracie Fields grin and a dropped chin. There is a lovely three quarter length serious one of me standing in front of the Watteau; and a glamorized profile. In the afternoon Miss Ward was in a vile temper and screamed at everyone, including me. She dragged out enormous books by girls who had done 100 words a minute in two terms and I said, "She must have bin a blinkin' miracle" sans penser! I have no tact. Had to wait half an hour for a packed tram. At home, found Lillian's car has come! Lillian has been left a thousand pounds by her father. She has already bought an opal ring, a new gold watch, an evening frock, two years of stockings and a day frock.

Friday 1st March: At lunch I rushed to Myers and bought a long, gloomy white overall for cooking, and a recipe book. I look like the secretary of the Ku Klux Klan.

Tuesday 5th March: The weather is exhilarating and the town is filled with A.I.F.'s on their last leave before sailing. I want to weep over everyone.

Wednesday 6th March: After tea, I went to cooking at the Gas Company; it is great fun - what Lillian would call "playing at cooking"; we sit in deep armchairs watching Mrs Newman cook and lecture in a miniature yellow-tiled kitchen; then in a huge kitchen we cooked scones and pastry canoes, with ovens each, cupboards each and everything well kept and arranged. My things are quite edible.

Thursday 7th March: The paper today is very "jubilant". Mr Menzies, the Prime Minister has announced that 50,000 men are being sent overseas after the others. By June next year, we mean to have sent 90,000 only in the Army! Apart from all these exciting young lives, where will Australia be for her own defence with over a million men - young men - away. And sheer egoism - what a dull world my daughters will have with no men - and where will be my husband? Where will Paris be? Where will our dreams be? Oh! This is hopeless.

Saturday 9th March: I went to dressmaking in my homemade frock and did a great deal of my nightie. I have been invited to two deb dances and with all these going off, I must not wear the same creation, however much the "Express and Journal" likes it. I had tea at the Brookman's, including the usual two soldiers from Woodside - Michael and his cousin David Brookman. Sibyl's friend, Wody Blackburn rang, asking Sibyl there and then me, as well. It was a coupling-off party. I met Sibyl's Tom Yates, a shy, little school boy. They took absolutely no notice of each other and yet they write three letters a week! Typical of adolescence. We listened to the gramophone on the lawn - Mike Tipping and Wody, Sibyl and Tom - I and the stars!

Thursday 14th March: This is a splendid day for soldiers to march in cool breezes and warm sun. A most unhappy day for 50,000 South Australian relatives. At a quarter to four we heard the drums and, filled with a kind of sick excitement, dashed down and saw the soldiers march past the saluting base. They went by - simply thousands (it seemed), very young, very unhappy, very brown and very ugly with their slouch hats and the "Rising Sun" badge. Many had lipstick on their cheeks and I wanted to weep, but afterwards felt weak and empty as though excitement had come and passed me by. I walked home and saw soldiers with babies in their arms and girls hanging onto their arms.

Friday 15th March: I forgot to mention that yesterday the Finns ceased fighting at 11a.m and Russia has taken great wads of brave little Finland. They swept all before and just when the Russians were gaining, they had to give in because their military conditions were worse than anyone dreamed. God! What a world we live in! Russian Republics along the coast of Finland. Ten thousand Finns with bundles on their backs and children in their arms tramping to a tiny little Finland. No doubt they said, "It can't happen here". Sibyl came to tea, we listened to records and got gloomy and morose about the War. David and Michael Brookman are going with the next A.I.F.'s.

Sunday 17th March: After lunch I bathed, dressed and went to Sunday school. I was in the middle of poetically describing the Garden of Gethsemane to the infants, "Dark, silent olive trees, white gowns, the pad of sandaled feet, moonlight on a centurion's armour and torch light flickering on bearded faces" - in fact I had just achieved poetic heights when one child said, "Gee, wouldn't ya be scared!" After tea, Richard and I listened to the wireless, Richard tapestrying, me sewing, and the others at church.

Monday 18th March: Arose at half past six after dreaming unhappy, cruel dreams of Daddy and felt awful - very tight inside and sick. Six weeks ago, two men from the Water Works came about eight pounds ten owing, Daddy having refused to pay. Darling Maman, another nasty business. They got all the family matrimonial troubles out of me. Oh!

It's all so unpleasant! They were rather decent, though. I am terrified of the world of my ambitions. I am terrified of apathy and competition and a talent that is not there and, selfishly enough, the excuse of family ties. When I want to go sailing over the world, flinging up jobs and security. What will Mother say, after slaving year after year to give them to me? Perhaps she will understand.

Saturday 23rd March: The world is still trying to answer the question of Finnish bravery. They made us believe that they were sweeping all before them (even Chamberlain believed) and then in the next second they are crushed and defeated. Otherwise we might have sent troops beforehand. They say the Finnish Ministry of Information lost the war.

Saturday 30th March: Edward Godfrey called for me and we drove down alone together to the Britten Jones deb dance. He is a darling - but I can never keep my own secrets and I pray they never get to him. The dance setting was delightful. A huge sunken garden in coloured light, like an arena with forest along the edge, open marquee, good partners, two with Edward, mucked up the supper dance with Sam Kerr and ended up with two partners. Sam Kerr terribly unhappy at compulsory training and vent his spleen on me. Edward and I both frightfully ill from supper on and we dashed home.

Sunday 31st March: I didn't get up till one and felt terribly sick. Yesterday was the most un-romantic drive I've had - Edward and I half asleep, ill and silent. He is a posthumous baby - father died in China before his birth. Staggered to Sunday school, taught them something and felt very (and unnecessarily) conscious of my red nails. Went to Sibyl's, told her every minute of the dance and vent my wrath on Sam Kerr's slight; he told me in all seriousness he loathed my nails, hated a threesome, detested the way I did my hair, thought my make-up appalling and was thoroughly disgusting. I walked home with Mrs Brookman's mother, Mrs Shiels, with her telling me of old dances and chaperones and bustles and what nots.

Tuesday 2nd April: There was a packet for me - a token of forgiveness from Sam Kerr. It was a copy (with the editor's compliments) of the "Phoenix" - university magazine. Max Harris, Sam himself, Charles Jury, Roger Willoughby all contributed. It sends cold aches through me - doubt feelings. Australia abounding with talent like this and it doesn't blossom - and I, with no talent…! I would give <u>anything</u> to go to the University. My education is so small and petty and <u>minute.</u>

Thursday 4th April: After tea I went to the University for my first Workers' Educational Association lecture on English literature. It will be interesting. Miss Morriss, M.A., meanders a great deal, but her subject and her knowledge of it is vast. I have discovered two new poets - always exciting - Chatterton who killed himself at eighteen and Gerard Manley Hopkins. I am disappointed in the crowd. I half expected to see <u>workers</u> striving for an education - instead the usual bourgeois high-class mob. In town after I saw the actor Frank Waters and was once again shocked at his common plebility. Yet he once thrilled me in a theatre!

Sunday 7th April: Arose early and walked to town through deserted streets and caught the 10 o'clock bus to the Oxford Group House Party at Holiday House. Read Steinbeck's "The Grapes of Wrath" going up to Mount Lofty as the scenery was grey and cold and monotonous. Every-one there, walking and enjoying themselves. Had lunch and begged to be introduced to a refugee called Georg Klimont. Everyone too shy. Later I was fiddling with the fire when he came and helped. We talked above the singing and playing and then went for a walk mile after mile after mile over lost roads, misty rain, sun on rain, swampy vegetable gardens, summits, cottages. Georg (pronounced Shorshe) is very naïve and Aus-trian. I taught him to cooee, to suck eucalyptus leaves, to speak Austra-lian. Oh! Lots of things. He lives in a boarding house in Buxton Street, North Adelaide. I must ask him to tea. He told me fairy tales in Austrian, laughed a good deal and I found he was one of the refugees of my Wilder-ness teacher, Miss Hassell, and he adjudicated a debate at our school. He's been here a year. Came back about three hours later, feeling guilty as we had missed meetings galore. I don't know what he's doing here. Rushed home and helped entertain the John Horners and the Clive Careys till I gave up the ghost at half past eight and went to bed.

Tuesday 9th April: After dinner, I was sitting in the dining room lis-tening to the wireless, when they said that Germany had invaded Norway and Denmark and that Norway had declared war on Germany. Denmark almost wholly occupied. Poor Norway! After losing her honour, month after month, by pampering and fawning to her most hated enemy - and then be spurned! I am beginning to have new ideas about a national honour - and no ideas at all about <u>inter</u>national honour.

Thursday 11th April: Today is windy and dark so that at half past nine one has to have the light on. I love these days. Yesterday, there was the biggest naval battle off the Norwegian coast, since the Battle of Jutland. Two German cruisers went down and two English destroyers were lost. What on earth happened today? I met a journalist editress who once more dampened my plans to be a journalist, which are losing their ardour. I don't much care what happens to me. The W.E.A. lecture on English literature was meandering and only taught me how little I know. Stewart Cockburn and Fay Sellick drove me home and we argued furiously against Stewart on Pacifism. He's a Pacifist in Camp! So nice to meet a boy with hope and foolish, vain, lovely dreams.

Friday 12th April: Last night Sam Kerr, primus, rang and asked me to the films. It was a great surprise, because he doesn't seem the sort of person to invite a seventeen year old teen to the pictures out of principle.

Saturday 13th April: Had a shower, dressed in grey coat and skirt, red jumper and red bow and Sam came in a taxi. He was very nervous at first. It seems strange that he should have such a bad inferiority complex at almost 21, a live spark at the University, terribly clever etc. etc. He was very nice tonight, in a pepper and salty tweed suit, just like a student should, much taller than me, lots of curly hair. The picture, upstairs, was quite good - both English, we went to the Vignola Café - very pseudo intellect, death masks, lamps etc. Had coffee and talked, talked on everything. Then we wended down the Arcades, looking through slot machines at films and home in a taxi. I am sure we both enjoyed it.

Monday 15th April: I apologized to Sam on Saturday about some platitude I had made and he said, "Good God! <u>You</u> never speak in platitudes", which was so much grander a compliment than being told I had lovely eyes (which I haven't). In the turmoil of smoothing out Wody Blackburn's romance with Mike Tipping, who after proposing to Wody and telling her what she's to call their children, then took Sibyl's other friend Anne Ayliffe out three times in a weekend and made tearful love to her; so, Sibyl didn't have much time to be impressed with my bits of news. My romances are much too intellectual for Sibyl.

Tuesday 16th April: At lunch time I had a fitting for my evening frock. It is delicious - a huge, bouffant skirt of pale pink tulle, stiffened with net, so that when I walk it flares out behind me, and, in contrast, a black velvet top with only two strings of pink pearls. I also bought some cute sandals to be tinted pink - flat heels and round toes and awfully comfortable. Mother and I had chocolate and biscuits and lunch at Judy's Coffee Shoppe, where you sit in a pseudo-Japanese atmosphere, and then I dashed back late to Ward's. It's a stinking hole although I have finished theory and am concentrating on speed. Through an amazing fluke I did 105 words per minute in the afternoon.

Wednesday 17th April: Received a letter from Sam asking me to go to a dance at the "college" - "St Mark's", I presume - which excited me greatly. I'm very fond of Sam - in an almost protective, intellectual sense. I'm sure I'm the only person who's bothered to understand him - and he was a bulldog during the Leaving exams! At quarter past eleven, I rushed to South Terrace and had my first official music lesson from Mrs Horner. She has offered to teach me music for nothing. I didn't know a thing and was terribly dumb and nervous. I came straight back and had another fitting for my frock and didn't have time for lunch but ate it surreptitiously during type-writing, while Miss Ward actually asked me if I'd like a job! I gulped and said "no". It's not much point getting a job before I'm good enough to be on a newspaper. At the moment at "The News" there is no journalistic position open for women, only two jobs open, a secretary for Mr Brown, the chief editor, and a library one. Quite honestly, I don't really care what happens to me much.

Thursday 18th April: Last night at cooking I made pasties and short-bread and this morning we ate pasties and shortbread. I am always feeling sick and when I do have a meal forced down on me, I am really sick, so I really ate nothing at all. I am sick always - always, and am always sick of being sick - even at Ward's. I went to the University for my W.E.A. lecture and it was much better than before - more coherent and more I knew about. Fay and Stewart drove me back and we read T. S. Eliot in the light of the car.

Friday 19th April: Feeling sick, as usual, so Mother rang the doctors and bought me some foul medicine which made me feel perfect for the dance - after three solid weeks of sickness! I had lunch with Judith Crase who was at school with me, at the University Refectory and every time I looked round, I wanted to weep. I was consumed with envy for her being there, and told Mother so when I saw her. I could have bitten my tongue out - Mother who gives me everything and then I have to be so tactless! Got ready for the dance, washed my hair, dressed in my perfect frock, Mother the angel, came home and did my hair. Four boys and Bizz Brookman called for Richard and me and half way to the Law Smith and Bowen dance at Gawler, we conked out! An Archdeacon picked Bizz and me up and we left the boys on the road. They were towed in, later. We came very late, everyone seemed full up, got my programme full somehow, dullish partners, but I loved it.

Sunday 21st April: After lunch I went to Sunday school and when I had nothing to do, I went out to put some rubbish in a tin - and heard loud, tremendous music. I followed it out of the back of the church, down a lane to an old, huge, cobwebby, pioneer coach shed. It was Grieg. I listened, then rushed back to my children, and after, went back again and knocked, not being able to resist. There stood Walter Desborough, in tight ballet trousers and a red ribbon round his hair, on a "property" trunk and three girls in ballet uniforms holding their arms to him - dancing to Grieg music, and Joe Siebert. There were planks and dust everywhere and sunlight shining through the holes in the iron roof, high up. Joe is building a theatre there for ballet.

Tuesday 23rd April: Peg Ayers told Mother that she was at the Vignola when I was there with Sam and one of the boys of about twenty five said to John (millionaire Sir Sidney Kidman's heir), "No, don't look at her. She's mine. She's the sweetest thing I've seen for a long time, and I'm going to wait till she grows up".

Thursday 25th April: This ANZAC is like every other I can remember, sitting by the fire with the window shutting out a grey day, the same voice

(Richard's) broadcasting the same service from the Cross of Sacrifice. Only this time, we pray to God that those men didn't die in vain, which is so aimless, because we know they did. We know the sons who marched today will die in vain.

Saturday 27th April: With Sibyl, we trammed to St Peter's College to watch Mike Brookman playing football for the Old Collegians Football Team. It was glorious weather, the architecture, the cloud effect, the boys playing on green fields everywhere. I saw and waved to Bob Cotton, a boy whom I had only told last night at a party that I wasn't the kind of girl who went to football matches and paraded - and he saw me the next day - about the only girl! Still I did know Mike Brookman who was playing.

Sunday 28th April: Everyone went to church but me, and I wrote an essay for the W.E.A. - not so bad but not so good and filled with platitudes. In "The Truth" newspaper, Fay Matters gave me a good write up saying I was developing Mama's "own grace and faultless taste" and looked like a ballerina.

Thursday 2nd May: Last night Sam Kerr and Billy Bray rang me, but I was out. Funny if I was asked to the St Mark's University dance and St Peter's College Boy's dance - two stages of one's life. I walked to town with Richard and typed for two and a quarter hours without a break while the more brilliant members of Miss Ward's did a Bookkeeping Exam. At lunch Zoe Gilbert from Miss Ward's, and I wandered down to North Terrace hoping beyond hope we'd meet someone terribly exciting who would brighten up our lives for one fleeting moment. Came home in the tram busily learning business phrases for the exam tomorrow. Miss Bottrill has just about told us what we are having. Sammy rang and asked me to the French film on Saturday but I'm going to a dance, tried to persuade me off it, but couldn't, so made it Monday.

Saturday 4th May: I went like mad till twenty five minutes to one today at dressmaking, trying to finish my frock, so that I can wear it on Monday night. I swayed home in the tram reading T. S. Eliot's "Hollow Men"; a wonderfully good, loose, almost coherent poem. Mother is feeling very unhappy about screaming customers and rows, and the hateful smallness of Myers. Lillian drove me in to a dance, late, programme filled with interesting men, two with Tommy Simpson, supper with Bob McDonald who gave me some encouraging remarks about Sibyl (she's thinking of having <u>him</u> next). I enjoyed it terrifically, Tommy kissed the hostess Mrs Davey goodbye as a bet, and she was terribly touched! Tommy drove me to the Tuxedo and paid fifteen shillings each to get in, very smoky, but great fun. I danced mostly with Tommy. He kissed me very affectionately a good many times. I remonstrated, but had to make his thirty shillings worthwhile.

Sunday 5th May: Dragged into church after I had told everyone each in turn about my night out, and decided in church that I was thinking and speaking too much of boys - not so much a teen-age "boy craze" but just because I was meeting more and going out with more. I certainly have no illusions about Tommy Simpson, however darling he is - he's flirtatious, spoilt and too rich. Went round to Sibyl's and told her about Bob and Tommy and the dance and the Tuxedo last night and then decided to give up thinking incessantly of dances and social whirls and partners and compliments. I must remember <u>that</u> Richard and Bryan say my conversation is getting boring.

Monday 6th May: Miss Ward's was just bearable because there are only four days in the week and I'm going out with Sam tonight. At lunch, Patsy Hunt from Miss Ward's and I wandered about town and pretended to be interested in each other's company and I walked home in almost unbelievably perfect weather and gave a grubby infant three pence to get home with. Sam called at about half past seven in a taxi and we saw "Returned at Dawn" with Danielle Darrieux, Pierre Dux, Pierre Armand, Jacques Duquesnil (Don't take my word for them). Excellent film, and rather immoral but Sam and I had plenty of "savoir-faire"! Went to the Vignola after and had to shriek intelligent conversations over the Adelaide Palladium which sat next to us. We talked for an hour, walked to King William Street through deserted arcades and home by taxi. We're always late and Sam gets gated. Great fun.

Tuesday 7th May: After Miss Ward's (when my life begins), I trammed home engrossed in T. S. Eliot and practised and Sibyl came round for me; we went to her place for tea and then on our usual, inevitable walk. We went past St Mark's and I felt I couldn't (or shouldn't) be enjoying myself with Sam gated for my sins. Still, I found I <u>could</u> enjoy myself nevertheless. Sibyl is beginning to quite like the sound of him in his pepper and salt tweed suit and his hand knitted socks and heavy shoes and platonic interest - rather different from Tommy! Dear me! And I swore not to talk about men so much. I'm meeting too many of them - have to make the most before-!!!!!

Thursday 9th May: The two nice Good boys, David and John, who were rather attentive at the Palais Royal last year, and who told me about their flying brother Squadron Leader Duncan Good of the R.A.F.; he has been seriously wounded so the paper said yesterday. Really the first "casualty" which has affected me this war. We are being forced out of Norway by Germany. We are losing this war - it is a huge Gallipoli and the Allied Countries are discontented and desperate with slow Governments. They are trying to kick Chamberlain, essentially a peace minister, out.

Friday 10th May: Sam sent me two tickets to a University debate. "To reply or not to reply, that is the question." I sewed desperately all afternoon until I could have torn my frock arm by arm because it is an awful failure. Sibyl came to tea and after playing the piano in the lamplight and singing raucously, we went to watch Bryan at Miss Nora Stewart's dancing class, bowing to little girls in half-length frocks and not saying a word.

Saturday 11th May: Germany has marched into Belgium, Holland and Luxembourg and is landing troops by parachute. These countries have appealed for help to England and France and, having been received, are now our Allies. Mr Chamberlain has resigned and Mr Churchill is now Prime Minister of England. He is expected to be very bellicose and, if we do win, I doubt if we will win with Mr Chamberlain's gentlemanly English honour.

Sunday 12th May: Today is "Mother's Day" and we gave Mother some flowers - I gave six pence - so did Bryan - and Richard gave seven shillings and six pence! Still, it is <u>all</u> we had unless we had asked for past arrears of Saturday money, which I'm sure would be more welcome to Mother in her purse than flowers on her dressing table - sentimental as she is. We trooped to church in white flowers and listened to a good service glorifying womanhood and everyone was there in families and I wondered if perhaps the church hadn't died, after all. Went to Sibyl's to tea, which I regret now, on Mother's Day. We made an awful mess of baked beans and Graham and Mike refused them. Listened to the wireless and laughed a lot and was made to feel very, very welcome.

Monday 13th May: Grey day, with birds twittering. Mr Anthony Eden has been made Secretary of War and I think he is too young and inexperienced. He has the unfortunate habit of rubbing people up the wrong way and losing countries like Italy, for us. Still....war news terrible. Heavy attacks on Brussels, Rotterdam, Amsterdam, Massey, Lyons. Oh! Everywhere - even the Maginot Line. Dead bodies of women and children and boy soldiers lying across the world. I wept over the paper today. It is not the only time. Sibyl took me to the films to see "Tarzan and his Son" or some equally awful title. It is a long time since I went to the films for the sake of the films. We shrieked with laughter during it and after, convulsed, tried to look stern and polite at an afternoon tea party of old ladies at the South. Then we trammed home.

Tuesday 14th May: I met Judith Crase and we trammed to Paradise, walked up to the Montacute Valley, through it, and had lunch by a stream. We crept into village churches and slid down hills and down the Corkscrew, down the Gorge Road, hitchhiked on old rabbit carts and stone-carrying lorries, and walked miles and miles. Home dead tired, feet in terrible condition, shoes worn out, happy, bath, dressed, Sibyl to tea, debate on whether canteens should be wet at the University on Sam's tickets. Enormous fun! Everyone there, including Mic Sandford, and Sam delicious and very amusing and I very proud of him. Other side, the Woman's Christian Temperance Union, won to everyone's amazement. The boys laughed at everything too much. I spoke to Sam afterwards.

Wednesday 15th May: Found that Holland had laid down arms to the Germans and various royal families were flying round Europe.

Friday 17th May: This awful sickness has begun all over again, spoiling my holidays. In the morning I wandered and pottered and in the afternoon went visiting and forgot as best I could, my inside. Dressed in my pink and black frock, my hair looked sleek and well-groomed and I wore

Mother's squirrel coat cape. Sam arrived early and we drove to St Mark's and talked in his attractive room - built in, cream bookshelves, chintz on curtains and cushions and bed, a cozy radiator, and tasteful prints. Had four dances with him, with Bruce Macklin, John Muirhead, Sam's brother Willy Kerr; etc. etc. Practically no supper and we had next dance too, so went to his room, Sam in an armchair by radiator and I on a stool and I eventually wheedled him into reading his poetry which is past my intelligence but sounds all right! It was so nice and then home in a taxi. He will be 21 next month and is getting a car - through Edward Godfrey! We are going on a hike on Monday.

Saturday 18th May: I awoke feeling simply awful. Too faint and weak to eat or walk. Eventually bucked up and cycled to Dr Wigg's who talked to me for a good while on psychology. There is nothing wrong with me, but my subconscious mind is making me vomit and feel generally ill because it wants to get me away from the things that consciously and unconsciously worry me - the war, Miss Ward's etc... It is called hysteria, though doesn't imply what it usually does - everyone has certain cases of it and it is only overcome by being aware of the reasons. I staggered home and tried to understand and explained to Mommy but I still felt rather terrible. I read and then went for a short walk with Mother, changed, had very little dinner and went to bed. Whereas all the time I would give anything for some good, old-fashioned medicine - thirsting for it, in fact.

Sunday 19th May: Lay in bed, feeling awful, rose, could hardly eat any-thing. Even when I do eat I'm sick after, so what's the point? Meanwhile I get weaker and weaker. Evidently the psychological truth hasn't dawned yet. At Sunday school I felt better and tried to teach some disbelieving children the book of Genesis which I don't believe either so we ended up by discussing jelly fish and apes and Darwin. Went to the Brookman's and recounted my troubles to Sibyl and when I went into eat, Graham carefully removed the bread knife and Mike stood over me reading "Hys-terical Fits" from a huge book. We had an uproarious meal and discussed golf after, played ping pong and Mike drove me home, me in the dicky seat. I pray to be well tomorrow.

Monday 20th May: Oh! Miserable day! Oh perfect, sunny, gentle autumn weather! Oh! Vile sickness! I tried to bear it but had to go round and tell Sam I couldn't make it. He looked so adorable in walking clothes and waiting to go with me - up through copper coloured trees and green hills and lunch at a hidden-away farm. I would give anything to have gone and yet I, myself, had to put it off. I felt sick and weak and unhappy and went back and crept to bed, while he went back, too, to read "Henry VIII" all alone, because I had spoiled his first day. He said he didn't mind, because he was polite but I think he did. The weather - everything was perfect. I read in a cold bed and howled a little secretly. Still, we are going again when I am better and I asked him to come and see me. Sibyl came to tea to cheer me up. She came and cheered me up.

Tuesday 21st May: Of course I awoke feeling bright and sunny to go to Ward's, which shows terrific self-control in the face of the enemy. Actually, the enemy is flooding into France, making successful advances towards Calais and Boulogne, having taken Brussels (old news) and Arras (we have that back again now), Abbeville (on the coast) and Amiens. They are slowly nearing Lille and only 75 miles from Paris. The papers are making no attempt to coddle us into imagining victory, now. In the evening I felt well, but restless and thinking of Donald, Curly, Sam Kerr which was silly but unhelpable. The family sat cosily and silently, by the fire which drove me, at length, into the streets in an old raincoat and I went to the Brookman's which is filled with noise and people coming and going and thick hunks of bread and butter. Michael walked home with me.

Wednesday 22nd May: Dull, dull Ward's, where I count the seconds, but seem to get miraculously over my sickness, which I am led to believe, causes it. At lunch I went to Radio 5AD but Richard was busy and in a hurry so I wandered unhappily about town thinking of Sam and imagining everyone I saw was him - and suddenly, there he was! He was shocked that I should wander the streets at lunch and, in order to get me off them, made a luncheon engagement on Friday. We talked and waited for a man to drive up in his prospective second-hand jalopy. Then I left. Coming home in the tram, there he was again, clutching Boswell and Donne and Milton and Swift to his chest and going home to study. Made the tea and went to cooking and made a vile Irish stew and thereby finished my cooking course.

Thursday 23rd May: The Germans have taken Boulogne and are advancing to Calais, which they will take, doubtless. Mr Law Smith, who drove me in, is convinced that they will make France another Czechoslovakia (let 'em try) and then, after collecting their forces, assail England and conquer us. Damn America! Went to the Doctor's after Ward's and was screened and examined for consumption, but it looks as though I won't be another La Dame aux Camélias. Walked home in the mist, finding on the way, that Sibyl has a five day fever and then, after dinner, dressed in evening clothes I went to the Corinthian Club, a swing, classical music Association, a sort of social, supper, music, speeches, dancing session. Bruce Macklin gave a dull, rather good speech and I had supper with Clive Carey and a young singer called May Cottle.

Friday 24th May: Felt rather ill again this morning but that's what Dr Wigg calls emotional sickness (as apart from hysterical sickness) and I'll say it was - founded on Sam. He was buried in an armchair in John Martin's foyer, reading Max Harris's first publication "The Gift of BLOOD" on a lurid red cover. Ate very little and talked till two which made me about half an hour late, and decided not to go back at all, and after humming and hahing about films, walked out of town and went to the Zoo! Sam simply horrified and glanced furtively up and down Frome Road to see if he was noticed. Great fun. Baboons showed themselves wrong way up and elephants made messes. Very smelly and unromantic but fun. Had afternoon tea and wandered home, footsore and quite happy and not quite so much in love.

Saturday 25th May: The Germans are still advancing and people are still sending out dance invitations and Richard has signed up papers as a first step to becoming a pilot for the R.A.A.F. Went to sewing and walked home with Mother across sunny, blue misty golf links. Had lunch and went to visit Sibyl, who rose on my advent and we read common film magazines in front of a fire and became saturated in guilt and commonness, had tea and Michael and David, in their new A.I.F. uniforms, drove me home early because at the last minute Mike Tipping rang Sibyl asking her out.

Sunday 26th May: The King has asked this Sunday to be set aside for praying for peace and the victory of goodness. It seems so strange that in this blasé twentieth century with one of the greatest wars of history abroad we should pray, as a whole Empire, for victory of good. People simply standing up and sitting in the aisles in all the churches. In a universal prayer we pray "to be saved from destruction" and "help us now!" We at this moment, are a losing side - as far as war, only, is concerned.

Tuesday 28th May: A letter arrived from Sam today with tickets asking me to go to Joe Siebert's ballet theatre on Saturday. I went alone to a delightful concert tonight, at the Elder Conservatorium, a farewell to Lloyd Davies, a violin teacher there who has joined up. It was a string quartet by Haydn, a sonata by Brahms and one by Delius (quite the best) and good singing by Hilda Gill and Max Worthley. I walked to the tram with Max and his wife Connie. Very amusing, but it brought me from the heights.

Wednesday 29th May: The war news is about the worst of any. The Belgians have surrendered, because Leopold the King, contrary to his leader's orders, has signed the truce, but Belgium is discussing charges against him and are disowning his act. It has left us in a critical position, hemmed in in France, with our allies unable to fire. A million men surrounded, in a position to be hacked to pieces. Considered a filthy trick. One can't think of one's own nation in such a crisis. Oh! We are so nearly lost! Raining gently - yet feeling rather happy, somehow - dressed in my green wool frock and red beads, I went out for dinner and to the films with a group of boys who never grow up. The boys are all terribly infantile after Sam but it was quite fun.

Thursday 30th May: Walked to town with Richard and was late; he was expounding his ideas on how Mother and I were to live after he had gone into the Air Force and Bryan had gone to sea. We were to live in a flat like Greenways or Sunningdale, and not have a maid but a hot dinner in town and a picnic meal at night, and Mother was to have his Bank Book which is almost one hundred pounds. I'd rather have him. I told Miss Ward I'd like to have a job now and that I was going to apply once again to the "News". I trammed to the Doctors, who skimmed me up and down and told me to come again in three weeks and charged half a guinea.

Friday 31st May: We are making our ghastly defeat in France into a glorious victory. The papers are full of the gallant withdrawal of French and British troops from France, the ruthless steady advance of German tanks and our soldiers swimming to boats in the channel, to get away. When they are all back home, what then? Sibyl came to tea. It was rather delightful, a small meal with only Bryan and then we sat by the fire and Sibyl knitted khaki scarves and I sewed my blouse which is rapidly acquiring shape. We talked war mostly, and people, and decided Leopold hadn't been worthy of having a crush on. Then I walked back with her with a handkerchief round my head to keep off the cold. The vines have been cut away for the winter and the moon shines nakedly onto my bed.

Saturday 1st June: Asked to three dances this weekend, going to none (The Junior Red Cross, St Peter's College Mission Dance and the Cornell's). Got through a good deal of sewing which I should have done last week, at class. After tea, Sam came in his new car (?) and we rattled off to the new Theatre Studio, where Joe Siebert is putting on his ballets. They danced beautifully and I knew them all, which was interesting. Theatre wooden looking, but, in spite of its minuteness, quite attractive. Afterwards, we chugged into town, round and about town, deciding where to have coffee, laughing an awful lot, went to the Athens Café in Hindley Street to see low life, had coffee and oysters, in murky surroundings, dusty coloured streamers, fly blown mirrors, smoked a cigarette under D.B.K's guidance, walked about town, got into the rattletrap, drove to the foothills, got lost, landed somewhere in Gawler (almost), I steered and eventually, laughing like mad, arrived back.

Sunday 2nd June: I tried to write an article plus review on the ballet last night on Sam's advice that I try a little freelancing. After Sunday school I went to the Studio Theatre to see Joe Siebert about the article but he said that there were representatives of the papers there - so there didn't seem to be much point. Joe was standing in his own theatre with all the props about him, with a smug expression on his face. I spent the rest of the afternoon at Sibyl's and came home for tea and laughed a lot with the family and drank Ovaltine.

Monday 3rd June: I experienced the unusualness of the compliment of being asked out by someone who you've only met once. I told Sam he had competition and we got awfully common like the Athens Café and said, "Ave some more coffee, duckie?" etc. etc. The great and wonderful B.A! Sam Kerr! Italy obviously coming into the war sometime during this week - Mussolini hasn't missed a war yet. Another severe blow to our family is that 5AD are thinking of sending Richard to Mount Gambier to broadcast until he is actually called up to go overseas. That means that even the few, few weeks we would have left are taken away. It's rather a rotten trick. We are sitting by the fire, discussing it now and Mother and Richard are particularly sick at heart. We've lost the war, we've lost Richard - we are losing them all. Darn the whole world structure. I am making vain attempts to write this while I am balancing the ink on the hearth rug.

Tuesday 4th June: The famed Battle of Dunkirk is nearing its end. They are getting soldiers onto boats to cross the channel. The beaches are swarming with soldiers burying themselves in sand, bombs bursting, and nurses binding up wounds. It's so horrible, and so futile, and of no earthly good whatever. I went and had lunch in a warm dressing room with Mother at Myers and hated Miss Ward's, and the weather is brutally cold, the coldest winter I have known. In the evening, Sam drove up in his rattletrap and drove Mother and me to the University Theatre Guild. The car stalled by the Cathedral, and had to be examined and cranked, and then drove on. There were three plays - J.M.Barrie's " The Old Lady Shows Her Medals" (amateurish) - "The Man Born to be Hanged" by Richard Hughes (eerie, good) - and Sam's play "The Proposal" by Tchekhov (screaming, Sam excellent as an actor). Interesting people there - Mic Sandford, actor Frank Waters, Joe Siebert, Barbara Salter, Alison Harvey etc.etc. We trammed home in the cold.

Wednesday 5th June: Walked to town as I often do and went to music. Had lunch with Mother at a new teashop called the "Teapot Inn" and had malted milk and toasted ham sandwiches. There was a march of the Air Force men, and they looked far nicer than the A.I.F.'s. They were younger, better uniforms, better looking lot, better type. Mother and I and Tony Gilbert heard the governor make a speech about War Bonds from the Commonwealth Bank steps and Richard broadcast it. I have decided, however, not to make over my millions to the Government. They want twenty million pounds in one week. Everyone went out - Mother to the opening night of the Colonel W. de Basil's Ballet Company with Lady Sandford, and Bryan and I to "Keep it Dark" at the Australia Hall on complimentary tickets. It was a rather common, but clean, musical comedy, with a very nice hero (so it was worth it, despite the numerous Shirley Temples).

Thursday 6th June: The statistics are coming out now about the battle of Dunkirk, which has ended - the last members of our army having been removed from France. Oh! Awful defeat, 350,000 men returned. Thirty thousand were "lost". I saw the headline in the streets and I wanted to be sick. "Lost". It is so expressive - not wounded - gone for nothing. Boys who wanted to write best sellers and become famous actors and marry pretty girls and dance and have children - all gone. "Lost".

Friday 7th June: After tea, Richard and I went to the ballet; it was simply delightful. "Les Sylphides" was danced by Paul Petroff and Tatiana Riabouchinska, better than I have ever seen. The music was excellent. The new ballet, "Paganini" with Dimitri Rostoff was weird, modern, full of good lighting and effects and dramatic. "Le Danube Bleu" - new version - was gay and infectious and dancer David Lichine extremely good.

Saturday 8th June: Received a rather sweet, rather long letter from Sam about nothing and demanding the supper dance on Friday next. After lunch, met Mother and Bryan at the station and trained down to the Crawfords at Brighton. We had afternoon tea, went for a walk with the sea laid out "like a patient etherized upon a table" (T. S. Eliot) and calm and infinite and steely. In the train coming back I suddenly felt very dissatisfied with myself, for being irritable, lazy, intolerant, always tired. I half slept in Mummy's fur collar.

Sunday 9th June: The ballet - its impressions, its subtlety, its movements, its beautiful, inhuman women, its exclusiveness - and that's a point which is amazingly powerful - a sort of binding to people in the theatre which is not there in a picture or even a church. Mother, Bryan and I went to church, were told Australians were flabby and apathetic - a point I, the most apathetic of them all, am trying to put across. Practised, odd jobbed and went to Sunday school and tried to stop the infants flirting with their little Bruce, who, in his tiny, wee pants, has plenty of Sex Appeal. Everyone is getting tea ready and Richard is in a very uproarious mood - he can't make up his mind whether to pay his bills or not - what with going off to the war and dying for his country which, of course, isn't the spirit. I had tea at the Brookman's, talked, dashed through the usual slapdash meal and went to Christ Church - very inspiring and prayed for a list of boys in the army I know.

Tuesday 11th June: Looking in the paper today, I see that Italia has declared war on the Allies without provocation, without excuse, and after waiting till France is almost beaten. Huge battles are raging across the whole of France within 60 miles of Paris. I listened before going to town, to President Roosevelt's speech which was meant to be important but he said the usual things - giving us arms etc but keeping out and letting us fight the battle for freedom and democracy. Still, they are only doing what we did at Munich. In town, the newspaper boys are calling out "French Government leaves Paris". It is frightful. It cannot be defeat!

Wednesday 12th June: Last night, until quite late, Richard and I sat by the fire and tried to thrash out the problems of the world - Why war? Why death? Is there heaven? Is there God? We found no answer, just as we knew we wouldn't - but we go on talking. Paris is being heavily bombed, Italy has advanced towards France, and America is straining to the utmost. I watched Air Force marches at lunch. I went back stage at the ballet for a few minutes unnoticed - a matinee on - lots of foreigners. This morning there were raids on Hindley Street in Adelaide for Italians. In the evening, Mother and I walked across the freezing park to the ballet. Met Richard. It was simply superb. "Swan Lake" disappointing, Tamara Toumanova very heavy; "Francesca da Rimini" lovely, classic, Botticellian; Paul Petroff in "Le Spectre de la Rose"; Tatiana Riabouchinska delightful in "Graduation Ball". Scintillating, irresistible, infectious, cute David Lichine, adorable subject – oh gay and amusing and catching.

Thursday 13th June: I am still half dancing to "Graduation Ball" - the naughty boy Lichine, clutching the crumpled blue hair ribbon from

Riabouchinska's pigtail, with his wicked eyes gleaming, his ridiculous mouth hung open, his slender, lithe figure half crumpled up - I can't help thinking of it. It is unforgettable. Walked to town across the frosty parks when everywhere is clean and covered with dew. At lunch I went to Myers and read English magazines in a dressing room with Mother. There was no letter from Mr Morley, the editor of the "News", which I was praying for. Miss Ward had helped me with my letter for a position to him. It began by a friendly little letter "of help" and ended with "qualifications enclosed". Today Richard has his medical test for the R.A.A.F., and he went, full of foreboding and spirited. It is a full day's test and quite an honour to be accepted. Sam rang up about the lift to the dance tomorrow. And I forgot to thank the little man - just accepted. Met Georg Klimont, and I talked to the Austrian refugee for twenty minutes. He's a darling. After the W.E.A. lecture, Stewart Cockburn showed me "The Advertiser" printing and took me to supper with Tom MacGregor King where we ate crumpets and drank coffee until ¼ past 11.

Friday 14th June: I had such fun last night and had promised Mother to be in bed by ½ past 9 - but what's a ¼ to 12 anyway? Stewart and Tom MacGregor King were such intellectual and handsome company. I felt sick all day - of course, there being a dance on! Everyone was marching about and waving les tricolores in a French Red Cross effort. Paris has fallen. The Swastika flies from the Eiffel Tower. The Germans goosestep down the Champs Elysees and salute the Arc de Triomphe. And I dance! Sam called in his car, now called "Petroff" and we landed somewhere at Belair, eventually getting late to the Mount Osmond Country Club, but programme full up to 5th extra in five minutes with thousands of perfect partners - Tony Gilbert, David and Mike Brookman, two with Stewart Cockburn, two with Sam, and so on, etc. "Chick" Robertson, my hasty flame, danced with me (the one who met me once and asked me to a dance which I sacrificed for Sam). A lovely dance. I swished about in my pink tulle and black velvet and fur. Sam drove me home and I gave him a lecture on posing.

Saturday 15th June: I lay immobile in bed until a quarter to one deciding that sewing lessons were for those who do not dance. Arose to go to the Ballet with Alison Harvey, B.A., but Mother for the first time in remembrance, put her foot down, so I rang up Alison and put her off - not very reluctantly. Sat by the fire and went for a walk to work off my sickness and buy some violets for Mrs Brookman's birthday. Still feeling like nothing on earth, dressed and went to a dance in North Adelaide and had the sixth, supper, seventh, eighth dance with "Chick" who is sweet and flirtatious and awfully fast (which is rather fun after Sam) and then the ninth and tenth with Dick Beresford who is not slow either and kept on telling me sleepily all evening that I was "wizard", wonderful and potent, and did I "need my love to keep me warm" - which I didn't in a stern voice. It was great fun in spite of Tommy Simpson not turning up. I was full up in a few minutes and parked my leftovers on José who is most pathetic. Chick Robertson went to a beer party after and couldn't walk home with me.

Sunday 16th June: Once again lay in bed and tried to remember all my compliments for Sibyl's boredom, and at the last minute dashed off to Sunday school, where not feeling at all in the spirit, I gave the children a lot of moralistic stories to chew. I wandered round to Sibyl's after and we discussed the war with a Mrs Craig who has just come back from England and is horrified at our apathy. Then Sibyl came to a very delicious tea and we sat alone by the fire and wrote a rather dippy poem on the dancer David Lichine for the weekly "Impromptu" magazine at Wilderness School. Awful rumours are circulating at school that Lichine doesn't bathe and so we wrote an Ode in Repudiation. It is hardly respectable so will be censored.

Tuesday 18th June: The French have given in! The French, the proudest of all nations, are being forced to eat the dust before a crowd of gangsters. An Englishman compared it to a beautiful, idealistic woman being maltreated by hooligans, and her lovers unable to assist her. It hung over me like a cloud all day - this horrible helplessness. There is a huge wave of feeling that the Nazi forces are insurmountable - that any little force will be crushed inevitably.

Saturday 22nd June: The lust for ballet celebrities has gotten into me. Sibyl rang and said we must meet them after the matinee; Sam is taking me tonight. I went to sewing and then was fitted for a skunk bolero for spring wear and a strange pale honey-coloured spring coat with mink lapels, to be made for me. Went into the Grand and beheld celebrities stuffing themselves at lunch. We saw Georges Skibine last night eating crumpets in a milk bar and Nina Verchinina in a fish shop. I sewed by the fire and Sibyl came. Walking past the city bridge in the twilight we met and talked to Antal Dorati, Italian conductor, who was a darling. Stood commonly outside the Grand and spoke to Denisova, Alberto Alonso, Orloff, Genevieve Moulin, Leskova, Razoumova, Volkova. All sweet, all tired, all polite. Nicolas Orloff stood dumbly and then said, "I do not speak English - good". Sam came, we went in the stalls, and saw "Aurora's Wedding" - "Le Coq d'Or", "Graduation Ball" - Oh! Still lovely! Went to Vignola and there was dancer Paul Petroff with Peggy Ayers. Poor Sam. I did nothing but discuss my adolescent pashes. Great fun.

Sunday 23rd June: I am still not even tired of ballet. They go tonight - so Georges Skibine said. I lay in bed while people marched backwards and forwards until eleven o'clock and then bathed and washed my hair. The news from Churchill has come through. "His Majesty's Government learn with regret and amazement that the French have accepted the terms imposed by the Germans." They are not known yet, as a peace with Italy must be made first. That rankles, because they have been beaten on every front so far and yet, through Germany, are the victors. After Sunday school I walked to Sibyl's and told her about Paul Petroff and discussed ballet and mentally wept over their departure for ever. Went to Judith Crase's and we had toasted crumpets and hot sausage rolls and tomato sauce, and coffee and fresh bread by a coal fire, in deep couches. Then we walked across the park and heard Reverend Ruth, the Baptist Minister preach on this "the darkest day of this war". I learnt much from him. He is a great mystic.

Monday 24th June: Someone drove me into town and thereby swept misty parks and gaunt grey trees out of my hands. At lunch I sat by myself and read Ezra Pound and fell in love with him. So far, and as far as I, in complete ignorance of poetic technique can judge, I like him better than Eliot. I bought a paper and read the conditions imposed on the French. They are awful. Treacherous. Yet, with all England calling them traitors, I don't seem to think them so. They made the mistake every nation makes when they are in a hole - they decided their own soil was greater than an ideal. Perhaps only fools have ideals these days and they were being business-like. Nearly all France is militarily occupied, under German Government.

Monday 1st July: I nearly completed my shirt, to have Mother say it was like a maternity gown and to take about a yard off my lovely seams. It's a soul destroying occupation. I think I'll marry Tommy and won't have to. Buried myself in "History of Literature" and found I had competition from Bryan, to my amazement and joy. Bryan is suddenly becoming interested in girls. Two. He goes as far as milk shakes after school.

Tuesday 2nd July: Somehow today was rotten. It was grey, dull, irritating weather to begin with and the alarm refused to go off. Then I felt terribly low, slight pains for no reason at all, slightly sick (and I am not getting neurotic about it), and a sniffly sort of cold. I walked in alone feeling self-conscious in my strap-over school shoes. I counted the minutes at Ward's and three times nearly walked out. Then the Germans have occupied the Channel Islands and things are tense in Japan. Then the Corinthian Club is on and I've paid my money but regret the whole thing. I shan't go. Stewart Cockburn rang and said he couldn't manage the Woodlands School's Red Cross Dance but asked me to the Law University Dance. I rang Edward and he backed out of my invitation on account of stomach pains. He then asked Richard and me to the pictures.

Wednesday 3rd July: I have definitely and finally renounced Edward Walter Godfrey. I could just hear his little soul recoiling last night and the great blow came when he asked Richard and me to go to the films! I have felt quite in love with Sam all day. At lunch I read "Outline of Literature" - story of "Odyssey" and "Iliad" which I should have read at my age. Trammed home and no letter from Mr Morley but a ticket to Joe Siebert's Bach ballet from Sam, and a sweet letter telling me to feel "under no obligation" to write - which I promptly did, covered with remorse over Edward. Sam's been treated awfully rough after all he's done for me - and Edward's done nothing and got all my luv. I'm feeling quite tender all of a sudden. Inevitable, of course.

Thursday 4th July: Somehow this week has been rotten. Restlessness over the non-appearance of Mr Morley's letter from "The News" and Miss Ward has not been very kind lately. I hate bickering with teachers - they are always right - only I wish Miss Ward would pick on someone her own size - which is being rather cruel. Sam had sent his member's ticket for the Theatre Guild so I clattered out in my high heels to the Hut which Joe's built, to see his ballet set to Bach, called "Harlequin, The Flute". It was wonderful, very crowded, terrific amount of work, definitely influenced by certain ballerinas of the Ballets Russes. Sat with Judith Crase and it poured with rain, so we dashed, sopping wet, to Rundle Street and I trammed home with her.

Friday 5th July: I felt sick again today on account of the dance tonight; it's very helpless. However, I dressed, was sick, made up and looked darned glamorous. Stewart Cockburn with Elliott Johnston and sister Marjorie Johnston came round and took me to the Waterhouse's, the opulent, ostentatious, white house on Lefevre Terrace, for a cocktail. A perfect party - Paul Pfeiffer, Max Harris (both poets) "spooky", lots of Teesdale Smiths - anyway crowds of nice people - and Sam. I was horrified to be there with someone else and he too. Made me unhappy and apparently him, too. But at supper Elliott Johnston said he had no hopes for the success of the evening as Stewart had turned up with Sam's girl and Sam had told him he was not asking her himself as it was going to be a terrible show - and so came without a partner - to see me. So Sam told me, too. He was a rather darling, jealous fool and spoiled the evening. I had every right to come with Stewart. Danced with Roger Willoughby at the Law University Dance after and also with Max Harris, Lance Burt, Captain John Yeatman, Elliott, Herbert Adams etc.

Saturday 6th July: Herbert Adams who I met last night has asked me to lunch on Monday. He is about thirty, bald, bloated, of Adams' Cakes and is quite popular, heaven only knows why; I despicably accepted. I don't know which is worse - too few boys or too many. Mr Morley from "The News" wrote saying there was no vacancy. I had to unpick every stitch of my completed shirt. Oh! I felt low. Sibyl asked me to the pictures, we went and saw "When Tomorrow Comes" with Charles Boyer and Irene Dunne and I had to walk out just when he was deciding between wife or Irene. Peter Gilbert drove me furiously home. Stewart and Richard were just leaving when I got there. I put on a green frock, lovely stockings, a beanie, high shoes, and my hair was beautifully done. I looked terribly smart and arrived half an hour late at Sam's 21st cocktail party. It was a great success and Sam was sweet, made up for last night and we are going to an Ignaz Friedman concert together and letting our rejective dances go. I spoke a good deal to the poet Charles Jury, Elliott, the poet Paul Pfeiffer, Sam, Dug Wighton, Louise Matison and Michael Quinn Young.

Monday 8th July: Met Herbert who was awful. We had lunch at the Oriental and he walked back with me and lured an invitation out of me to go to his flat after Ward's and hear his records. All afternoon I sat in stunned silence imagining orgies in the worst taste taking place at Herbert's flat. Sam sort of developed a halo during the afternoon. After Ward's I marched up to Herbert; said I couldn't go with him as I didn't know him and he asked if I thought he intended to attack me in broad daylight. It was awful. He tried to gauge my freedom on every night this week. Went to Sibyl's for tea and jitterbugged and went crazy, then wrote letters and listened to the radio.

Tuesday 9th July: It poured with rain all day and in my brown school shoes, my swagger raincoat, muff and pixie hat, I trailed round town, "job hunting". First to Mr Roberts, Chief Accountant of the News. No vacancy. My name on the list. Next Mrs Fitzmaurice to put off my sewing lessons. I'm sick of her. Then Mr Kinnear of 5AD. No vacancy. Put my name on the list. Informed me there was no glamour in a radio station - a fact I have learnt. I went to music in the afternoon and, owing to colds and not practising, couldn't play a thing. At home there was no thank you letter from Sam - he never was a very polite sort of bloke. I'm dreading a call from Herbert whom I dislike. He's quite an innocent little man but has assumed evil proportions. He rang up. He can't take a hint. I refused the films tomorrow and said I was booked up for fourteen weeks.

Wednesday 10th July: Yesterday I got a letter from America. Today I caressed my French letters from my French correspondent and lamented the disunity of the Entente. It is one of the saddest things of the war -

fighting an ally - the ally. Richard's photograph is all over the covers of the Radio Call newspaper in the city.

Thursday 11th July: I spent all lunch time vainly fitting on shoes which wouldn't fit and ending up still wearing my old navy and white sport brogues. The shoes, Sam calls "ridiculous". It seems foolish and small-minded to write a diary on one's minute proceedings when History is being made. Air battles are fought with more furious violence every day. Today, a hundred planes were engaged in the fight to block the Dover Straits. We won, as we always do in the air. The Italians are losing on every front. I went to the W.E.A. and had my essay on "Defence of Sour Sobs" read out to the road makers and journalists as the best, "a literary gem in a tiny way". This is encouraging yet not enough to win Fleet Street.

Friday 12th July: Sweet letter from Sam. Sibyl rang through the pouring rain and asked me to tea. Lillian drove me in her car as the rain didn't stop. Had tea and we decided at ten, I should stay the night, although the rain had cleared. Sibyl lent me a short nightie, a dressing gown and Michael lent me his bed. He dragged it into Sibyl's room, where we giggled a lot and felt almost as though we were on our honeymoon and eventually went to bed and talked. Nearly fell out of bed three times during the night.

Saturday 13th July: Awoke in Sibyl's room, had a shower, cleaned my teeth with my finger and dressed. Had grapefruit and Mexican rice for breakfast, listened to the ballet "Petroushka" on the gramophone after, dashed home, changed, came back and went to the pictures to see Ginger Rogers in "Fifth Avenue Girl". Rushed home in tram, changed, dinner, Sam rolled up, went to Ignaz Friedman, Polish pianist, greatest player of Chopin, had no stage manner, little sympathy between him and the audience, yet played divinely particularly the Chopin pieces and a Beethoven. Talked to Max Harris, Dugald Wighton, Mick Quinn Young, Paul Pfeiffer, etc. then went to the Greek Club, had most interesting conversation with Greeks and an A.I.F. from Indo China. Lovely Greek coffee, smoked, got on well with Greeks, conversation got too dangerous politically so asked us to leave and waved us goodbye down Hindley Street. Motored round a bit, stopped by the river, nothing silly, just talked late, home.

Monday 15th July: At lunch I suggested to Mother that until I got a job I spend the afternoon at home, studying the things I want to study and she accepted. I flew to Miss Ward's, told her, and walked home, completely happy. I shall really enjoy Miss Ward's in the morning now, almost. The only fear is that I get a job too soon! My first afternoon to myself! I did French grammar; I practised; I ate oranges on the lawn; I found some old school magazines of Richard's and discover screaming pictures of Sammy and "Chick" etc. etc. Sam was rather a hero at my age in spite of football boots and shorts.

Tuesday 16th July: I shall write to my French school friend correspondent, Hélène, and see if my letter can penetrate into German occupied areas; penetrate into what is complete darkness to the rest of the world. There has been an air-raid on Rennes killing 4,200 people. This is where Hélène fled, on capture of Lille where she was living.

Thursday 18th July: After lunch practised and went through piles of old schoolbooks and thought what a pity I haven't time to learn Greek and Latin and German and am full of wonder that I once read Virgil in the original. During the W.E.A. lecture we studied the satirists in the early nineteenth century. We looked at Max Harris's photo in Preece's window with Stewart and Fay. Max seems to be taking his place in Australian literature.

Friday 19th July: This morning was grey and it rained periodically. However, in blue suit and raincoat I met Sam and we rode up to Montacute Valley in "Petroff", couldn't find anywhere for lunch, bought a packet of biscuits and chocolate and walked along the hill road to Marble Hill; softly misty with vague rain, that cleared and the sun came out on the wet trees. We branched off to Cherryville, found it was a dead end, climbed up an almost vertical hill for an hour, through brush and bracken and slippery bark and found I had left my bag behind! Truly femine. Plodded down and a few hours later reached the top again. It was almost dark, walked back, sucked some ginger beer, dashed home wrapped in Sam's coat, scarf, etc. Had a bath, changed and arrived late at Sibyl's small sixteenth birthday party. Pat Pinder, Barby Salter, Judith Crase and Judith Stokes and Wody were there. Felt tired and unsociable, talked by the fire, had tea and listened to records. I curled up in an armchair with a cat asleep in my arms. Pinder drove me home.

Saturday 20th July: Wasted the whole morning fooling round in and on bed. Read the paper. Hitler's boast to be in London by Friday the 19th unfounded. He is trying to lower the morale by peace offensives. There was an invitation asking me to go to the South Australian Hotel to assist the Countess Bective in a Red Cross Mannequin Show. I was dressed in evening clothes for the dress circle with Judith Crase to see Georg Schnéevoigt, Finnish conductor when Tommy Simpson rang at seven asking me to go to the Ballet, couldn't, and so is taking me to the Tuxedo after. The concert was lovely, a Dvorak, lovely Sibelius, Concerto and a Symphony. A bit early for Tom, so Stewart Cockburn showed me around "The Advertiser" where I sat in the editor's chair. Then he took me to Tommy. We couldn't get into the Tuxedo so we went, Henry Martin, Molly Stokes, "Chickie" and I, and danced at the "Blue Grotto". Came home in Tommy's huge car in his trench coat and balaclava. He kissed me about 100 times and I didn't care. He is rather a darling.

Sunday 21st July: Snoozed until 10. Was crowed over by Lillian who knows all about my love affairs, because when she came last year I did not believe in kissing as an occupation, now I realize it is the most harmless of habits. Two infants (17 and 21) smooching in a car! I feel, all the same, I'm not the most exemplary of Baptist Sunday School teachers. Georg Klimont called during the day and left his card. Very thrilled.

Monday 22nd July: Georg's visit has thrilled me tremendously. Tonight I rang Georg and asked him and his sister to tea next Sunday. He can come but is in doubt about Gertrude. It was awful being conversational over the phone because he is so difficult to understand.

Tuesday 23rd July: I went to a very social, slightly snobbish gathering at the South, presided over by the Countess of Bective, for a general committee of the Red Cross Parade at the Theatre Royal, helped by Lady Gowrie. I didn't do much but sat with Ros Dumas, Sue Yeatman and Joan Brennan and put my name down for the usher's committee. Why I was asked I don't know. All much older and all notorious butterflies.

Thursday 25th July: My name is now on the list of all the more interesting offices in Adelaide, for work. This morning went comparatively fast and smoothly. Speckled sunshine, a cold blue sky, faint wind, and almost blossom and irises. I adore irises. Everybody in the News these days are making wonderful speeches about that villain Hitler and trusting in God and waiting for the forces of evil, which we will combat. Soothing to one's nerves. Wrapped up in a grey coat and skirt and scarlet scarf I went to Joe's ballet with Sammy to see "Harlequin, the Flute" again. We had coffee in town at Vignola's and talked until midnight. Sammy said, " I wasn't beautiful but I was active in mind and body, a bit nervy, fiddled and blushed, sensitive, attractive, eyes changed colour, eyebrows darker than my hair; mobile mouth" - rather fun and then I analyzed him.

Friday 26th July: I had lunch with Judith Crase listening to the Carnegie Gramophone at the Conservatorium. We listened by a Russian stove in a large deserted, padded room to Beethoven. Clive Carey, a teacher there, popped in. Clive and his black Homburg hat are rather nice. I was sent to Sargood, Gardiner Pty Ltd, Charles Street for an interview. It went quite well, but asked if I could do arithmetic. Gave me some invoices (2 yards at 14½ shillings) which got me stonkered. Spoilt chances.

Sunday 28th July: It is pouring with rain and has been doing so all day and night. The almond blossom is limp and soaked. Sibyl and Georg Klimont came for tea. He was very charming, very plain and his accent was intelligible. Sibyl and Georg and I sat by the fire with the lamp on and listened to the gramophone. He went to the opera in Vienna once a fortnight. He told us some amusing stories about the Nazi invasion of Austria. He got slightly more political than usual. We had supper and he walked home with Sibyl. It was interesting and he was delightful but I was disappointed about something.

Monday 29th July: I didn't make another date with Sam. I hope he doesn't jilt me. He hinted that he had thought about it more than once as he felt I didn't much care about him. I didn't then probably, but when he says things like that, I do immediately. Home to lunch with the housekeeper and washerwoman. All take a very dark view of an enemy alien's visit here last night. After tea I strode up to O'Connell Street, was forced into buying some Herbert Adams' Cakes and trammed to Mr Hackworthy's, the minister, where we had a Sunday school teachers meeting. It went with a swing. I perched on Mr Hackworthy's arm of his chair by the fire and we had supper.

Tuesday 30th July: My music lesson was awful. Mrs Horner was as patient as she could be, but I simply don't seem able to come down the minor scales once I'm up there. I feel guilty and at a disadvantage as I don't pay. Still, I'm used to that feeling after five years of free education.

Wednesday 31st July: Went to the South for the second Red Cross Show. Did nothing but eat with the other girls. Cleared the tables, we did! All the family walked across the park to see "Gone with the Wind". It lasted from half past seven until twenty past eleven, and was simply wonderful throughout. Vivien Leigh as the famed Scarlett O' Hara was superb, Clark Gable, Leslie Howard, Olivia de Havilland all perfect in their parts. Came home in a sort of daze across the park again. The war scenes made me think of Richard the whole time - writhing on the ground! In three weeks Mummy is going to Sydney to actually get the divorce after six years of waiting. And I've got the job!

Thursday 1st August: Went to Mr Stevens of Sargood, Gardiner Pty Ltd and was officially given the job. Twenty five shillings a week, rise soon, bonuses, only seven commercial travellers, and an office boy under me. Everything arranged. Don't like the hours, nine to five thirty, but...... money in the bank. Every hour spent there means an extra hour swimming in Lake Como some day. Dashed back to Miss Ward's, told her, told everyone, grabbed my books and danced down the dark old stairs grinning like a Cheshire cat. Came home and there was a book from Sam Beviss Kerr of Andrew Marvell's poems and a sweet poem by him in the front. At the W.E.A., it was on Byron and Lear and Carroll and Beerbohm and "Gone with the Wind". Lots of tearing about for trams.

Sunday 4th August: Last night I went to Tommy Simpson's 21st sherry party. It was rather fun and I talked most of the time to Geoffrey Anderson and got a date with him and then to the Tuxedo where I danced a terrible lot with Derry Paterson of another party. I made a date with him too. We are going riding on two of his 21 horses on the beach. He is a darling. He said I was a "damned good sort". This morning I slept till ten, and missed bus to Holiday House Youth Movement. Pat Moore, a school friend, had told me about a Youth Movement run on the Nazi one, and begun by Charlie Price, but with higher ideals. I caught the 2.30 train, dozed, and chewed gum. Gorgeous people up there - Varsity crowd and Oxford Group though not together. Hiked round hills with "Beetle" Teesdale-Smith, Pat Moore, Margaret Cowell, etc...over quarries, views, good air, red cheeks, huge eucalyptuses. Tea with Beetle and Peter Hopton etc...after sat by the fire and was told details by Peter and Alison's brother Alain Harvey (a surprise). Two hour meeting on beds and floor with Charlie Price being proper dictator's type. Others there were Peter Anderson, Willy Kerr, Shirley Eyles, Elizabeth Carter who had invited me, etc. It was on education and doing summaries for Charlie's book on the show. I am very keen. It gives me something to think about outside myself. We careered down to the station in Charlie's awful car, all hanging on the sides. I slept and chatted to Beetle, home by train at 11.30. Very late. I am not looking forward to the job - too tired to think about it.

Monday 5th August: I grew up today. I left schooldays behind and caught a train at quarter to nine and strap hung with ten million others and walked into an office and took off my coat and hat and took a letter and typed it back and filed and invoiced. After lunch, I arranged flowers - oh, strange first duty - curling yellow and brown nasturtiums in a pottery vase. The office boy is Alf Slarks. Dickensian? I learnt a whole lot which I hope I shan't forget. The place is cold and I shall be lonely and a bit bored with the little work at present. "Got off" at five o'clock and trammed back with the bored workers.

Tuesday 6th August: Rather more fun today. I was duly presented with the office and safe keys which hang over my head like the safe itself. Mr Stevens is going to Melbourne tonight, which means nothing to do for three days. Alf Slarks, the office boy, still reticent and Miss Pudney, the private secretary, still helpful, although there is a faint hardness in her voice after I've asked the same question more than seven times.

Wednesday 7th August: My letter to my correspondent, Hélène Magnier in France, returned heavily censored. Derry Paterson, the polo player, rang at seven and asked me to the Tuxedo and at half past nine (half an hour after he should have rolled up) he rang from a Service Station. Lights had fused. So I trammed to the Napoleon Hotel, went to Room 6 and found Dick Wills (of G and R Wills Wholesalers fame), "Pup" Beaumont, Derry and Peter Anderson. They were parked on Dick's (from Melbourne, Anthony Eden moustache, English etc) bed, flinging hot water bottles around. I parked too. Tuxedo at ten thirty. Very few there. Art Maskell, our best drummer, played everything we wanted and drank our wine. I drank fruit cup. Peter asked me to the Tuxedo on Saturday week. I accepted. Derry asked me too. Nasty looks thrown around. Derry bribed me into refusing. Peter, didn't, of course. We drove everyone home, sitting on everyone else. Derry very sweet and young. Kissed me at great length and told me I was a "bloody nice girl".

Thursday 8th August: Having arrived home at 4.a.m last night, I felt weary and the office lay heavy on my heart. Lillian has gone to stay with her aunt as German measles have set in, which means numerous meals in town - we being a particularly helpless family. Had lunch, lazing in the sun on the balcony on North Terrace of the Oxford Group Rooms, with Pat Short and Pat Moore. Tommy Simpson strolled by and I whistled blatantly but was unanswered. I went back to the office, dithered over phone calls, mucked orders, learned a little more, and knitted an Air Force scarf. Walked home from work and instead of going to the W.E.A., struggled into bed and daydreamed until I slept. I still have lovely peaceful day dreams but there is always something missing - the absolute peace that can't be with war - even though 12,000 miles away.

Friday 9th August: Mr Clark and Mr Veitch, the two Commercial travellers came back today and seem awfully decent and very easy to get on with and good company - awful phrases but they cover a lot of ground. I had lunch at the Arcadia with Derry and he walked back along North Terrace with me. I was horribly late and Miss Pudney and Alf were waiting grimly to get in. Derry and I talked horses and decided to get married and shock everyone. Richard swears I will get involved in "Breach of Promise" if I accept any proposal. After work, stayed in town for tea with my family. Art Maskell played "What are little girls made of" for me at John Martin's. It is my theme song. Met Sam and walked down to "Gone with the Wind". It was very hot upstairs. I loved it the second time, but dialogue is weak and seldom soars and is very mournful. We had supper at Vignola's and Sam got Socialist and said enough to intern him. We were shadowed by a policeman but drove off unmolested and cruised around. We talked on the weir for a long, long time and came home. He is rather a darling.

Saturday 10th August: At seven Georg Klimont called and we decided to go to Unley to see "Juarez" with Bette Davis, Paul Muni and Brian Aherne. Excellent, though not a good film story. Brian Aherne stole the scene in everything. The Chamberlain twins were there and my refugee scored a great hit and interest wherever we went. He nearly stood up in the film when they played the Austrian National Anthem. We walked home from O'Connell Street. He is amusing.

Sunday 11th August: I like the Chamberlain twins immensely, but I dare not think what their opinion of me is. They have seen me three nights this week with a different boy each time. I'm terrified of getting a reputation. One does if one has more than three particular men. Also, I'm becoming rather boy-mad.

Monday 12th August: There was a letter from Sam, very brief and enclosing two love poems to me "If you should go" and "The Spring is Quick" - very intelligent and unintelligible. Sam's not the sort to go slinging poems about to a kid of seventeen. Very dear of him, though.

ST. MARK'S COLLEGE
NORTH ADELAIDE

Dear Carys,

I have a suspicion it's quite appallingly indiscreet of me to send you these. However, there's always the w.p.b.

Sam.

P.S.   I'm feeling very bored already.

IF YOU SHOULD GO.

What ripening fair thy beauty
In me bears must fortify the core,
And stay a rampart where
False lights naked signals I ignore;
But might be shaken from me as a fire
If all beggars prisoners you restore,
All willing traitors you have captured there.
Yet since there was much purity of these
In the exchange, and more
Than my quick-sand government
Has learned to explore,
I could then foreswear peace,
Having won from war
Full balance in my humble fall.

THE SPRING IS QUICK.

Memory, in worlds for every wind
Uniting spring and fall,
Like grace in silent trees
Now stirs my parasite mind.

It is memory and I have come by steps,
And I the maker servant since
The sparks at setting out were struck
In the place those hands made of themselves,
Extended both by night and day as these
Of the memory before all desire,
Which burns at once in touch and thought.

Therefore my way is the ploughing
This slow enduring desert up,
And braver spring.
Scatter then the appalling stars,
As gaudy wolves, which cozen me.

Let thy mercy arm the flowers.

Tuesday 13th August: Today at Sargoods, all my errors (tiny, minute ones) grew black and heavy round my bowed head. I did begin a business letter to Sam but ripped it out of the machine when Mr Stevens pranced in like a canary. At lunch, I had mine in the Oxford Group Rooms with Pauline Bruce and Pat Moore, and didn't sling anything at all onto passersby. At Sibyl's, I read and ate almonds and raisins and Mrs Brookman, by slow and embarrassed degrees, confessed that she was writing her memoirs for the sake of her two girl children - and I was allowed to read the Almighty Work - very interesting.

Wednesday 14th August: Today I made mistake after mistake. I have probably lost the firm hundreds of pounds by now. My friends are faithful, however. Peter Anderson rang, asking me to go to a Paul Muni film on Saturday and the Tuxedo. Then Geoffrey Anderson rang and we made a date for next Wednesday and then Georg Klimont rang and we are going to the Repertory on Saturday week. After this deluge I must write a real letter to Sam. Men!

Thursday 15th August: As a matter of fact Sam rang last night too and we decided to go to Majestic Vaudeville tomorrow night, so after four different boys had rung me within one hour, I felt I was decidedly a Woman with a Reputation. I danced happily into town, having arisen at seven o'clock, and walked blindly into the black void of the basement of Sargood and Gardiner. Mr Pearce, Deputy Manager, told me the Vaudeville was unfunny and crude, so I rang Sam and he relievedly agreed to an Ozone picture theatre.

Friday 16th August: Mr Stevens drove off with Mr Veitch to sell trousers to the Kapundian natives and left me in charge of the office and

Al Slarks. I typed a letter to Daddy telling him to be good to Mummy during the divorce proceedings and to give her a good time. Home to tea. Sam came to take me to the pictures but we decided to go for a moonlight walk instead. We drove down to the beach, bought chocolate and gum, took a look at the shivering sea and got back into Petroff. We drove to Hallett's Cove, leant on a gate and talked and saw the lights glowing along the coast. Then we drove back to town. I renovated and we went to the new restaurant, "Quality Inn" and drank coffee and ate cinnamon toast, Sam being rather low in funds at that time. We talked until midnight - rather flighty, flirtatious talk and drove slowly home.

Saturday 17th August: This is the most perfect day I can remember. Mummy and I walked to town through green trees and blue mists and sparkling dew and slanting sun rays. I was paid at Sargoods - £2.10.0 and it was my first salary of all time - apart from pennies for killing snails and 5/- for my first published story. Peter Anderson called for me in a huge car, and we went to the Regent to see Paul Muni in "We Are Not Alone". We had lounge seats, I had a sweet partner, very happy, wonderful film, I wept. Then we went to the Tuxedo. I wore a navy blue and white check cotton frock with scarlet beads and trimming. I looked rather nice. It was the Tuxedo's first birthday. Reluctantly joined up with Alan Pilgrim and Po Bruce. Just danced with Alan and Peter, but didn't mind a scrap. I'm a little in love with Peter. We drove home at three thirty, chewing gum and waving balloons.

Monday 19th August: I nearly flung the Adelaide Branch into prison today, which would have disrupted the whole firm in every part of the world. I mucked up the banking and blissfully (and dumbly) altered the bank receipt after it had been stamped, to set things right. Mr Stevens sat over it for some time and then rang up the Australasian bank and got another receipt. Henry Martin, Tommy Simpson's friend, rang and asked me to go to a show tonight. Bed was dropped. He turned up in a Sailors uniform (joined for duration). We saw the Vaudeville, very weak and unfunny. Vignola's for asparagus and supper. Home in his car. He kissed me, unfortunately. I don't want to have to kiss every boy I go out with - 5 a week.

Wednesday 21st August: I went to the "Orfice" dressed up to the teeth in high heeled shoes, smart wool frock with scarlet trimmings and a small cocktail skull hat. After Sargoods, I met Geoffrey Anderson outside - all togged out in Air Force uniform with ridiculous peaked cap and wings. We drank advocaats at the Oriental and were about to stay to dinner there but went to a dive called Carr's Café where we had lobster and drank a toast "Mo Morituri, te Salutamus" (Hail, Emperor! Those who are about to die salute you) in Chablis. We had a wonderfully intellectual conversation in which I held my own. We beat Sam without a doubt. We had good seats in the lounge for Deanna Durbin in a good show called "First Love". Then we had coffee at the Athens Café. There was no time to go to the Tuxedo with friends, so trammed home as he had to be in barracks at twelve.

Thursday 22nd August: I received a note from Sammy telling me when he was calling tonight to take me to "Dido and Aeneas" - Clive Carey's opera, and telling me he would take me to anything I wanted to see if the opera didn't appeal. I replied by ringing him up and saying I couldn't make it tonight as I was chronically tired - the truth. He was extremely disappointed (wrote and said so). I went to the office. Felt very cold down "there". Like going back to Hades, further further into the gloom without even a Cerberus to talk to - only Alf. I struggled to bed early after practising, had no regrets about Sam (having grown by this time into a Scarlett O'Hara) and slept. Nothing lovelier than cool sheets and a long empty night ahead.

Friday 23rd August: Peter Anderson came into the office (we have been carrying on correspondence purely businesslike through our office boys) and giggled at me over my counter and arranged about tonight. Arrived in his luxurious car, took me to dinner at the South, drank Chablis and talked too much, and then drove to the Regent to see "Rebecca". We chatted to Richard and his friend Barb Kelly during the interval. The film was excellent, theatre packed, perfect seats, perfect partner, terribly tired both of us. We were egged into going to the Tuxedo with others there, so drove blearily round. Artie played my tune and had some drinks with us. Derry came about twenty minutes before we left at one o'clock. Had time only for one dance with me, and he begged me to stay on. He nobly drove the rest home, and I went alone with Peter.

Saturday 24th August: I am in love with Peter partly because, in spite of Derry's lurid stories to the contrary, he is difficult to get. I am becoming awfully spoilt. I don't understand how it happens, but I have so many boys all of a sudden, and I'm not a dazzling beauty. If a day goes by without at least two boys ringing up I feel like an old maid. Georg Klimont came at seven dressed in perfect evening clothes. I dashed off and changed into blue evening clothes too and Lillian drove us to the Repertory. It was a good show; and we could both understand the Irish accents. It was called "Spring Meeting"- an Irish comedy. Came home in the tram although last night Peter offered me his own car, a sweet but impossible offer.

Monday 26th August: I went to Sargoods and Mr Stevens told me very nicely that this job of mine had been a trial and a not very successful trial and he had found me a position with a Mr Reed. The maths, he felt, had stumped, and always would, stump me. I felt rather sorry about things because, although I didn't care two pence about leaving the job, I felt I had been getting on fairly well, apart from banking and extensions. At lunchtime, Richard lectured me harshly while I wept into my milkshake.

Tuesday 27th August: I went to see Mr Reed, the lawyer. He seems terribly nice. Carpets, a window with some real live sun, good furniture and an absence of commercial travellers and soft goods. I'm a joint secretary to a K.C. and Sir Lavington Bonython. I had lunch with Sammy and he is breaking his heart over me. He won't pass any exams in his state. He thinks I treat him as a habit - worse than a piece of furniture. It's not true. He works himself up; he will know about his chances for a Rhodes scholarship on Friday.

Thursday 29th August: In the morning, I saw Peter walking to town while I was on the tram and he took off his hat and waved it all the way down the street. At lunch I had it at Mr Reed's while a Miss Conroy showed me the works and buzzed switchboards in my ear. Derry is very thrilled because his father's office is just downstairs in the Steamship buildings, where I am to work, and so he will visit his father a lot. Gosh! I can't help being fired! Dashed home, dressed in tulle and velvet and furs, and sold lucky matchboxes at the Miller Anderson Red Cross Parade at the Royal. The most fashionable audience I have seen in Adelaide - from Lady Gowrie down to me. Mummy went with Lady Sandford, and I sat on the steps by her, and in a vacant chair with the Chamberlain twins. There were huge crowds selling flowers, orchids from Java and Burma, debutantes in white frocks - Vice- Regal Parties are awfully slow but amusing though, and patriotic. The whole theatre shouted "There'll always be an England" at the end.

Friday 30th August: Derry rang saying he couldn't take me to the pictures because his father was taking his car to a bird meeting. The thought interests and intrigues me. I have been jilted because of a canary! I persuaded Alf to watch the office and went for the mail. I saw Peter going into the Town Hall to humbly pay a fine. He meekly gave his money in and they took it with drawn brows. Poor darling, I do love him. After lunch, I walked back to the University to see if Sammy had won the Rhodes scholarship. There is no news. After work, I wandered home across the links. I rang Sammy at St Mark's and Andrew Wells of all people has won it. Sam was a bit depressed, I think, but I hope my ringing and saying I had thought of him all day helped. Settling down for the evening, Henry Martin rang asking me to the films. It was teeming with rain. I dashed to the sports car with him and fell in on Tommy. They both took me to the Regent. I felt very proud of Henry and Tommy on either side. At least I don't have to kiss two goodnight.

Saturday 31st August: Peter and Derry and Billy Bray asked me to go out tonight. I am going to a Thomas Beecham concert with Sam. A sunny afternoon. I slept in Mummy's bed, practised, Sammy turned up after Peter had rung again urging me to go to the Tuxedo after Beecham. I couldn't, of course. Perfect Beecham concert. He is a most spectacular, thrilling conductor, huge crowds, Mozart, Haydn, Sibelius, a splendid Delius, and Wagner. It thrilled and fascinated me. Then on to Vignola. There it began. Sammy told me quite frankly he couldn't go on in this "friendly" fashion. He was terribly in love with me and the self-control was over-coming him. He was foolishly jealous of every boy I looked at; he never dreamed of going out with anyone else yet I went out every night with someone different. We had a proper bust up. He said he couldn't go on without kissing me and so on, and now, after this, it was quite impossible. He wanted to give the whole thing up but I persuaded him against this. He was most unhappy. I hate hurting him, but I can't do anything about it. I don't love him.

Sunday 1st September: Sammy, last night, was talking about my friends, sweet, rather empty headed people when Tommy Simpson and two boys I know, Eddie and Spog came in. That just about finished it. They greeted me as old friends, and so after a bit Sammy and I left. He took them as examples and said I was worthy of something better. I disagree. I want fun at seventeen, not a husband. They give it to me - good, unspoilt fun. I'm not keen on any of them (bare Peter) and they are not on me, I think. Slept, during the morning, dressed, practised, lunch, diary, Sunday school. Poor Sammy! I can't stop thinking of him being unhappy. I went to Sibyl's for afternoon tea and wound army wool. The family bickered and nagged a lot, Mrs Brookman tired and untidy, Mrs Shiels harping, Sibyl harping and Michael (the cause) in bed with this "Woodside Throat". We had tea, and Graham tore back on his motorbike with me pillion, hanging round his waist, while I put on decent clothes and Sibyl and I went to Christ Church. I felt waves of sleep surging over me every few minutes. The service was good, the choir boys sang Handel, and the sermon as usual was uninspired.

Monday 2nd September: I walked to town to be at Mr Reed, K.C. and Sir Lavington Bonython's office at half past nine. I had a chat with Mr Reed about secrecy and diplomacy and became very fond of him. I like Sir Lavington and Miss Gilbert and Miss Conroy (a rough, pleasant, blunt creature) but don't seem to stick Mr John Bonython, Sir Lavington's son. He is rather bloated and casual. I went for quite a lot of walks getting things, and made quite a lot of tea in blue china cups. I walked home and after tea caught a taxi to the station and saw Richard off to Sydney for two months. He swears he will never come back to Adelaide to live, and he might not, because he is going to the war immediately after this. He kissed me goodbye. We walked back and it is very cold. Sammy sent me "a peace offering" - "Portrait of the Artist as a Young Man" by James

Joyce. Thrilling. I am expecting a telephone call from a young man with an abrupt voice. Peter!

Tuesday 3rd September: I picked flowers for the office and sauntered to town across the links with dew and mist everywhere and birds walking around in it. I arranged lavender and freesias and ranunculi, and put scarlet and yellow nasturtiums in a green vase for Miss Gilbert. I took down long notes on an opinion most of the day and typed them back. A smooth pad, a smooth pencil, a slow voice, a carpet, a window, and a big oak desk make the performance rather pleasant. Lady Bonython came in and surveyed me and told me I "had grown" which is polite but not true. At lunch I had a fitting for a Liberty silk floral frock for Saturday night, when I am having dinner at the Anderson's. I want the parents to like me!

Wednesday 4th September: I never mention the war. It is not egotism. Every day the headlines are the same - violent raids on England - bombs dropped on Berlin - Southampton under fire - Cologne destroyed. It goes on in an unholy cycle. I met Derry by chance at morning teatime, and we consumed milk and coffee, chatted and parted with the usual promises that are always broken. Sibyl wrote to me in the night and said she loved Billy Bray after fourteen years of feuding with him. Could she have him? I shall write and give him to her. She swears he's keen on me.

Thursday 5th September: I had an intellectual lunch with Sammy at the Quality Inn, and instead of being difficult the atmosphere was quite gentle. He asked me once if I had got over his onslaught. I nodded between an asparagus and egg salad. We discussed Milton and Joyce and Tolstoy and Vice-Chancellors and Socialism and the two debs at the same table thought we were showing off and sniggered but I didn't care. Philistine versus Dilettante. That evening, I returned to the fold once more from my literary lapse, owing to Sargood- Gardiner and too many Tommies, and went to the W.E.A. after some months.

Saturday 7th September: I spent the afternoon getting ready and making sprays for Mummy and me. She is going to the films with Lady Bruce. Dressed in my lovely new Liberty silk frock, grey coat, yellow spray of tuber roses, Peter came in the car that awes me; huge, lovely home; his father is eighty! His mother is sweet. We had a grand five course dinner, maids serving with silver dishes, finger bowls, had claret, sherry, coffee. Saw naked photos of Peter aged one. We then drove to see "Pinocchio", Disney's second full length cartoon. The film is amazing and flawless. Jiminy Cricket, the "conscience", a skit on a Hollywood publicity agent, stole the show - "acted well!" Then to the Tuxedo. We stayed until four o'clock.

Sunday 8th September: I slept until ten to one and Peter rang to apologize to Mother (who adores him) for keeping me out so late. Apparently, he too, slept until ten to one. It is mutual sympathy and telepathy. I promised him to go to bed early tonight. In the evening, after tea (of asparagus dripping with butter) we went to church because the King "said so". It was a National Day of Prayer and everyone marched about the Adelaide Oval in uniforms and sang hymns and asked God to win the war for the Empire - a very laudable and good move.

Monday 9th September: Derry, to my surprise, came to see me and threatened in the nastiest voice, to kill Peter. He hates him now. He had a proper bust up with Peter over me. England is being bombed mercilessly but she is hanging on - the main result is that the English are filled with hate and revenge. Seven hour raids over London nearly every day; factories have decided to go on working during alarms. The thing will never stop; there is no ending - bomb for bomb - building for building - civilian for civilian. It will go on until someone breaks, but human powers of endurance are amazingly strong. I had dinner at the Brookman's where Wody Blackburn is staying; we talked and knitted and shrieked over "Petroushka" playing on the gramophone, Sibyl having not yet become fully freed of it. The two, whom I adore, strolled back with me. They think I have grown up terribly suddenly; from the virginity of the Leaving. They think the Tuxedo and Art Maskell and my friends are the height of wickedness - but exciting and something to be coveted.

Tuesday 10th September: I met Derry in town looking extremely woeful, because it was his birthday and everyone had forgotten. All he received was one packet of cigarettes from an anonymous donor. His mother is far too busy with the horses to remember. I tried to buck him up, but I keep thinking of Peter, and can't.

Wednesday 11th September: There is never anything to do at Mr Reed's. I have taken to dusting his books and reading the most interesting parts, only, as Mr Bonython said, "they are heavy without and heavy within". At lunch I revelled among dress materials, choosing stuff for shorts and blouses and sea coats. Everything is very gay and American and in extremely bad taste. I chose things that are "cute". Tonight I actually went to bed early, hoping no-one would come round. Sam rang up, dithered over the phone and made me tired and intolerant, simply furious. I read Joyce for an hour and slept.

Friday 13th September: Georg called for me and Lillian drove us in. I was a little cross because I had to put Henry and Tommy off. We saw "Raffles" with David Niven and an Irish tragedy. Both were excellent. We raced for a tram, and Georg was very sweet and interesting and Austrian and refugee-like but I think I shall stick to Henrys and Tommies.

Saturday 14th September: Peter drove me home from work. I walked to the Orient Line where his father is the agent, and got into his dreadful car. It rattles, is badly painted a staring white, you have to hold the doors on and things fall off. I made him dash down King William Street and we saw everyone we knew including Sibyl and Wody sniggering after us. I am restless and unhappy because I love him. He is going to the same picture tonight in Po Bruce's party with Joan Brennan and me with Sam! Oh! Darn Sam. I shall smile politely at Peter, and feel guilty. I've a good mind to chuck everyone up for Peter. I'm terribly tired of Sam. I'm tired. Sam came for me in a terrible mood. He reminded me of a minor Heathcliff. We saw the film "Balalaika" with Nelson Eddy and lovely Ilona Massey. Sam loathed it, I liked it. I evaded Peter although he was looking out for me. I told Sam I didn't want to have supper with him in his present mood, so he darkly turned the car and took me home, saying he was feeling exactly as he did a fortnight ago. I told him I couldn't do anything; I was fond of him, but not in love with him. He said he was disappointed in me and that he apparently could keep his intellectual integrity whereas I couldn't. That infuriated me. I pointed out that I couldn't be one mass of intellect; he wasn't and that it was ten times easier at a University, than an office. So we parted for good - a strange "world without Sam".

Sunday 15th September: "Worlds without Sam". I felt rather unhappy about him last night, because he is so wildly miserable, and in earnest, and unusual and brilliant. But there is sun in the streets and blue, blue, blue sky and green things all over the trees. I taught a solitary and un-tempted child about Isaiah. I wore my new navy and white knotted sandals, a blue linen frock and spring coat with musk lapels. I can't help being unmoved and empty and utterly shallow. Yesterday, the King and Queen were bombed out of Buckingham Palace, St Paul's was threatened by bombs and fire, and the House of Lords with a great many other famous landmarks has been harmed. There is a new fund for helping the British civilian casualties - first for the Poles and the Czechs and now England. It makes me want to scream out "There'll always be an England" from the top of the world. A kind of prayer in the subjunctive.

Monday 16th September: Thus begins the second week of the Blitzkrieg on England. I walked to town rather unhappily and past the low doorway where three Italians are machining suits, and in my office arranged lavender and ranunculi. I did nothing else all day, except make morning and afternoon tea and tell Mr Reed my opinion on an interesting case. His wife told Mother that he had said of me, "She is very young, but intelligent, which is a change. Yesterday I gave her a book of legal phrases and the result was amazing". Gratifying, although I only remember asking a few dumb questions about reformatories. I lunched with the Chamberlain twins who are unspoiled and innocent and credulous. All day I read James Joyce until I am fired to write again in his peculiar style.

Tuesday 17th September: To my amazement Sam wrote - a very sincere, sweet letter and Lillian is dying to see it. I shall answer it. It is a light, summer evening. I shall write.

Wednesday 18th September: It is dark and wintery again with a few summer frocks hiding beneath dripping umbrellas. The newsboys always shout louder when the streets are wet. This time it is the Italian advance in Egypt. I trammed home and saw Peter drive past in his car "Maurice", having tied the doors on with greasy strips of rag, searching the tram for me.

Thursday 19th September: The last few days have been quite full of opinions. Mr Reed, quite seriously, even asked my opinion on one today. I gave it to him, quite seriously. Peter rang and asked me to lunch with him. I have seen or heard from him every day this week. Looking as glamorous as possible, I met him at Birks and ate Lobster Mayonnaise and drank milk and had nothing else. He said he was worried because I had "renounced" so many people lately (Georg, Sam, Derry, Herbert). Would he be next? I didn't tell the little fool it was only because of him, that most of them had parted from me.

Friday 20th September: I awoke with a happy sensation, thinking it was my birthday then remembered it was Peter's. I sent him a packet of chewing gum, labeled, sealed, gummed and strung and he rang, thanking me in mirth and saying he had joined the A.I.F. and had been passed medically as well. A patriotic gesture on immediately coming to the right (or wrong) age of twenty. Peter came at seven thirty in the Hudson (Not Maurice, according to promise). We saw the film "Four Sons" - about the Nazi occupation of Czechoslovakia with Eugenie Leontovich and Don Ameche - harrowing with Peter bound for war in Egypt, and Richard for the war in Europe. We went to the Tuxedo as it was his birthday. A few there; we danced for an hour, I drank milk and every one of the waiters collected to see how much it cost! Drove home and sat in the car talking for some time. I think he is very fond of me; he definitely wants a photograph. He didn't kiss me. I am not a little vixen but I want him to.

Sunday 22nd September: Peter came in Maurice and I introduced him to Mummy at last. Mic Sandford came then and we smoked and drank sherry and had a lovely High Tea with the two on either side. Nine days ago I met Mic in town and after saluting me, I had asked him to tea. He simply suffuses you with his personality without allowing you to fall in love with him. He was very clever and entertaining and made the most embarrassing remarks to both Peter and me. Peter quiet but easy to manage, and shy. In spite of Mic, in comparison with Mic, he was still enchanting. We talked and smoked by the fire and had supper. Peter's rattletrap Maurice wouldn't go so, after cranking it furiously, we pushed him down the hill.

Monday 23rd September: Peter completely rules my life. Even my work. Messages become exciting, because I might see him. Telephones are the most exciting things of all. I see or hear from him every day. Today his office boy came round with a letter - a cutting from a Classified Ad about a Viennese boy wanting to meet an English girl. Was it Georg looking for my successor? I wanted to answer it. Yet there was no boy of my own and his car was not in its usual place. An Adelaide Steamship boy took a letter to him with "As though I care!" on a large sheet of paper. It wasn't meant to be squashing. Sorry diary, but this is becoming more and more boring. I am in love.

Tuesday 24th September: Yesterday a refugee ship going to America, carrying London children, was torpedoed and sunk. Ninety four children were drowned. They were marvellous. They actually sang, children of ten, while they pushed the dead bodies of other children into the sea from the life boats. I think it is the worst thing of the war. I heard the King's speech. He has created the George Cross for civilian bravery, coming after the Victoria Cross. Peter rang, asking me to lunch tomorrow and we made a date, involving Maurice and the Torrens and lunch in paper bags! As I was walking home, Peter emerged out of a very hot sun, tie flying, and hat in hand. He walked home with me, carrying my silly little suitcase, because at lunch I went to music and needed it. I mustn't lose Peter. Mummy adores him and is terribly keen to marry me off. He wrote her a sweet letter of thanks today.

Thursday 26th September: Oscar Symon, extraordinary son of Sir Josiah Symon, had a long talk with me this morning about writing, philosophy and psychology. He has some excellent ideas, one of them is to keep a diary of the things that interested him during the day - small things. I decided to try but knew it would be the same as this - Peter. Had a fitting at lunch time and Mummy told me she might become Head of the Misses Frock salon at Myers and a Melbourne buyer. Lady Sandford persuaded me to go with Mummy and her to the Symphony concert at the Town Hall, though I was sorry to miss the W.E.A. I arrived, dripping furs and gingham, and saw Sammy. Instead of blushing furiously I waved eagerly to him at the gathering of St Mark's in the gallery and sailed in -

poor Sammy - with Mic Sandford. William Cade was the conductor and Oscar Natzke was the bass baritone. Lovely Vaughan Williams, Beethoven, Liszt and Verdi. The audience was thrilled. Grinning at Sam, I went home with the Sandfords.

Friday 27th September: I met Peter at the National Bank and waited while he staggered out with the Orient Line takings. I had lunch with the Chamberlain twins. They are very sweet and very popular. I can't keep my own secrets. I bumped into Dick Wills and Pup Beaumont (of the Derry, Peter, Tux night) and Dick, looking like Anthony Eden, was walking blithely through town with two white feathers in his lapels - gifts from some Old Lady. He is getting Peter and me to join them at the Tuxedo after the dance tomorrow. They are a fast, faintly dissolute, but decent pair.

Saturday 28th September: After working in the morning I came home and found Mummy dashing wildly up and down the hall, getting ready for her trip to Sydney tonight. She has some lovely things. I dithered and got excited with her. After dinner (our last together for a month) I put on the freshly ironed tulle and black velvet, a veil round my hair and we drove to the station. I saw the darling off and left her in Colonel Blackburn's charge, as the troops were leaving. Peter and Alain Harvey were on the ramp. We drove down to a Brighton Local Dance, to Good-Walters party. I was wild with happiness. Had thousands of partners, including locals. I adored and adored it. We drove the others home and went to the Grotto and met up with Dick Wills, Derry Paterson and Pup Beaumont. Foul place, mauling drunk people, crowds, and fug. Peter said he loved me in the middle of it. He was terribly ashamed at bringing me there but I wouldn't leave under two hours. We drove home slowly and were terribly in love with each other. It was quite different from anything I had known before; it wasn't even like a magnified pash. A new feeling. I shan't go into it. I wrote Mummy a long, long letter, and there are things - I felt madly happy, and so did he. This is a difficult day to write about in cold blood and black ink.

Tuesday 1st October: I am shivering with excitement because I shall see Peter tonight. I evaded him in town when I saw him today by darting down a side street. I suddenly felt scared at seeing him, as though his love might not live up to hot streets, and hurrying people and bank pay-in books. He came after dinner and there were cigarettes and a fire and a nice supper and bowls of roses, and lamp light. He wound wool for me and we talked. He held me so tightly I could scarcely breathe. I adore him. He is mad to marry me, but we are such children. We cursed our age. I felt terribly unhappy and in love when he had gone.

Wednesday 2nd October: I had lunch with friends but I tell no-one about proposals, although I unburden myself to Mummy in huge letters. Lillian knows and I am angry with myself. I should not discuss these things with her. Her outlook is warped and mercenary. "I have made a good catch." I shan't in future, but I break these good intentions, just as I don't practise the piano. Peter walked home with me slowly across the links and I trembled with excitement to have him with me. Yet, I feel the thing to be scared of is not Peter ceasing to love me, but I stop loving him. It is a strange thought, but I have learnt to distrust my feelings. It makes me feel wretchedly unhappy. I told Sibyl I had had a proposal. After all, she is my best friend.

Friday 4th October: Peter came in the Hudson (Maurice has gone out of action for all time, Amen) and took me back for dinner. Only Mrs Anderson for dinner. Very grand but it doesn't frighten me now, because it is Peter's home. Upstairs in her bedroom, Mrs Anderson put her arm round me and said we were such babies, but she was glad it was me and that already I had been so good for Peter. She kissed us both goodbye when we left. I shall not see Peter for three days because he is going away.

Saturday 5th October: I went to the Wilderness Old Scholar's Garden Party, ate a huge afternoon tea, saw the old rooms decorated with flowers and sang a little and met everyone. I came home laden with flowers, including four lily of the valley which Sammy promised me. He wrote to me yesterday and said he must see me. What can I do? I don't go out with anyone but Peter now. I have refused Billy Bray, and the Tuxedo tonight. I will refuse.

Sunday 6th October: I gardened during the morning in the heat in the old sandals and dirndl and sun hat. There is even a faint difference in the Estate. Bryan is away camping at Victor Harbor. At Sunday school we rehearsed a screaming play in which the whole class show off with appalling zeal. I practised the piano at home and had tea at the Brookman's. Mr Brookman is very ill; in fact, they are convinced that he is dying. He totters round in a white, doped way. At home, Lillian is entertaining friends in the dining room.

Monday 7th October: I odd jobbed and Sibyl came, after Lillian had cleared out, looking like Dietrich, in slacks and sunglasses. We got our lunch and darned and read old diaries and went to her place in dirndls and sandals. Found Mrs Brookman really hysterical over Mr Brookman, which amazes me as they are hardly ever on speaking terms. We got an eggy-asparagus tea, had the usual arguments about the war and I came home early to write letters. At midnight a call came from Sydney. It was Daddy to tell me he had kept his promise and was being good to Mummy during the divorce. It was so strange hearing Daddy's voice. It was ponderous and of deep quality and ended always with a sort of cough, as though he wanted to know if I were still there. I found it difficult to talk - yet we rushed through nine minutes.

Saturday 12th October: Peter dined at the Brookman's. They attempted to be very grand with squashed grapefruit in tall glasses, but broke down under the strain and finished in true Brookman manner, with Betty Bagot, a frequent guest, spilling the sugar down Peter's neck and slinging food and dishes about and Sibyl yanking out the finest plates and saying they "would be covered in dust".

Wednesday 16th October: I had lunch with Peter at the Maple Leaf where we always go now. The darling, with true youthful vigour, had written poems about me and kept them in utter pride and secrecy in his wallet. They reminded me of Sam's - clever, unintelligible, and very intelligent. I love Peter's better - the ones I haven't seen because they are "so bad". They are getting to know us at the Maple Leaf. The waitresses regard us sympathetically and with profound, professional understanding. Peter says our meals are getting cheaper every day.

Thursday 17th October: Peter has a present for me and he is going to give it to me tomorrow night. We had lunch at the Maple Leaf and he changed his mind and gave it to me there, across the table. It is a pendant that belonged to his grandmother - very old, very lovely, with a diamond coronet with two pearl sprigged pendants, holding aquamarine stones. It is delicate and splendid and wonderful. I can't get over it. I want to cry all afternoon with happiness - that Peter gave it to me and that his mother in turn gave it to him for me.

Friday 18th October: I had a large breakfast but was violently sick after it, and have felt pretty sick ever since. It must be too many late nights, excitement and worry and Mummy coming home. I had lunch with Peter and I always fall even more in love with him every time I see him. He is so young and serious and happy alternatively. He felt today that he had been terribly selfish and nothing would make him change his mind. In the evening Peter called for me. I wore the blue taffeta frock and pendant and felt terribly sick. I nearly didn't go. Peter is too sympathetic. He spoils me. I went to the Andersons and didn't eat a thing. They were all very concerned. I feel very weak and empty but am not hungry.

Saturday 19th October: Peter rang at eight and called for Bryan and me in a taxi which was simply adorable of him. I felt terribly low but better when they arrived - Mummy as smart as ever and lovely and Richard, brown and good looking and younger than Peter! After some thought, I went to the office although I still couldn't eat any breakfast. I saw Peter a good many times during the morning, mainly banking. Kym Bonython, the younger son of Sir Lavington, came in as a Pilot Officer and saluted me a lot and said he had had dinner on the train with the family. He is a darling. When I arrived home, I received heavenly presents from the family; a soft, white squashy bag of kid from Richard, a white, twisted string of beads from Mother and some American rough weave green and white shorts and a Hawaiian top, too. I proudly presented my pendant.

Sunday 20th October: As a family we are having such fun together again. The boys are slinking about in coloured American coolie coats and Richard said he gave me a very special kiss on the platform just so as Peter would know he had a right, too!

Wednesday 23rd October: I had one of the worst nights I remember. I was sick and sick and sick, about seven times during the night. It wretched me to bits. The doctor suggested ice at eleven o'clock. It was a help.

Thursday 24th October: I stayed in bed till the doctor came, and Mummy waited although her job is important now. She might be made a Head of her Department at Myers. The doctor examined me and said he was going to see the thing through to the hilt and I was to go to Hospital and not see or hear from a soul. Peter, Peter is all I think of. My mother too, but somehow, Peter... The expense worries me. I rang the office and Peter rang me. When I told him I was getting dressed to go to Hospital, he said he shook at the knees and his voice was strained and scared. Lillian drove us in and they stuck me in a high, white hard bed with an old woman called Mrs Jarman of about 300, in another bed. Miss Gilbert from the office brightened my lonely existence by sending me carnations. My eyes sting and I am tired and lonely. I am only allowed to drink liquids today. I read magazines a little, slept and cried myself to sleep.

Friday 25th October: They make the day very long here by waking us at six o'clock and swabbing us down and rubbing us in methylated spirits. I ate a large breakfast heartily and Dr Wigg came and told me I could write one letter. I wrote a long letter to Peter. Some flowers - lupins, carnations, cornflowers and Canterbury bells arrived from him, with a veiled note because he cannot write to me! Old Mrs Jarman's friends are most amusing. I thought only voices like theirs existed in Australian satires.

Saturday 26th October: They took a long time to wash the decks today and when they weighed me I was only six stone and ten ounces. Dr Wigg came and said they would not operate or stick tubes down me, just fatten me up. Peter's flowers are everywhere. Some yellow tulips arrived - nameless. They do not tell me now who even sends things. When I am all mussed up and tearful and hot they are good company - tall, cool, long, smooth stemmed. I think they are Peter's.

Sunday 27th October: Nothing happened. No one came. I read and knitted a little and slept a little and listened to old Mrs Jarman making a nuisance of herself. Even Doctor Wigg didn't come today. And in the evening with the night-light on, and washed and brushed, I howled and howled damp salt tears into my pillow out of sheer loneliness. I knew I had nothing to sob about - no pain - but it gave me immense pleasure and I went triumphantly through three handkerchiefs.

Monday 28th October: This was a happy day. I felt sparking, ate a lot, and read hundreds of pages of "Outline of Literature". I was weighed again and taken in a wheelchair and had put on 2 lbs in two days. Happily weary so got tidied up early and, all cosy, went to sleep. I was vaguely dreaming about Peter in the night-light when I looked up and there was Peter at the other end of my bed! He had brought some magazines, a letter and a photo and himself. He had broken all his promises and there he was. I could hardly breathe; it was so dark and silent. He threw himself down by me and kissed me, and he was so cool and rough and gentle. Then he said he would have gone mad if he had not seen me; and left. He came and went in about a minute. I still can't believe it. I laughed myself to sleep. He must have been a dream.

Tuesday 29th October: I awoke with laryngitis, a headache, aching eyes and my legs ached as well through disuse. So perhaps Doctor Wigg was right. What do I care? I have that memory - and no more doubts. It makes me shiver with excitement at my adventure - our guilty adventure! Some more anonymous flowers came - carnations and roses. I have given up wondering who they are from. I lay in bed for hours in the evening, day dreaming.

Wednesday 30th October: You may notice that I don't mention treatment or pain or anything - because there isn't any. All I can dig up is a sore throat. They are just fattening me up and won't let me waste any energy whatever. I must reach a certain weight - 14 stone! They took Mrs Jarman home so I am by the window in the room alone. The tulips are almost withered. They let me go out on the verandah so I lay all afternoon with my eyes glued on the cloud effects and the gate. Sure enough, at 5.15pm Peter walked in and talked to me for half an hour from the garden like Romeo. I had numerous unofficial visits and Mummy. Yet I feel on air. There is a very sweet, wired posy of miniature roses from someone.

Thursday 31st October: Dr Wigg disappointed me by not coming. He may be hard but he is a sort of visitor. And I had rather a guilty conscience to unburden. They decided I had better not go on the verandah again as my guests were noted and viewed with disapproval. Mrs Snell, who is now with me in Mrs Jarman's place, is pretty ill and probably finds me a boisterous room-mate. I am getting restless and gay. She disapproves of me, I think. I have lead them all to believe that sheer dissipation landed me where I am! Sleep in my hard, white bed.

Friday 1st November: I went for a walk today, shakily up to the bathroom and shakily back again. Mrs Snell is terribly prejudiced and intolerant. She appears to think education is the curse of modern child upbringing, that their eye sight is more important, and the waste of electric light! She insisted on the waste of electric light. More flowers. I know they are Sibyl's by the colouring.

Saturday 2nd November: The doctor came and blew Sibyl up for a most ridiculous, and highly diverting note she sent which didn't get past the censors. She condemned the Memorial Hospital - "this dump" and the doctor in one breath of humorous invective, but it was taken darkly by her victims! I told Mrs Snell she wasn't a Christian because she condemned all natives who dared imagine themselves equal to the Great White Race. I boiled and seethed, but remained comparatively quiet. Mummy came to see me, my first official visit, but I cannot go home until tomorrow; so here I sit, in a blanketed chair, on the balcony, watching the cloud effects and the gate.....I found out that there was another war in Greece, invaded by Mussolini, but everything turned against him.

Sunday 3rd November: Today Bryan and Mummy drove up in Lillian's car and I came joyfully home. I noted a few changes, dithered happily and shakily, entertained Sibyl for afternoon tea and washed my hair. I sat in smug satisfaction by my own hearth once more, was terrified I would be sick again and sent back to Hospital. Was sick again. Peter came and after tea the rest rather obviously returned - Church, homework, radio programmes. Peter and I sat by the fire and he got it into his silly head that I didn't love him so much. He was so unhappy.

Monday 4th November: I awoke sick today, and feeling fed up because of it. I lay in bed for half the morning, pecking at my food again and cursing high heaven. In the garden, I talked to Richard while he drew me. We had some interesting discussions.

Wednesday 6th November: I was given a fairly good reception at the office. Miss Conroy is almost a nervous wreck and is quickly acquiring a warped outlook. Mr Reed was very decent and suggested I stay away a bit longer to really recuperate - then immediately loaded me with all the work he had saved for me. Later I met Peter in the middle of Wellington Square, and he was there, in the ridiculous suede shoes with the round toes, a silk scarf, a sport's tweed coat and an open shirt. We dashed along, holding hands, to the river and along the banks under the willows away from the city. We sat on park gates and the greens on the links and picked grass seeds out of our socks. He is delightfully sentimental for a boy of his sort. Yesterday, I gave him a very small curl of my hair for him. He is fast collecting a museum, kept in all his pockets and beginning from a short hand message that I wrote him at room No 9, Napoleon Hotel, when I met him with Derry, many, many weeks ago.

Thursday 7th November: It is my birthday and I am eighteen years old. I dashed home after work, felt sick, dressed and Lillian drove us into the South Australian Hotel where we met Peter. We had dinner - a celebration of my birthday and a party for Richard who is leaving on Saturday by train for Pearce in Western Australia, to an aviation camp. It is a long, filthy journey. The war has begun for him.

Friday 8th November: Mr Chamberlain, former British Prime Minister, has died, aged 72. He tried so hard, but he just faded out with almost no talk. All talk, when we do talk of it, is of the Greek's wonderful advance into Italy, and Roosevelt's third term.

Sunday 10th November: I rang the Baptist Church today and suggested that I put Sunday school teaching off for a while - general idea being to recuperate but main reason being that now Peter and I can only have a short weekend together in future. I suppose it is weak. I can't spare a whole afternoon. They agreed. I suppose it is weak; I'm not very strong minded. I love Peter.

Tuesday 12th November: Coventry, in England, has been horribly wrecked, and the Cathedral bombed beyond repair. They show us pictures of the Cathedral as it was, and I want to strangle every war monger. They give us a list of people killed in Germany by our planes - 200 casualties in Bremen, etc. After being so desperately "tolerant", all I think of such figures is, "A bit of their own medicine". We got a letter from Richard on

Y.M.C.A. paper and crowded with morals on the letterhead. He says it is a marvellous life and says the only good part of war is the meeting of fine men you would not have come in contact with in private life.

Thursday 14th November: Today Peter and I lunched at the Vignola and at the table where Sammy and I had our first bust up. In four days time Peter will be in civilian clothes for the last time. It is a good thing that he should go to Woodside. We both feel that we have been seeing each other far too much - yet wouldn't have it otherwise. Michael Brookman is leaving for overseas in four days time to the Middle East. John Langdon Bonython from my office is going into camp; Peter's I think. Captain Bonython and Gunner Anderson.

Tuesday 26th November: Today is the opening of the exams and Bryan has taken the whole thing with unheard of calm, when Richard and I were in a blue funk. Peter came. He looks so awful in his shapeless uniform, but so awfully dear, with a sunburnt nose that makes him look about five years younger. Yesterday, he had the day off for examinations for the A.I.F. which he has passed.

Thursday 28th November: Last night, Mrs Brookman went to the pack-a war mania, to send parcels overseas to Michael's regiment. Sibyl doesn't think Peter is worthy of me. She thinks he is nice, but effeminate. She likes hefty athletes. Sam wrote a brief and clever answer to my congratulations. He has won the main award at University for English literature, the John Howard Clark prize. He evidently is still suffering over me; Sam, like the proverbial elephant, is not one to forget too easily - and very careful not to put himself in a position to be snubbed again.

Thursday 5th December: Today was heavy, hot and headachy; the sky was yellow with dust and grit, and it swirled up in driving eddies under one's skirts and into one's eyes - crossing a road was the extreme of irritation. I had a rather enjoyable morning, sitting at my desk in a cool room, writing up Acts, which come pouring out of a prolific State Parliament, now that it has finished sitting. At lunch, I bought more Xmas presents and during the afternoon wrote letters. Things are quiet and I get sick of making tea for other people and washing up like a cafeteria waitress. There is something very petty about the Bonython clan and their retainers. Miss

Gilbert is the worst crawler I know. Today Pilot Officer Colin Chapman, a friend of Graham's, was reported missing, on his first bombing raid with the R.A.F., aged nineteen. It has upset me beyond words. He was just beginning his "party" stage with girls a year ago - an absolute baby.

Friday 6th December: Peter made his will yesterday. He told me his assets are four thousand pounds and that he has left everything to his trustee, his father and before he leaves he will direct that it be transferred to me. I love his generosity; I hate his blood money.

Sunday 8th December: Peter admitted with shame last night that he didn't much like the A.I.F. The fellows were all as hard and tough as nails and the discipline was terribly severe. He was homesick and confessed that for the first time in years he had been near crying last night. That was apparently his greatest shame of all! He is pretty patriotic in a quiet sort of way. He had to go back to camp early. Today he rang and said that, unexpectedly, he could come down tonight. I told him I was going to Sibyl's to tea, and Mummy said I sounded a bit curt. That worried me; I hope he does come, so that I can allay the usual fears that arise. He rang, saying he couldn't come after all and apparently the fears hadn't arisen because I had to overcome his ideas on A.W.L. (Absent without Leave). Went to Sibyl's and after dinner, we had a reckless drive in her sports car which was once Michael's, along lonely hill roads and I came home, a wind-blown wreck.

Monday 9th December: There was a letter from Richard on my return from work. He adores the two letters I have written and begs for more. I am glad because I am always a little self-conscious writing to him, fearing he will think I am trying to impress him with my style. There are tremendous military scandals going on in the Italian Army. Every week an average of two generals resign and two today have been mysteriously killed. Mussolini must be biting his lip to think he started this wretched war which might someday, be Peter's war. Visited Mr Brookman in hospital with Sibyl and Aunt Polly and Bizz Brookman. He is getting better since he's had a brunette nurse.

Friday 13th December: Another hot day, but with a cooling breeze later on. I trammed (it being Pay Day) and worked pretty hard the whole time, feeling a little snappy continually. At lunch I walked out hastily, always a little scared that "they" will ask me to "just hurry this off", and went to Mummy; ate lunch reading a "Vogue" in her little dressing room and went with her to drink iced coffee at Judy's. There Sammy rolled in, and was not nearly as dithery as I should have expected, though I had to hold myself in severely to stop blushing. Chatted about exams, and the Air Force. I left him with Mummy, quite at his ease, drinking soured coffee, thinking how much more restful Peter was.

Sunday 15th December: Up at a quarter past eight, shooting windows into their sockets to keep the heat out, and wrote letters - Xmas ones. In the afternoon, two of my Sunday school children arrived, dangling a blue hanky in cellophane. Mr Ernst Mühlstein, Mother's refugee from Czechoslovakia, came and Mrs John Horner, and after a delicious Sunday tea, decamped to the lounge and talked, perspiring heavily. Ernst and Marjorie shouted musical terms at the tops of their voices and I outdid her on art. I excelled on art. Mother remained quiet throughout, watching Marjorie vamping Ernst. She made no attempt to stave off defeat. Feeling terribly tired, I retired after supper and stood at the door, my tongue in my cheek, listening to Ernst saying I was "veevacious" and "good-informed".

Tuesday 17th December: Still the Greeks advance, but they are over-shadowed by our advance in Egypt and the almost amusing number of prisoners taken - and the Italian tents filled with wine and scent. I like that. And the Australians are in it, too, causing speeches from Up Above about Our Part in this Ghastly War, and doing Our Bit in the Theatre of Victory. Good old Aussies! I am getting almost intolerant now. At dinner I said something to Lillian about being lucky that her Stan wasn't in uniform. She recognised a bitterness that really wasn't meant to be there. But why should men like Stan, nearly thirty, who have lived and have no one to live for of their own, stay here while babies like Colin and Peter fight for them? You see, war changes one. I was frantically, even pro-Germany, tolerant in the beginning.

Wednesday 18th December: All day I was thinking of eight days leave when Peter could stay with me almost as long as we liked. And I kept singing "There's a Boy Coming Home on Leave" - a good tune. It occurred to me that Xmas was in a week today. I must think about getting another diary; this time an exercise book with only the things that particularly interested me; a rather more literary one than this and Oscar Symon's idea with more details that should make it better than this. Peter came late after dinner, in summer khaki shorts and looked like a Sudanese soldier. He was very tired and very adorable and quite worth all my love - when he smiles. I walked to the corner with him and it is so wonderful to love someone so entirely my own. Bryan has broken up and hopes he has left school. A milestone, perhaps. He is too young.

Wednesday 25th December: It was a lovely Christmas Day. I had some lovely presents but the best present of all, two days ago, walked in on four legs followed by a short tail, with a white nose and paws like raisin buns. It was Gavin himself with Peter. A lovely little thoroughbred with a pedigree as long as his namesake. Peter Gavin Anderson. Peter brought him round in the car and after making a puddle on the carpet, settled in. Today Sibyl came, I put on shorts, packed and we were driven to the Adelaide Hills. We swam at Silver Lake in Mylor - my first of the season - boated, played with Gavin who adores the water, and ate huge quantities of salad, and ice cream and dried fruit. After tea, we boated and watched the reflections and the prow making marks, and we sailed over golden trees. Then we drove to "The Rest" at Mount Lofty and dropped me there. Mother is sending me there for my holidays. It seems a most attractive place. I unpacked in my little room and walked in the dark.

Thursday 26th December: Awoke for early morning tea, arose in my floral silk nightie 'a la Miss Fitzmaurice, had a warm shower, put on shorts and wandered about the huge garden in indescribable wonder and weather. There is sun in all the trees and shadows under them and a blue, blue sky. After lunch Peter came and we walked to "Duncraig", Peter's perfect old home. We stayed to afternoon tea at the Wissells and heard their dislike and distaste of the present owners. They said, "They wished to God, Mister Peter still lived there". The rooms were hung with Christmas decorations and old photos and they were such dears and so kind. In the evening after Peter left, I read in the drawing room. After dinner I walked to "Hathaway" and had coffee on the verandah with Mic and Lady Sandford. He shocked me beyond words by, later on a walk, telling me that he was disappointed to hear that Sammy only wanted to kiss me, instead of me having to protect my virtue. He also told me I should get engaged to Peter but it wasn't fair to him. He would come back changed after the war. He also analyzed love and said, "The sooner you learn that love is a matter of bods the better". Disgusting. But he is most amusing.

Friday 27th December: Bryan came after lunch and we walked for miles along a white road, through a wooden gate and along a valley path, up a mountain side and back along a high white road watching chequered ploughed fields and men with hand scythes and ploughs. Bryan stayed to tea and left after; then I sewed and read a book here, called "Literary Taste" by Bennett. I also played "Fiddlesticks", the latest "all the rage" game, with middle aged men leaning forward, fingers curled and bottoms stuck out.

Saturday 28th December: Sibyl came up by a morning train. I had gone before she came for a lovely, lonely walk along Birch Road with faint sun on shivering poplar trees. We lay on my bed under an eiderdown, eating chocolates and talking about my - our - party we want to have at Silver Lake and Peter. I miss not seeing him for days. After lunch we sat on the verandah and sewed and then walked to Stirling and had tea, scones, loganberry jam and cream; then returned to Sibyl's train. I am praying that Peter will ring tonight. He did so. He came round and we saw the film "Rebecca'" again in the village hall. Before, I sat on the bandstand and did his mending. Chewed gum sitting on his trench coat and holding hands hotly. Stood talking miserably to Elliott Johnston, Sammy and Willy Kerr and said at last, "Let's go, Peter, this is cold", and Elliott said, "Yes, and that's frigid". I hated Elliott for making a situation more awkward than it was already. My remark hadn't sounded so bad, because we were all dithering round in true Kerr style.

Sunday 29th December: I was on edge last night with love for Peter. After lunch Mother and Bryan came, and we walked, looked at views and daisies, and then had afternoon tea at "Hathaway" with Lady Sandford, Mic and Charles Jury, the diffident poet. Yesterday the "News" rang, offering me a journalist job. I am in turmoil. I don't know what to take - known security and happiness and non-competitiveness versus vague ideals.

Tuesday 31st December: After lunch began to walk to Loftia Park and met Peter in Alick Downer's car, and we proceeded together. We reviewed Loftia Park and walked on down a white road bordered by white blossoms, gums and hawthorn. We lay in a rye field and kissed each other, among the stalks, like babes in a wood. After dinner at "The Rest", Peter sat on my bed and I made up, fiddled in vain with my hair, while dressed in a check frock with red wooden jewellery, and a red dahlia in my hair. Until nine, we reminisced happily in the car and then went to the Institute. It was very rowdy, very crude, and very plebeian - and that is truth beyond snobbery. I liked it; Peter hated it, and for a quarter of an hour was sulky and mean to me. So we left, I in bewilderment and as it was too late to go to Sibyl's party at the South, we sat in the car and I told Peter a fairy tale and we were very happy, after he had apologised for his sulkiness; I managed to persuade him to tell me that he regarded the country folk present too pleb to see us holding hands so firmly and I annoyed him, because I did so. Geelong Grammar School has given him feelings like that, and he was awfully ashamed of himself. He is a darling. We watched the New Year tick in, sitting in Alick's car, with the wind and trees about us. It is a happy 1940 for me, but what agony to the world!

1941

Wednesday 1st January 1941: This year began with one of the most passionate kisses I have experienced. It left me weak and ecstatic, and yet vaguely unhappy. It is a strange sensation watching a year trekking out and another trekking in. Soon after, Peter went back to camp. Later in the morning I walked down into Montrose valley, where wild daisies are white like snow across it, and putting them in my hair and clothes walked up onto the hill among the gums. Then to the Summit, watching Piccadilly Valley except when the Hawthorns hid it. "Carminow" and "Eurilla", the Bonython mansions, hid the valley for a while, and I actually hated the Bonythons for their extravagance. After lunch I rushed for my train, hat over one eye, racquets and parcels dropping after me, and pursued by the house boy with my luggage tied up in ropes; and in the train and the taxi I read Cellini, a new acquaintance, a present from Mr Mühlstein. Daddy sent me a pair of green scanties, which are laid in lavender carefully. I entertained Sibyl and her school friend Margaret Waterhouse in my nightie and summer dressing-gown, and Sibyl lay on my bed and wept, because she is in love with David Law Smith who is at Woodside with Peter. I forgot to listen, and thought of Peter. There were no raids over London on New Year's Eve, but the capital is still disentangling itself from the ruins of Sunday night's windfall. The Guildhall has been razed to the ground and St Paul's, the Abbey, Buckingham Palace, stations, and the House of Lords have been hit. It is only causing a tremendous national hate.

Thursday 2nd January: I went to "The News" and interviewed Mr Brown, the one-armed editor. The position he wants me to consider is a telephonist one, taking down cable news from reporters stationed all over Australia. It would be shattering, but, as he says, all newspaper work is shattering. Also there is the sacrifice of Saturday afternoons and dinners at the South, and all public holidays. I am in very little doubt about it. Peter versus Lord Northcliffe is an unequal contest.

Friday 3rd January: Sibyl and I had reached a dead-lock as to dates for our dance and so once again had put off ringing people. However, tonight at Sibyl's, surrounded by her Victor Harbor holiday luggage, I rang our guests and on the first call to Alain Harvey, received a rebuff. All he said was "Good God!" and that he didn't know. However, after that things brightened, causing considerable excitement and wonder at an original idea - at last. So, clutching addresses, telephone numbers and Gavin under my arm, I strolled home. That night I dreamed fitfully of the dance. We had no food an hour before it began; people turned up in their sandshoes; the ball room was covered in dust and littered with dead flowers. The right people failed to arrive and we were besieged by wall flowers demanding full programmes, and the boys withdrew.

Wednesday 8th January: Bardia in Libya has officially surrendered. The English-Australian and naval advance continues to Tobruk, which has been attacked. An aerodrome by Tobruk has fallen into our hands. Our losses were "fewer than 600" at Bardia. It is in these words that our losses are always given..."fewer than". Oh, Peter. I waited all day for tonight. I wrote you two letters and bought expensive cakes, and tore up the letters. And at seven o'clock, when everything was ready and you should have walked in, you rang, saying you were on picket duty. The wireless in my room broke into "There'll always be an England" and I almost didn't care if it were true or not. This fever is eating into me and making me detest and loathe war. Aunt Polly is the same; it is soul destroying and unfair to people who have to make even greater sacrifices - Richard, Peter and Colin Chapman. I was restless, and silent with disappointment. I felt it would be wiser after all to take Graham's friend, Brice McMichael's advice and go out with others and forget how much I love him for a while. Which means hurting him. Which isn't worth a hundred Tommies, or Henrys, or Edwards. Did Pepys fall in love?

Thursday 9th January: After work, there was a number of letters on my return. Aunt Lucy sent me one all about God, and Daddy sent me one all about Woman. He offered himself as a father confessor, but I know - or fear - that if I ever get into a tangle, I should unquestionably end with countless bastard children and a deservedly ruined reputation if I took his advice. Sibyl wrote, in an atmosphere of Anne Ayliffe cigarette smoke and jazz, from Victor Harbor, telling me how nice it was to have a "sensible, grown-up and patriotic" soldier awaiting her in the A.I.F. and not a despised school boy.

Friday 10th January: Miss Conroy muttering to herself. Miss Gilbert thinking that because I spend one day reading queer books, I am at a loose end the next. I, with the imagination of a Dante, assigning them both to regions of frustration. Mr John Bonython, on an hour's leave, dictating "two short letters" which will take me at least two long days to type. Mr Reed "coming up for air" behind his law library, accumulating on the desk. I left it all and fled to Mother, and we bought a pair of walking shoes, which symbolised the completion of a week's pay. And all this while, Bryan was playing with Gaby (Gavin) and rolling about together on the lawn, and Lillian was picking peaches and drying her hair in the sun. I am at home now, in my room, and I feel a little dissatisfied with staying at home on so many nights of the weeks, waiting for Peter at the end of it. And I wonder again if Brice is not right. But I washed my hair in shampoo and brushed it for hours till it shone - for the end of the week.

Saturday 11th January: Went to the pictures in the evening. The film was the first Australian picture made for world consumption and was Chauvel's "Forty Thousand Horsemen" - an "epic" in Hollywood style of the first A.I.F. on horses. I believe we would do better if we followed French methods, but as a nation we are as inartistic as the Americans. However, the film was good and filled me with an ardour for Australia, Australian things and scenes and people. We walked home in a hot night that was almost as bright as day.

Sunday 12th January: Peter came to tea and sat politely drinking sherry and playing with Gaby until Mother and Bryan departed to Church. We sat on the floor while the room got darker and darker. When they came back it was quite dark. After supper we strolled through the links, and all the greens were occupied. Other people's love disgusts me and makes me self-conscious. But we lay on our backs on the grass between an avenue of plane trees, and watched the infinite sky and the stars tangled up in their own veil of light. I have said goodbye so often.

Monday 13th January: Mother and I chose my wallpaper today. My room is on the eve of construction. My soul hankers after the most expensive, and Mother says she loves it too, while all the time her brain is working terribly fast....Money from England...that twenty pounds from my sister May...twenty five shillings off from my white handbag (Carys might lend me hers when I wear the blue frock)... How I love her. How I would give her twenty white handbags. How I still like the most expensive wallpapers! By the way, the newspaper "Truth" voted me No. 1 of my particular generation for good dress sense. However rashly false, it is pleasant for the world to know. It is pleasant that, in Sammy's gingham, I am a person of account. Unlike the second Mrs de Winter I am not swayed by black velvet and pearls, preferring wooden beads and wedge heels. I wrote to Daddy to thank him for the ten shillings and rather meanly turned on him. I flung his shattered life at his face, and pitied him standing rather tragically among his old destructive ideas. I said I didn't agree with them, being consistently old fashioned, and that sex rather embarrassed me. I should probably have a few children as politely as I could.

Tuesday 14th January: Mother was at a party so I cut up a sugared peach for her and put a rose on her pillow sentimentally. I know there was too much sugar and the peaches were warm, and I know that fat aphids were beginning to stroll about the sheets, but nevertheless she loved them. And I knew she would.

Wednesday 15th January: "The Memoirs of Benvenuto Cellini" are a little tiring to read at my desk. He insists on concentration - conceited wretch. Besides, although the whole thing is concerned one way or the other with antagonism, you always know who will appear on top. Today a far more important piece of literature than Cellini was sent to me - on Y.M.C.A. paper. He certainly doesn't write celebrated letters, but Sam, who did, suffers in comparison. The whole symbol of my "affair" with Sam is in our letters - we always wrote rough copies first! At lunch time I watched a march of machine-gunners, hundreds upon hundreds of them. They wore khaki shorts and open necked shirts with steel hats. I have never seen a more responsive crowd. The old soldiers urged them on with the old remarks and girls from second storey windows yelled and sang. And I wept in King William Street.

Friday 17th January: Bryan is sixteen today. He came in looking tousled and a little shy, so I kissed him and gave him some money which made him shyer still. To celebrate, Peter and Bryan and Mother and I had dinner at John Martin's, and, leaving Maman to earn our gate money, we went to "Under Your Hat" - an English comedy film with Cicely Court-neidge and Jack Hulbert. The audience consisted almost entirely of personal friends and I was rather proud to be able to display my youngest brother for the first time. He looked very tall and extraordinarily handsome, and didn't utter a word. Peter and I sat clutching hands shamelessly in rather clammy weather.

Monday 20th January: I feel urgently that I must write. Yet even that sounds insincere. It is terribly true. It is a feeling I used to have when I was a child that I must create something that wasn't there before, like a pudding or a poem. But even then I knew I couldn't, and the creative urge went on eating into me, with nothing to pacify it. It is the same today. I cast round in my mind for something to seize on, and merely describe a fat boy in the tram, or an idle sensation. And it is exciting and exhilarating until I remember a series of empty pages and crossed out words and dictionaries and people who never lived. It is exciting until I attempt to trap it. Then it is suddenly drab and hollow. The urge goes, and with it, the excitement. Henry James (Jimmy Pope), Tommy Simpson's great friend, died in a New South Wales air training crash. He is the same rank as Richard – Leading Aircraftman.

Tuesday 21st January: I went to welcome Sibyl home from Victor, expecting to find her lying on the carpet, chewing gum and getting emotional over David. On the contrary, she was very quiet, and merely said she believed she was rather in love with him and that she liked being kissed by David, only she always spoilt it by wanting to go to the lavatory. We went for a hot walk together in shorts and lay on the lawns at Montefiore Hill, watching the city turn blue. Later we sat on the hall floor and tried to concentrate on our wretched dance.

Thursday 23rd January: Mother was combing my hair and said, "You aren't at all the nice child you used to be. You are getting quite difficult to live with and I hate seeing you morose and self-centred and apathetic." Which, although I had spoken thus to myself before, made me think. So, spurred on with almost religious fervour, I went to Myers during the day and gave her ten shillings I owed her as a peace offering. Sibyl and I had lunch at Balfours, meaning to discuss our party list over asparagus and milk, but, following precedent, we didn't get very far. We ate a good deal and talked a good deal and I departed with my list. I spent the evening shouting hoarsely into the phone and then my nose bled bloodily for over two hours. There was blood over the bed and the floor and the basin and on Bryan's handkerchiefs. And dry blood all over my face and ears. At such times I generally breathe a prayer and add with exasperation, "Though why pick on me...!" I eventually fell asleep with my legs thrust up on three cushions and my head lolling over the side of the bed.

Friday 24th January: South Australia is experiencing the worst floods of its history. Roads and towns and railways have been swept away. Hundreds of miles are underwater and people are drowning. Well, the sky is clogged up with clouds and rain has been falling all day. Rather, it is falling when I look out of my window, but it beats down, in the street. I swam to meet Barbara Kelly at lunch and we ate lamb and lemon pudding at Myers. I can't put the show off now because my guests have all sacrificed a far more enticing invitation from Bill Wills because of it. So I sit here, looking out of the window, at the tops of buildings with their wet roofs shining and their walls dark grey with rain. It will never end - I dined at the Brookman's and Sibyl and I descended on town, buying fruit, cakes, biscuits, serviettes and sandwiches. We returned, soggy and laden, and shouting with laughter.

Saturday 25th January: At half past seven I crawled out of bed and rang Sibyl, begging her to put it off. The sky was grey and the ground dark and splodged with rain. We cursed and, after much thought and financial arrangements, switched the whole thing over to dinner at the Gresham, a show after (thanks to "Uncle George") and supper and dancing at the Brookman's. Oh, how we slaved! Mr Reed gave me half the morning and then closed up the shop. We bought tickets and ordered thirty dinners, extra supper, drinks, and cigarettes. After lunch we rang the Mob and by four, had caught them all before they set off for Silver Lake; all but Bizz Brookman and her brother Nigel, who are caught at Meadows by floods. We moved furniture and carpets, skidded happily over floors, showering cheap talcum powder till the place resembled London after a smoke bomb, and a poison gas raid. We buttered Viennese rolls, carted glasses and records, pacified Aunt Polly, and arranged flowers. Bryan, Graham, Sibyl and I dressed hastily and drove to the Gresham, where the Mob met. After dinner we rushed through the rain to "The Naughty Nineties" - a Will Mahoney show at the Majestic. It was gay, well put on, riotously funny and horrifyingly coarse. We all loved it. We piled in cars and had supper, danced and played ping pong. When everything was going uproariously, Peter and I slipped away. We sat in Alain's car and Peter was tired and not very well. He lent his head against me and his hair was damp and tangled, like a little calf. At one o'clock he left for Woodside, with David and Bob Fisher, in a taxi. After that I had a long dance with Derry and he told me (strictly confidentially) that I could always go back to him, that I had spoilt him for other women, that at last he had met his match and lost, eventually blessing our engagement, although he doubted if Peter could even afford the ring. Tony Gilbert and Kenny Price drove me home. A wonderful party!

Sunday 26th January: A telephone woke me at eleven and I dashed off to the Brookman's and found everything in an uproar. Aunt Polly was about to have a mental nervous breakdown, Sibyl was grumbling with good cause and Graham kept on breaking things. So I forgot them all, lugged carpets and chairs, washed glasses and drove home with all my goods leaving Gaby howling among the pop corn. I partook of afternoon tea among a much pacified family and found that all I owed on last night was £3.18.3. Mr Ernst Mühlstein came for dinner. I decided that I was a confirmed drunkard, because I lapped up the sherry when I brought the glasses out. It is interesting stuff. After dinner we played "Chinese Checkers" and ate the rest of my party, talked, discussed the interior decoration of my room at length, and then I broke up the party by going to bed at ten. Thus the charming Mr Mühlstein departed and left "Crime and Punishment" by Fyodor Mikhailovich Dostoevsky.

Monday 27th January: We dined at the South, Peter in uniform, I in furs and velvet, just as it should be. I somehow felt that Peter was bored tonight, but he drove home with me in a taxi and wandered for a few minutes in the garden. I knew he wasn't. I probably expect too much of him.

Tuesday 28th January: All day I was groping for something to found my ideas on. I wanted a plot. I had the characters and several scenes and undoubtedly the desire. But no plot. I thought of past plots (with pride) because although I blushed with shame at them all, they were at least something accomplished. At home, I drifted in and out of manuscripts and read Lillian the Alfred de Musset short story and the Meg novel. She preferred the last, because it had a greater publishing value. I have given up selling my stories before I write them. The hopeless part is that I have given up writing them. But the Brookman family stuck, and some remarks of Lillian. And on such a basis is founded the Great Australian novel.

Wednesday 29th January: Mother and I had lunch at "Judy's", watching people walking through James Place behind net curtains. It was a soft blue day and a soft blue night, shrouded in stars. The liftman, clanging up and down all day in his cage, kept on saying what "a waste it all is" and rolling French tobacco. Peter came unexpectedly, although he was tired and silent. We talked alone in the lounge as the family went out; then we walked through the links and felt the dew rising coldly from the grass. We sat among the roots of a Morton Bay fig, leaning against the trunk and watching the stars. Cunningham's Comet was up there, with a shower of light behind it, utterly unaware of Mr Bromley, our weather forecaster. All evening a terrible dread lest I should lose Peter took hold of me. But he killed it, by loving me to an almost dangerous degree. He was trembling and breathless and angry because he wanted me so badly, and couldn't have me. Then he was ashamed of saying so. Poor darling. There is so much to come before us yet.

Friday 31st January: My characters, the Osbournes are becoming a united family. There is Margaret, their mother, and Clive, their father, and Richard and Simon and Penelope and Polly and Michael. I told Bryan and Lillian all about them at dinner, but they kept eyeing each other sceptically and being generally non-commitent. I admit there is nothing extraordinary about them, but that is merely a sign of my approaching adulthood. This family is simply a result of my Urge to Create.

Saturday 1st February: This evening I dressed and walked to Fitzroy Terrace where the Lisle Johnson's sherry show was in full swing, convinced I should be bored. However, Peter dashed in late, just as I had almost snared a young man called John Goodfellow, R.A.A.F. (an interesting experiment because I was beginning to regard myself as passé). Mrs Anderson has put her foot down about engagements. Mother, I think, is furious with her, but I really can't be bothered to fight about it. After all, we are very young.

Sunday 2nd February: Peter is going to a Victorian Military Camp in a few weeks' time, until his pre-embarkation leave. It sends me sick and cold and helpless, but there is no earthly use in struggling against this war. The only thing to save one is to get swept along with it, in the blood and the loneliness and the futility of it all. And I once use to regard war as breathless, exciting - uniforms, one's heroes fighting but never dying, romantic, of self importance, of history, even when I was a pacifist. They were evil, secret thoughts we all had, and we lost them after the first few months. It became drab and for granted and empty. Oh God! God! Why war?

Monday 3rd February: I have had to go out, away from myself, to stop my silly worries and consequent sickness. Sibyl forgot that I was asked to dinner there, and went out, so I dined at home and went there later. Margo Waterhouse, Aunt Polly, Sibyl and I lay about in the sitting room gossiping above Schumann and Rimsky-Korsakov. Margaret, an inveterate gossiper, told us lurid and confidential stories about peoples' babies and peoples' brothers - occasionally they merged into one anecdote

- and generally ended on the same note - "However you can forgive him he's got Pots..." I was informed that Peter "had Pots", too. We drove her home in "Winston" (Michael's little car with the dicky seat) and drifted out to Parafield, discussing our "girlish secrets" (Aunt Pol) and finally sat together, looking over the railway lines to Bowden. Occasionally my hand would steal forgetfully out to Sibyl's...and then realize...and hastily withdraw. Midnight.

Wednesday 5th February: I came racing home, hair flying, panting down the drive and into my room. It is finished. Six days ago I stood among the glue pots and stripped paper in my room and tried to visualize it, while Gaby walked in and out, tripping over paint buckets and chewing the wall paper up and marching grandly out across the hall carpet, leaving cream footprints. It is now like an illustration from an English "Homes and Gardens", full of sun and freshness. There is a deep blue carpet that you can roll about on, right up to the skirting; and sun streaming through filmy net curtains and over the ceiling and along the walls. The furniture is Burmese Ivory with dulled silver handles and alive with my things - a blue leather blotting pad, ink wells, writing case, a few good books and a crystal powder bowl. And chintz everywhere - on the bed, the dressing table and windows and arm chair. There is a tiny bowl of Dresden china flowers on the dressing table and a bowl of Lorraine Lee roses. Somehow, though, there wasn't exactly the same excitement of possessing it that I had imagined, because Peter spoiled it a little by not ringing. I am so filled with doubts and, for all my love, have such little faith in him.

Thursday 6th February: Sir Lavington informed me, a little pinkly, that he knew Daddy's woman and the Other Family, which amazed me. I had thought that those three were safely buried away in a cottage along the Sydney coast line. Daddy, by the way, is now in Melbourne, but can no longer disturb Mummy's peace of mind. I felt definitely depressed so I rang Aunt Polly and said I had been jilted and was coming to dinner and she said that she was feeling exactly like cheering someone up who had been jilted, so I went. But before I went, Peter rang, apologised profusely, cleared himself and then rather tactlessly asked me why he was apologising anyway. When I arrived for dinner I was told I had come under false pretences. The nurse said I would lose him if I were possessive (she knew), so I was filled immediately with contrition, and fearfully worried. We tore into town half an hour late to see the film comedy "Charlie McCarthy, Detective" - with a little wooden ventriloquist doll as a hero. America is now a little tired of her wooden doll; perhaps because he lacks Sex Appeal.

Friday 7th February: I'm sick of everything. I'm sick of myself and my weakness and my lack of self-control. I'm sick of my hateful inside. I'm sick of being sick. I despise myself and the fact that I don't seem to be able to do anything about it. I'm tired to death of being eighteen and not enjoying it. I'm not egotistical and I'm not neurotic. I'm just weak. I tried to snap out of it at lunch by swimming with Bryan at the Pool, and it was fun, lying in the sun almost naked in the middle of the city and slipping through the water, and taking in Vitamin D. The Japanese situation is increasingly bad, and we are warned to sit tight and not give way to fear. There is a good deal of nerve mongering going on. Dr Grenfell Price, Master of St Mark's College, however is anticipating a Japanese attack in six weeks. It all seems words - words to me.

Saturday 8th February: Judith Crase came to dinner and we talked and sewed in my room. She is a little entangled with a young Jew from a Jewish communal camp in Palestine, who regards Sex as Natural. He is writing a book about a family also, with a slight difference. Mine concerns the effect of war on an ordinary family. The young Jew's concerns the effect of sex on an ordinary family. Which is worse? There is extra training of troops - militia - going on. They must stay an additional three months in camp for home defence. Perhaps Peter and Richard will have to chase little men round gum trees.

Sunday 9th February: Sibyl and I went to church together and I was impressed. Sibyl read the "Lest We Forget" list. I lunched at her home and we wandered about Bowden in the sun, sucking pink sweets. There are houses there smaller than the size of my room, but somehow Bowden did not depress me today. Peter rang, saying he couldn't get down to dinner but would come after. Mummy and Bryan went to church and left me waiting, striving to be gay and unconcerned and undoubting. But it was a failure. When he came I wasn't reassured; it is my own silly emotions convincing me, above all logical proof that Peter is beginning to stop loving me. I know it is false, but I can't persuade myself. What a fool I am! Of course I will lose him if I go on like this, never laughing at anything. I crawled up near Mummy after and cried my heart out. She made me promise – and so did Peter - that I would go out with other people during the week. I know it is the only sensible thing to do at eighteen but who will ask me now? I couldn't sleep, and was fearfully sick all night.

Wednesday 12th February: The City is hung with flags celebrating a victory - Benghazi, I think, although I have forgotten. How bitter to the men who died for it! If this were Italy (and we had a victory to celebrate.....) we would dance in the streets and there would be pale faces in the dark, and guitars and flying skirts. As it is, we look up at the flags and weep.

Friday 14th February: At eight, Mother and I met Gordon Heaslip (a boy who is fond of Mummy) at Pirie Bush's rooms behind the "Quality Inn" and discussed frocks and cosmetics and flats with long legged women with cigarette holders. Frocks of Molyneux and Adrian were hanging about the room and one sent old Pirie into ecstasies. He sprang up, pivoted round on his toes, slipped his hand down a disdainful side - to give "line" - and flung his arms out in a circular. Whereupon John Hammill, the Manager of "Quality Inn", began feverishly zipping open moth bags to show us Adrian's and we all fell back on our sofas, shuddering with delight and drinking iced beer. After supper we bought the Red Cross flower shop for two shillings and arrived home buried in flowers at midnight.

Monday 17th February: Peter came for ten minutes to say "goodbye" and left me restless and unhappy. It will be a definite relief when he leaves on Friday morning for Puckapunyal Camp. Damn. Love shouldn't be like this.

Tuesday 18th February: Barbara Kelly, Richard's friend came to dinner and to stay the night, for the express purpose of a Chat. We curled up on the floor, with a low lamp light and talked until one. We shifted from subject to subject yet always reverted back to the same one - Richard, strangely enough. For six years she has adored him and now, when she wants to love Alain Harvey (who could make her far happier) those six years stand in the way. It surprised me. I have never realized before their feelings. Richard has firmly stood out against it, knowing that it would interfere with anything he strove for, while I, womanlike, have only one end to strive for, which has trampled all the old dreams into dead shapes. But Richard, like Francis Bacon, believes that "They do best who, if they cannot but admit love, yet make it keep quarter, and sever it wholly from their serious affairs and actions of life; for if it check once with business it troubleth men's fortunes, and maketh men that they can no ways be true to their own ends."

Wednesday 19th February: We both were hoarse this morning, but walked slowly into town through the parks, which were clean and washed, and trampled sunny leaves across the lawns to the river. "It is this," said Barbara, "that we are fighting for - for peace and cathedral spires and gardens." I wonder if those other people believe that they are fighting, in such a way, for wide rivers and craggy clouded slopes and rocks built in the air. For Europe. At half past six I went to bed and slept fitfully until Peter called at eight. I dressed and went to him for a few minutes, cursing my sickness which came the moment I heard his step on the verandah. And now he has gone for a month.

Thursday 20th February: Mr Bonython dropped in from camp and began to work at five minutes to one, so I said, firmly, I was busy and walked off to lunch. Nothing was to stop me seeing the 2/14 Australian Field Regiment March. Barbara Kelly, Barb Matters, Tony Osborn and I watched in excitement, and I was fighting against crying. Then they came round the corner, feeling like heroes, with the band in front playing war songs, and Paddy Ryan swinging along in front in the cap I wore at Sue Yeatman's tennis party only a few days ago, and three hundred men in shorts. A child ran out from under my legs and flung itself at its father, clinging to his shoulders. And Peter, and Jim Hodge, and John Dunstan and Bill Bullock and David Law Smith and Peter Butler behind, self-conscious at our clapping. Peter said quietly "Hallo" and that was the last goodbye.

Saturday 22nd February: Oscar Symon and I bumped into each other while I was buying an Orphan Appeal Badge. He said he never bought badges On Principle, and when I suggested the Kingdom of Orphans was not a happy one, he said (thinking of his notoriously hostile family) that he didn't know....that anyway, the Magill Home was better than the Salvation Army, and walked into the Executor Trustee to sue another brother. Oscar is responsible for this diary. David "Nob" Good drove me to Alain Harvey's in dull helpless heat and we drifted about the gardens drinking sherry and rustling long frocks about the lawns. There was something almost Fragonard about it, faintly misty and high white houses with idle creepers about the pillars. We danced at the Parade Ground Barracks among khaki and heat, with hula wreaths around our necks and later returned at midnight to the Harvey's and lay on the lawn, talking in strange deep whispers that floated in the garden like shadows. When I came home, I hung my hula wreath about Peter's photo, because I enjoyed it so much.

Thursday 27th February: I was strap hanging in the tram coming home. Suddenly a small cream car shot by, a head stuck out and Sibyl shrieked, "Come to tea!" to the whole tram. I leapt out of the Men's Compartment, under the rail and into "Winston". Sibyl has a letter from David, and there is none for me. I am blazing with envy.

Friday 28th February: Suddenly I felt that I wanted a tremendously deep conversation with someone, so that everything is revamped by beauty of words or the unboundlessness of argument, so abstract that one is not always forcing oneself into it. Knowing that I was incapable of such talk, I wrote to Sam - a rather fine letter - and suggested he come and have a chat about Elizabethans, although I knew that "vegetable" love was dead. It took a good deal of courage to post it.

Sunday 2nd March: The Parafield Air Carnival has been cancelled, because the Police Commissioner says bran pies in a side show with alcohol, for raising money for the war effort, are illegal. Instead of tipping the bran pies out, the Countess of Bective has gone to live in Melbourne, saying all her efforts are frustrated. It poured grey rain all day. We drifted about the house, looking though smeared windows and reading in idle, straddling positions. In the evening the grey rain stopped us from going to church, so we listened to the radio play, "George and Margaret" and giggled and ate chocolates and thought we were rather a nice family. Which we are.

Tuesday 4th March: I walk home these days, stealing myself against the dreariness of an empty letter plate. I pretend that I am so used to it that it won't hurt, and think hard of other things until I get to the corner and then run, and it still isn't there. After that I can't do anything; reading and mending are impossible and I can't go to Sibyl's because I am afraid that she will have a second letter from David. I wonder why he doesn't write?

Thursday 6th March: The world was shattered today and built up again and shattered once more. It left me with a little less faith and a mad sense of having grown up, past all my friends. It was the letter which - o-irony! - I had wanted so much. It was very tender and sincere and inevitable. It meant the end of the Gumnut baby and other dreams, and the end of all this misery. Peter had stopped loving me. Sibyl came round and shook me out of a wild nightmare. She walked me round, told me the letter was empty and that Peter was shabby. She drove me round, gave me ice cream and lavender sweets and didn't convince me. He was fine; he had done everything according to our arrangement, and he could not stop himself from feeling as he did. So Sibyl in desperation gave me David Law Smith's second letter. It was sickening and made filthy all that faith that Peter had given me. I gave myself completely to him, and now I know he was not worth it. He had found it irksome and trying. His family were opposed to our engagement because they believed I was weak and delicate and couldn't give him children. He used me as a bulwark against which to hurl his passions, over which he had little control, and not satisfied with that, went to another girl he felt nothing for. And that last, more than wounding my pride, killed any love I had left for him. He disgusts me. He deceived me for months, hardly being able to tolerate me.

Friday 7th March: Well, it hurt like hell, but it doesn't any more. It was a splendid day and I almost danced to town, feeling that it was all over. People ask me about him and I just smile rather absently. An American woman permed my hair and it is delightful, all gently curly and short and soft, like a child's. Actress and writer, Clare Boothe Luce says that when a man is fed up he changes his wife and a woman, changes her hair.

Saturday 8th March: I played tennis at the Salters with my old school friends. It is so difficult to know what to talk about. Pinder has gone all vivacious and popular; Pat Short has drifted away from the Oxford Group; Pat Moore is silent, as though her love for "John" is too wonderful to chatter about. Stevie is the same. Completely boy crazy. It all seemed rather empty to me, and they are all so young. This feeling, I hope, will not last. We listened to a Beethoven Symphony and then Sibyl and I drove home in Winston.

Sunday 9th March: Mrs Crafter - Lillian has departed on holiday - crept out onto the verandah wrapt in sun and speckled grape shadows. She had a little penny exercise book and read us some of her poetry. We sniggered inwardly at first, but then realized that there was something in them almost akin to talent. I felt she was far greater than I when she said, "M' daughter, Merle - she says as how I should take up some learning about ....you know, what things goes into what ...." Rhyme! And "All those scribbles on them pages are what I copied down at the Library," with a sketch of a statue's rear in the Botanic Gardens. I can't express the respect I feel for that spark of creativeness that is there after sixty-eight years. It will have gone in me when I reach that age. Sibyl came to tea and taught me to drive Winston – key, ignition, throttle, clutch, accelerator, hand-brake, first gear and let the clutch out slowly - and a dead thing comes to life under you. I came home and found Mrs Crafter hugging her knees on her bed, composing an ode on "Freda, my friend". I sit at my desk, and can't write, so I read Dostoyevsky's "Crime and Punishment" to Mother.

Monday 10th March: Oh why can't I describe it - this most splendid of days! Mummy and I lay on the grass by the river eating peaches. There was suddenly no war. Everyone laughed and was silent with content. The gardeners touched their caps and said it would last. The white birds floated on the river like flowers and shadows of the poplars shuddered in the water. Aunty Moree rang from Melbourne saying they wanted me to stay at Hamilton within the next few days. I have wanted to go for so long that now I am hesitant. It might mean giving up Mr Reed, and is it worth it? I certainly feel better since Peter stumbled off. I look back on it all as a pathetic nightmare - that sitting waiting for him in the lounge, determined to be gay and indifferent and irresistible, and failing every time, like the girl in a comedy. So I shall go.

Tuesday 11th March: I wandered back from work across the park, with the city hanging like a blue cloud on the other side, not caring about letters. But there was a cable for Mummy - the one I have dreaded for so many years, saying that Nain had died. I waited until she had changed and then said, "A cable came from England for you". She said, "Mammy's dead" and flung herself on the bed before I had verified it. She took it well. Dear old Welsh Nain, you were pretty marvellous.

Wednesday 12th March: Bryan, Mummy and I went to Calvary Hospital with some dahlias to see the wife of Richard's best aviation friend. She has just had a baby, all pink and comfortable and covered in blanket and blue ribbons. All my inside sort of dissolved because I wanted one so badly. Damn Peter.

Thursday 13th March: There was something familiar about tonight. I changed, arranged some flowers and supper and sat knitting in the lounge with only the lamp on, waiting for someone. The fundamental difference was that this time I was not sick. Sammy came, clutching his latest edition wrapped in brown paper, holding them out to me, saying "Have one" as though they were chocolates. Among his poems is "If you should go" and he blushed as I read it and muttered something about "it should not be there…perhaps…" We did not talk about ourselves, nor of anything that mattered. His teaching, my novel, our friends. Sam lying on the couch, smoking a stream of cigarettes, handsome in his coarse, Byronic way, never finishing his sentences, filling his words with suggestion. And grinding off in Petroff and lights falling drunkenly round the corner.

Friday 14th March: I wandered to Sibyl's, and Joan Clift from her class, who lived in India was there, so we all lay about in the dark listening to "Scheherazade" and a quaint little thing called "Ondine" by Ravel. Nothing seemed to matter then; that old lifting feeling came back of yearning for something - something that Charlie Price and Sam and Charles Jury want. It is a feeling that is as comfortable as religion, but it doesn't desert one. There was a huge moon above Dr Smeaton's chimneys next door and it came in through the window and lay in pools about the darkness. We drank coffee in O'Connell Street and roared at each other about Adelaide poets.

Saturday 15th March: At four in the afternoon David "Nob" Good and Ninette Trott arrived in his car "Liz" and so, with Ros Dumas, rugs, baskets of grapes and tomatoes, sticks of celery and the collected parts of Liz that she dispensed with on the way up, we arrived at Sue Yeatman's cottage under the Summit - (backwards, because Liz has not much pulling powers). Later Charlie Price, Elizabeth Carter, Sue, Barb Kelly, Alain and Herries Harvey, Geoff Dutton, Tony Gilbert and others turned up. We shouted through the undergrowth, and built a hot fire at the end of the sitting room, which is long and polished, with long windows looking down over the city. We ate far too much - salads, fruit, nuts, cake, rolls, figs ad infinitum - and cleared away, danced till two in the morning and walked to the Summit, arm in arm, singing and stood in Heaven with the grey clouds swirling at our feet and mists as tangible as nets freezing our breathing. We were eating nuts by the fire when Ben "Chick" Robertson dashed in, after a party. However, he went to sleep in one of the bedrooms and only awoke when anyone went in to adjust a corset suspender or powder a nose. Charlie and I cracked nuts and discussed Culture - I regarding Charlie as though he held it in the palm of his hand. We pushed Liz up a hill, settled in, rugged ourselves into cocoons and, letting the brakes go, shot down the Greenhill Road.

Sunday 16th March: There was rain all day, smashing about the house and coming in grey sweeps, like last night's mists. I spent the day in bed, through weariness, exhaustion and pains. I read and slept intermittently and felt slovenly. I adored last night and it taught me something - that there are other exciting people, even here in Adelaide - Charlie in his slippers, his University jumper pulled down over his behind, his socks down and his hair untidy; Geoff Dutton spoilt and moody and handsome; Tony Gilbert who teases me. All of them.

Monday 17th March: I promised Mr Reed to wait until Mr Bonython returned from Melbourne. When I told Aunt Polly, she said, "Why, has John Bonython been jilted too?" So I sit here reading, champing at the reins and answering the telephone. I read "Round the World in Eleven Years" by the Abbe children, this evening. That's the sort of living I should like my children to do, instead of staying in one town till every foot of it is familiar, while out there is the world to do things in. What's the use of going out to it when your habits are formed and, to quote Clare Boothe Luce, your character has "jelled"? If I wasn't such a thoughtful child, I'd take my seven pounds after leaving Hamilton and wander from Melbourne through Sydney to Queensland, eating bananas and typing.

Wednesday 19th March: In the evening Mother and I, both in velvet and furs, sat politely in the Salter drawing room, listening to various Salter friends rendering vocal and instrumental music. It was very peaceful and inconsequential, like a comedy of manners, and cost two shillings. I liked it. We later ate cocktail tomatoes and egg sandwiches among other velveted friends; Mrs Someone made a speech on behalf of the Red Cross; Mrs Salter replied amid laughter. We said "goodbye" and "thank you" to everyone and departed. And this was once going to be so crazily happy. Peter came back from Puckapunyal army camp tonight.

Saturday 22nd March: It's a good feeling - leaving something behind - saying goodbye, with the books balanced and the place as it was when you first came. I felt all afternoon as though it was the beginning of the Christmas holidays. And I had seven pounds and courage and a peaceful world to investigate now that I am eighteen! I packed my bags while Judith Crase darned my stockings like a good friend. My clothes are in a trunk, mended, washed and ironed, and I can't wait.

Sunday 23rd March: Sibyl has jilted David, because he only loves her car.

Monday 24th March: After taxis and staggering porters and trains and silly women with streamers and smoke; tearless goodbyes; magazines and butterscotch; long galvanised roofs and familiar old women asking "Who are you" and taking out beer and sandwiches as the train moves out - "D'you see Mag with them two sailors?"; "My, doin' some fast work." "'Ave some, dear," "Y' sure?" forever and ever. I sat on my case in the corridor, watching the blackness, hurling by - da-da, da-da, da-day,da-da. - long jazzy rushes of sound and wind. The train was filled with troops, sleeping in the corridors and talking on their rucksacks. Two dashing aviators insisted on coming into my carriage, so I went to sleep between them, alternatively wrapped up in relays. They were warm and better than cushions, and paid for my coffee. The dawn crept along the edge of the land, and gnarled grey trees caught it, and so did the grey sheep and frozen grey earth.

Tuesday 25th March: In Hamilton, I was handed over to Major (Dr Sam) Fitzpatrick, by a Lieutenant Keith Lovett to the accompaniment of clicks and salutes and military bows. Uncle Sam and Aunt Moree's home is glorious, like a Renaissance house inside with polished wood, high painted windows, sloping carpeted stairs lit up by iron lamps, tapestries and mandolins. I slept during the afternoon and read dear old Anatole France by the fire with Elise, their daughter.

Wednesday 26th March: Cold, grey day with wind howling in the pines and rain prickling your face. Coffee and eggs in my Renaissance bedroom, a bath in my yellow bathroom, a long walk in a coat and skirt through the town, with a dog. And I am writing this in the studio-study. There is an easel here with a yellow smock on a peg, two violins and a mandolin and a music stand; a table with earthenware painting bowls from Holland and a highly polished beer barrel filled with etchings. When Elise came home from school we went out on the horses along the creek.

Friday 28th March: I walked through the streets of Hamilton - the paper shops with strange newspapers, the large leather traders and the station hands leaning against their horses in the streets. There is a good deal of exaggerated excitement over the bloodless coup d'état in Yugo-slavia, where the leaders under Regent Prince Paul who signed the Axis Agreement with Germany have been overthrown. A new crowd under the seventeen year old King Peter II are now with us. I don't believe this will help us much; Belgium did the same thing and where is Belgium?

Saturday 29th March: Elise and I and some of her friends met at one of those old verandahed houses by the pine forest on bicycles and horses, in breeches and boots, with baskets and rucksacks. We swept out along the roads and through paddocks filling the baskets with mushrooms and arrived by a creek in a shallow valley. We cooked chops and mush-rooms and ate them in huge chunks of bread, lying on our backs in the shade. We tethered the horses and spread out over the paddocks, with my horse Dookie madly chasing hares across the flax fields. Lieutenant Keith Lovett, who I met on the train to Hamilton, came visiting. Aunt Moree says he is like Daddy when he was young. He is very dark and alive, rather flirtatious, and unexpectedly filled with dated ideals. Most people with dated ideals haven't the courage to express them, and he makes me feel a coward. I wish I could believe emphatically and fanatically in some one thing and hurl my whole strength into it. Look at this diary - it is shallow and insincere. Oscar Symon told me on Monday that a diary is useless if it is not frank and cruelly honest. Is this?

Sunday 30th March: Uncle Sam, Aunty Moree, Elise and I piled into the car and drove towards the Grampians. We passed through Dunkeld, a struggling Scotch village at the foot of a scraggy volcanic crag and mowed down scrub in the car till we came to a low lake with pines and wheat fields on one side and the Grampians on the other, mirrored in the water. Elise and I swam, plumped up and down in it, raced for a mile around it, rolling in the grass while Uncle Sam painted us and Aunty Moree sketched. It is a wonderful place. I can see some of it vaguely from my window, pale blue crags leaping straight up from the wheat lands and the grazing paddocks. We were all in a mad mood and shouted with laughter and leapt out of the car when we saw a mushroom, racing towards them like wild things, afraid lest they escape. We fried them for tea and dragged ourselves to bed, falling asleep immediately.

Tuesday 1st April: After baking in the sun during the morning, I dragged Dookie along the river in an effort to urge back some of the energy the sun had sapped during the morning, but instead gave myself up to it and half slept in the grass. Being naturally lazy, I have to fight against Aunt Moree who wants me to sleep all through the day. Anyway, I did play tennis by the Presbyterian Church just before the sun went down miles away across the grazing lands. I have seldom seen such a sun; it was heavy and rather overripe. Just as it fell into the sea a magpie fled out of the grey church and cut my eyes that were dulled by the red mass, with its strong black and white. Like eating lemon after sugar, and as nice.

Thursday 3rd April: Today Dookie and I went for another walk towards a hill that I never reach, like El Dorado. A soft grey rain drove us on, smacking against my raincoat and bare legs but it drove us back later, wet and vanquished. I was taken unawares and had to go to a Red

Cross afternoon to sew buttons on shirts. The Town hall was filled with middle aged station women and bank managers' wives. As I came in their voices seemed to surge towards one and through and past one. And there they all were, sewing button holes, drinking three pence cups of tea and winning the war.

Friday 4th April: Aunt Moree is making me into a perfect social worker. This afternoon I visited two homes for afternoon tea and tried not to eat too much, dangled small rebellious babies, discussed sheep and rainfall with young mothers and cooed over new engagement rings. Everyone in Hamilton when they go visiting take a pot of jam jelly, a bunch of dilapidated flowers, a new apple tart (always apple) or a crayfish from Portland. In exchange they are given kisses and afternoon tea.

Saturday 5th April: The children from the Western District gave a display on the Oval. Elise is disgusted; she thinks it's a Nazi idea and that we present our children as young Pagans and worthy soldiers for future greatness. Nevertheless they looked splendid - thousands of them from Convents, High Schools, Colleges and State schools. I sat in the Official box with the daughter of the School Commissioner and watched the babies dance in the Maypoles. There was a small Japanese child by me with sloped brown eyes and dark shining hair. It would be worth marrying a Japanese to have a child like that. Afterwards the daughter and others came to the pictures and saw a Dr Kildare film. We drank milk shakes, while the nurses in our midst yelled with laughter about the picture. Jimmie Kildares are rare.

Sunday 6th April: Somehow, just as we are told that we are safe in the Balkans and that Libya, Africa etc are ours forever, and that the Mediterranean itself is under our rule, the Germans come —there is something invincible about them. They have invaded Yugoslavia and are helping the Italians in Greece. Yugoslavia is not in a position to oppose Germany. Greece is fighting like the gallant little country she is. Today, I was told to pack at once and go to Melbourne. Somewhat surprised I did so. I packed, bundled into Uncle Sam's car with Aunt Moree and drove off within a couple of hours. An aunt of theirs is dying and both are called in to mourn and consult respectively. It was a great ride. The road came up out of the blackness and hit the footlights; there was flat country on both sides and once or twice a glow in a small house. Rabbits and hares lost their nerve and flung themselves under the car like suicide squads. The dull thud always made us jump and throw up our hands. It is a horrible thing to kill these days - with so much killing. We passed through Ballarat and then on to the Refshauges to stay. Supper by a fire in a small kitchen and sleep in a double bed with frost outside as white as moonlight.

Monday 7th April: Driving on again with the Refshauges through rich country with black soil and apple trees. And then Melbourne through stinging tired eyes. Flowers for the sick, a little weeping and visiting and then oysters for lunch. I met Mary again, the Fitzpatrick's older daughter, and we were left at the Alexander Hotel together and the Fitzpatricks returned to Hamilton. As we walked up Collins Street a voice said, "Why, it's Carys, isn't it?" and there was a small round man in a loud check suit and a French hat. It was Daddy. I was disgusted; after seven years of romancing to be presented with this! We gazed at each other self consciously for a few seconds, shook hands and strolled on together. After afternoon tea at "Elizabeth Collins" we both made our escapes in different directions and I had my hair shampooed at Buckley's. I felt that all Melbourne was lying in the sun ready to be looked at and discovered. It was an independent feeling that made me love her - a Casanova eager to make another conquest, although he in turn would be conquered and tied to her by her tidy suburban gardens, her Italian book sellers and the string of Neon lights down Swanson Street. My father and I dined at Mario's (where good women don't eat alone) drank Sauterne and put flowers in our button holes. And then to the Berrimans, to bed.

Tuesday 8th April: Maudie, Jeanne Berriman and I wandered through Melbourne looking at everything and buying nothing. I dined again with Daddy. We couldn't afford dinner so we went in search of George, a journalist who writes the war leader in "Truth". We found him in a café under his boarding house, a little drunk. We yelled at each other about everything - Anatole France is all I can remember - until the waiters became a Union and turned out the lights. We stumbled out in the dark and strolled arm in arm along Swanson Street, bursting with good company and our own brilliance. The last we saw of our darling George was him standing under a street lamp, his fist clenched in the air, Fascist fashion. It was Pop's birthday so we trained to Kew and saw the film "All This, and Heaven Too" with Bette Davis and Charles Boyer. It has swept the world and us too. After flinging off my hates and prejudices at Mario's yesterday, I feel better now, and Daddy and I get on well. I see now that taking sides is a lazy way out, that I can like Daddy without impairing at all my love for Mother.

Friday 11th April: Daddy and I wandered arm in arm through the sun and the Botanical Gardens. All Melbourne was about, as this is Good Friday. Important people played with their boats on the lake and little girls chased swans over the lawns. We sucked rotten ginger beer through straws and discussed life, lying on our backs. We dined at a Lyon's Café and I had to lend him money to pay for it. Crossing the road, we sat on the Christening steps at St Paul's and listened to Stainer's "Crucifixion", trying not to catch someone's eye all the time, while sleep swept about me in waves. And on to the Crow's with my case. I slept in a high cream room, with a thick pink carpet and heavy taffeta curtains that run along rods when you pull a cord. The furniture is genuine antique mahogany, with a Royal Copenhagen mermaid who looks out from a desk into the garden, wondering —. There are twin beds with heavy green brocade covers and a bathroom of my own, with a sea-faring bath without salt water. Quite frankly, I feel a swell.

Saturday 12th April: These John Crows are wonderful people. I like the gentle ease of the place and their befriending of my father who is deserted by everyone as a "rotter" and not a nice man to meet. These Plymouth Brethrens are fine Christians! Mr and Mrs Crow, Daddy, Madame Gregor Wood and I drove to the Dandenongs where tree ferns grow thick and dark in the valleys and the gums are tall and slim like pines. We walked into a Russian forest where sound is deadened by pine needles and there was an unearthly feeling of being alone and apart from the world. We visited William Ricketts in his studio which is filled with his aboriginal pottery of legendary inspiration. Daddy wrote an article on his work at one time and today became an author again meeting his subject.

Ricketts is a queer little fellow with large blue eyes and a lost small face, and his body quivers like a squirrel's. The opossums come to his studio at night and when they cease to come, he goes out on a man hunt with a rifle. I have never seen a man talk of murder before with any sincerity. He gave me a wild violet but it died; next week he is leaving for Central Australia to meet "his people" and to find if they approve of the little violinist turned artist. How I should love to go with him! We dined at "The Pig and Whistle", the only perfect replica I have seen of an English Inn, and our host returned to the fire after every serve to read "The Architects' Journal". Madame Gregor Wood sang "Where'er You Walk" and I sat by the window looking down a valley to a moon and many trees and another valley. We talked of deep things in that room. There was a wonderful feeling of having come home to something —

Sunday 13th April: Daddy and I strolled down to see Aunty Lucy and Grandfather. I had a wretched sick cold and could hardly go on, but I found Aunty Lucy an unexpected surprise. She lay bedridden in a large sunny room surrounded by texts and the Royal Family, but also a wireless, a scamp of a brother who is leading – my dear! – the old woman to the devil and the racing track, and good old Irish courage. Mary Fitzpatrick and I bought some roly poly and went to the Rubbo's flat. Syd (Dr Dattilo Rubbo) showed me round it while Ellen sat on a box in blue slacks, combing her hair which is honey coloured and reaches thickly to her knees. I fell in love with them both - dark Italian Sydney, 27, Doctor of Philosophy, lecturer in Bacteriology and a fourth year medical student, black hair, white boyish smile, son of a famous R.A. and a fine painter himself – Ellen, a lost fair little face in wonderful hair, and a greater painter still. And of course Michael - two 'n a half, fair hair cut like Christopher Robin and in love with moons. They have all done amazing things – danced in London for two years, kept themselves on paintings alone, cycled round Europe and boated down the Danube. We took a boat today and rowed down the Yarra past green banks and blue gums and people kissing. We lay on our backs eating cold meat sandwiches, then chased the moon over hills till we caught it and brought it back with us, Michael leaning over the bow saying "Oh you boo-i-ful moon, come 'ome with

Michael", and it did. We sat about in the Rubbo's flat, drinking coffee and reading books and laughing a great deal while Syd pretended to be a doctor, listening to our insides. We argued fiercely about the impossibility of such a thing as an individual, and I came home in a happy daze to find the Crows in great anxiety.

Monday 14th April: We sat in green chairs under a Magnolia tree, reading and writing and throwing clumps of earth at spiders in a web, while the Crows pretended I was their daughter, which was pleasant for both of us. I was introduced to gardens, fondled crocuses so yellow that they dazzled one's eyes in the shadows and was told that autumn is the best season of the year because death in a garden is a wonderful thing. Later we watched their sons Tom and Peter showing off at the Melbourne Baths. Tom is delicious. He stands on the diving board, head turned towards you, eyes and mouth in a huge self-conscious beam – and dives. And somehow he appears out of the water again with the selfsame beam, huge and self-conscious. We read at night in the study, fighting and playing ping pong and listening to my brother Richard as a bomber pilot in the radio play "Coast Patrol" and tickling each other behind chairs. I think they would like a sister.

Tuesday 15th April: After an indecent lunch at "Elizabeth Collins" I staggered round the Art Gallery, Public Library and Museum with Daddy, and developed an absorbing passion for Venetian glass and Sappho's homosexual poetry. I wish I lived in Melbourne among all this glass and with all these people. Mary Fitzpatrick was to take me to a Life Class but as we were locked out we saw two poor films instead, sitting high up near the ceiling. On the way home, I picked up a deserted "Herald" from the seat and read it. On all sides we are facing defeat...defeat...defeat. Bombed here, ousted here and here by these invincible maniacs, yet all we are told of are our petty victories, their losses and our men with Thumbs Up. This nation is decadent, I am told; the spirit is defeatism and even apathetic. We are not allowed to face facts, even though we know. And suddenly the whole blasted world blew up. Nothing was tangible. The excitement of being young and fairly attractive and faintly intelligent counted for nothing. The thought that this sky and earth and tram and the sleeping

Accountancy Student would desert me was enormous. But then the world collected its bits and settled down again. It always does, thank God.

Thursday 17th April: Jeanne Berriman and I stormed the Public Library, mentally bowing before dear Sir Redmond Barry, the founder, as we passed in. I fought my way through galleries of Lionel Lindsay, Sir William Osler and aeroplanes till I stood in rapture in front of a Dégas painting, whose poor little dancer is almost bent double with fatigue and misery, hair falling over her fingers from the nape of her neck. Jeanne liked everything I liked and was not too keen on the people I was not too keen on. Jeanne is beautiful and dumb. We lunched at the Gallery among Art Students at small separate tables and by walls hung with jilted pictures from the higher regions. Then Daddy, and out again with him to the Fitzroy Gardens, hot houses rich and heavy with camellias, bronze gates of St Patrick's and high incensed ceilings footed by tiny brass boxes where men of no experience hear confessionals. Nevertheless I believe in confession, but I shall never enter the Roman Church in my life as I once believed, because in the past few years - and the past few days - I have discovered surprising mental honesty in myself. We trammed to St Kilda and ate grapes along the promenade by ourselves, while beside was the sea in Hobsons Bay, all blue and pale towards Geelong.

Friday 18th April: I left Melbourne today. I packed my bags, bade the Crows and my own bathroom goodbye and left without breaking the Royal Copenhagen mermaid. Daddy and I stuffed ourselves with lobster at the Victoria and I was positive I saw Peter through a window. It was not Peter, but I felt suddenly sick and feverish. Damn Peter, because I'm still in love with him. The Hamilton train drew out and left my poor father standing on the platform by himself, conscious probably of the futility of us all loving each other and yet being apart. I wonder if I shall ever see him again. Aunt Moree met Mary and me at Hamilton.

Saturday 19th April: Hamilton has possessed us again, and country towns can be possessive. We have been put back into its fairs and gymkhanas; we watched its men marching, its stalls and wheat tossing competitions taking money for the new hospital. We gave pony rides to the children for three pence all afternoon and took it in relays to eat afternoon tea under the grandstand, buy lucky handkerchiefs and throw hoops and watch the young men racing.

Tuesday 22nd April: Pop has a job - the job for which he would have committed murder, I believe. He is now in an administrative position with the Royal (English) Air Force in the Mediterranean or Malay, in a blue uniform, his sense of failure removed and an extra two pounds ten for us. I immediately put myself into the University but, decided money in the Bank was more adventurous. Aunt Moree and I bought plants from a nursery and I was tempted to pay 3/6 for a Poplar and send it to Richard who can talk of nothing else but trees, because he sees none. I romped about in breeches all day and sit here again in the studio while Mary is painting in the large yellow smock and trying to get me to pose in the nude. I remain adamant.

Monday 28th April: This was a splendid day. Aunty Moree, Mary and I - this time with a notebook - spun along the road to a station, fifty miles away. We lay about on rubber cushions and rugs, while outside grazing land and coaching villages, waterfalls, long blue plains and gum bush bowled past. We ran the whole gamut of the Australian scene and the sun dazzled the road, polished up the leaves and generally pansied up the world for us. Aunt Moree streamed on about people until my notebook was a giggling mass of character studies. In we went through high white gates, under miles of trees to the homestead. Our friends were pretty girls in striped shirts and breeches who had come home from Melbourne to muster and crutch, whose brothers were in Palestine and who danced together at night but never minded. It amazes me how deeply war has sunk into the country. At night, taking pity on two men from the army, we dragged down mattresses and fur rugs and let the army sleep its last night in peace for they depart tomorrow and have only a freezing paddock and pigs' pens to sleep in tonight. They crept out early this morning leaving everything in order and a legion of fleas.

Saturday 2nd May: Mary left early for Melbourne, where she is finishing her domestic course, and left me here alone. Riding Dookie, I walked round to the Calvary camp and saw the men in leather breeches and plumed hats, and their horses herded together in polished saddles and bits. From the camp you can look down on Hamilton in an evening mist, its steeples and colleges and green trees. I was taken to "Forty Thousand Horsemen" which I had seen. The theatre was packed with small boys and many of the cavalry men who had ridden in the film. The excitement was intense. It was queer seeing the same uniform when you turned to go, training for the same fight against their old enemy in Egyptian deserts.

Sunday 4th May: Up early and away in the car to Mount Gambier. The mist was dull and swirling about us all the way there, covering everything. It was pleasant being in South Australia again, as though I had come home. We went to church to hear an unsympathetic preacher - the object of our visit, as the Presbyterian elders are badly in need of someone. I should hate to doom them for five years to this humourless Man of God. After a lunch of oysters, kippers, asparagus and cranberry pie we drove straight back before I had seen the lakes and caves. The drive back was splendid because the sky reflected blue on everything, the earth was smooth and emerald green and white clouds lay in long shadows across it. But it was depressing in its loveliness and its sense of life because, picking up a South Australian newspaper to see what parties I was missing, I read that Nob's heroic brother, Duncan Good, is again missing, that Bryan Carter, an ABC radio compere, has not returned from Greece, and that Peter Ingoldby, a friend aged 19, is dead - smashed up in his plane. It was not very long ago since he and I ate roly poly in the pictures and the sailor in front told us to take our "bloody tarts from off me Neck." I dreamed of them all last night, until the crashes became one crash and the three men Richard, and I hated this murdering world.

Thursday 8th May: Aunty Moree said she was tired of eating afternoon teas with healthy people, so we staggered along the railway line with a pineapple on a string, and a bag of bananas, and into a tiny wooden house smelling dank, and of oil cloth. An old man, white haired and deaf and mumbling, sat in a corner of the kitchen holding two poppies, while a fat filthy Irish woman dangled the pineapple in front of him. A few of their seven adult children hung about in the doorway, arms hanging limply at their sides. The youngest boy was black with coal from a foundry and smiled at me with a white smile and bright eyes. Arranging chrysanthemums and rosemary in my room later, I thought a lot of them and thanked God I was not one of them.

Monday 12th May: Yesterday, I went to bed early, for the last time in my Renaissance bedroom. Today, more chaos and packing and sitting on trunks; a formal dinner with Mr Glyn Jones, the departing pastor, amid candles and steam from the roast; a walk through Hamilton saying "goodbye" to people in the street and shopping for odds and ends; a conversation by the fire on Aunty Moree's favourite topic - love affairs; irritating farewells and a long train journey through the night to Ararat, reading the socialistic book "The Ragged Trousered Philanthropists".

Tuesday 13th May: The time drags by and this hateful train tears on forever. The carriage is full of girls asleep with young men and legs and stuffiness. My eyes sting and my hair is knotted. I sat on my case watching the autumnal leaves through the hills; then darling Adelaide and Mummy and Bryan and the end of that inhuman train. Sibyl lunched with me and tried to entice me to the films but I held out firmly and dropped asleep on my bed. Later Sibyl came and left early after dinner so that I lay in my dear little bed with Mother knitting me a blue jumper and Bryan sitting on the floor, while I told them about the holiday that is ended.

Thursday 15th May: Bryan and I gardened steadily after plunging ourselves into the earth for fifteen minutes to "get the feel". We laid the garden bare of autumn leaves with the neighbour's secateurs, and annihilated Bryan's Thistle Farm, and in the afternoon I went domesticated in a gingham apron.

Friday 16th May: All morning Sibyl and I drove backwards and forwards from O'Connell Street, carting melons. We cut them up all day, only stopping for nourishment and then on again. Nob Good asked me to a dance, as Rosslyn Dumas has decided to wait for someone else, so we drove down to the Luxmoore's Red Cross Dance at Glenelg in "Liz". There was no lid and we each had to hold a door on, which is fun, even with velvet and tulle and a fur. The dance was small and rather dull and I danced a succession of fox-trots with beery soldiers out on the loose. Later we drank champagne at the Luxmoore's, lying by a fire until three o'clock.

Saturday 17th May: Alain Harvey gave a dance to the nicest people in Adelaide so that we were all bursting with good feeling and good living. Tony and Peter Gilbert drove me there and we met Nob Good, Barbara Kelly, Alison Harvey and her sister Herries, John and Margo Walters, Sue Bowen among others; and a John Portus (on whom I have developed a nice old fashioned pash). We sat on cushions and couches by a fire at one end of the room and danced at the other to a gramophone, under the high Georgian ceiling. We toasted buns, danced mad ballets, climbed pomegranate trees in the moon light. The boys were all in uniform, but there was not a war that night. We were much too happy and the night was far too beautiful and we all drove home in Nob's car and John Portus told Barb that I fascinated him. Peter is very far away. John is nine years older than I am and has been on a walking tour through Wales - not with Lloyd George but with the miners, and he is, as Sibyl says, "unobtainable".

Thursday 22nd May: Elise Fitzpatrick arrived today from Hamilton and slept all morning in my room. Yesterday evening, I filled the house with flowers for her - poinsettias in brass bowls and roses and lavender in crystal vases and irises in my blue porcelain bowl. Barbara Kelly took Bryan, Elise and me to the Youth Theatre, a Communist group run by such passionate creatures as Elliott Johnston (who was dispensing subversive pamphlets in his orange tie), Max Harris (who was in the play, acting in his crude, hateful way), and Billy Bray (who will be everything before he's twenty) and the former prodigy of the piano, Philip Hargrave. We sat on the backs of chairs among curious University students and interested socialists from Hindmarsh, while everyone shouted hymns of hate, with rollicking tunes like the Salvation Army. It will obviously be banned at the start, but it only cost one shilling and "Squaring the Circle" is quite amusing, even when acted atrociously.

Sunday 25th May: I arranged a walking party for Nob Good. At two his car "Liz" arrived with the walking party comprising Alain and Alison Harvey, Barbara Kelly and my adorable John Portus, Nob and I. We wrapped ourselves in rugs and army coats and drove to Montacute, causing enormous hilarity wherever we went. We walked up Black Hill and down Black Hill which is no easy task. The boys wore tweeds and forgot about uniforms and we tore our stockings and shoes to shreds, carried kangaroo tail plants, slid down stony heights, swung from tree to tree and arrived late in the afternoon at the foot, filthy and delighted. We marched back to the car banging rusty tins, shouting songs and making music with a comb and a pound note. John walked in front twirling a kangaroo tail, as band master. We roared home to my place, washed, brushed, had a sherry and sat down to one of Lillian's magnificent high teas. We staggered to the fire, sat round it playing Noel Coward's game, acted titles and scenes in old clothes, scarlet cloaks and made merry generally. The house was in an uproar, so we danced in the vestibule and the back verandah to the gramophone and everyone departed tearfully at eleven. I lay in bed with a happy feeling inside me, feeling that these were my friends.

Monday 26th May: I have bought two winter frocks, a pale blue wool frock with navy spots and navy trimmings, and a deep blue angora with embroidered flowers on the belt, round neck and sleeves. Blue, blue - Elise and I had afternoon tea in town and I bought three of Tchekov's plays for eleven pence. We drifted home across the links in the misty twilight, but I can't seem to make her love Adelaide as I do. And why, after Melbourne?

Wednesday 28th May: Elise and I walked through North Adelaide to the Botanical Gardens and everywhere were golden trees and dried leaves about our feet so that we felt very young indeed and flung leaves in the air which the gardeners were burning in blue smoke. We trailed back through the Cathedral, leaving a track of peanuts, and I arranged flowers during the day for Peter Cotter. A Mrs O'Sullivan from Casterton, near Hamilton wrote to me about one, Peter Cotter, a landowner, twenty four, orphan, Air Force, Geelong Grammar, much travelled and utterly charming. She wants me to adopt him in his loneliness which seems no hard task. He dined with us and is indeed a Mother's Delight. He is tall and strong and good looking; he is steady and secure and conservative; he is wealthy and independent. He is not very exciting.

Thursday 29th May: The sky was blue, like delphiniums, so Elise and I went down to the river where the trees are like showers of blossoms at the edge. The leaves seemed polished and solid gold and the ground is heavy with them. We lay along a grey trunk out into the water with Gaby on my tummy. He kept on forgetting where he was and eventually fell in, so we took him home across the park and washed him. We saw two crazy films at the Theatre Royal, where there is such an atmosphere of ballet and plays and Gilbert and Sullivan. I read Tchekov by the fire. They do nothing but theorize, these Russians, so I wonder how they ever got a Revolution going.

Friday 30th May: Elise and I lay in a tangle of sheets and unfinished packing, reading poetry aloud and listening to my worn out records. After lunch we left her luggage at the station and Elise at the Public Library and I went and interviewed Mr Reed. He was terribly courteous, jumping about and wringing my hand and pushing chairs under me till I felt he really wanted me back. I gather that is the position but office etiquette forbids stripping a secretary out for no apparent reason. He will ring me. He will see what he can do. He will talk to his friends. He is a dear. We tracked round town, dustying ourselves in second hand bookshops and ate a large meal with Mother and Bryan at John Martin's. Bryan and I walked home across the park, thanking our Destinies that we were not on that jazzy train to Victoria.

Saturday 31st May: I played Cinderella tonight and sat in the cinders while Mummy went and danced with a tall young Englishman. I sat alone, writing, weaving splendid tales of balls that did not end at midnight. This is an obvious case of repression. The next day, Bryan and I forced Mummy into Church looking very bloodshot and dopey. She lurched home at two this morning and I trust she did not "sit in cars" with the tall young Englishman. What it is to have an unmarried Mother!

Monday 2nd June: I lay in my pansy bedroom, like Little Lotus Bud, and read a ghastly murder story called "The Advertiser". It is about Cretan hills bloody with slain Englishmen and German boys; it is about heroic and futile sinkings of two giant ships - the "Hood" and the "Bismarck". It is about a world streaked and smeared with evil, and little men doing courageous things for nothing, except that man is a courageous animal. But so shallow are we that we forget and go on living as though our brothers were not dead in Crete, and London a charred shell. I wrote in the sun during the afternoon and when I say "writing" I mean no diaries and letters, but My Great Australian Novel.

Wednesday 4th June: The Crete battle has ended and the public is mad at the Home Office and calls then "dithering fools" and weeps at the useless wastage. Yes, we have been at war for so long that we can call thousands of hacked up boys - "wastage".

Friday 6th June: There is trouble brewing with the French over Syria - the next step to the Suez. The Vichy Government in France is reported as working hand in glove with the Germans there.

Wednesday 11th June: The Americans will procrastinate forever, probably. We are pottering around in Libya, and casualty lists are fantastic. We are still advancing in Syria. An American ship has been torpedoed by a Nazi. Someone says the war will go on for thirty years. We are greatly depressed because Richard will be leaving shortly for overseas, while most of his friends are remaining behind as instructors. They drew from a hat and Richard was unlucky. He is elated but we —. To draw life or death out of a hat! Michael Brookman is in the offence of Sollum in Egypt.

Friday 13th June: I interviewed the Women's Royal Australian Naval Service about enlisting and cadged a letter of introduction from Sir Lavington to Mr Dumas, Managing Director of "The Advertiser". I dined at Myers for lunch with Gordon Heaslip and two Hungarians who have a doll factory which is in its infancy. I applied for a job as stuffer but was told I would do more disorganisation than dolls. We were interrupted continually by clever looking foreigners who kept rushing in to return books or three pences. They all appear to be poverty stricken doctors of Something.

Thursday 19th June: We are at the gates of Damascus looking down on her gardens and minarets, but the French Government refuses to give in. We are being held up in other parts of Syria and in Libya.

Friday 20th June: The Casualty Lists are printed closely like examination results. They are the results of Man's Selfishness and innate stupidity. But we forget. I fiddled about with sherry, fruit cup, flowers and savouries all day and waited for my friends, sitting on the stool by the fire with the bright lights shining on the sherry glasses and the cherries in the fruit cup, and the room was good; leather chairs and a thick green rug and lustre jugs, and I wearing a pink tulle frock and pale pearls. Sibyl came in floral taffeta, and twins Don and Ron Sawers, and Alain, and Barbara Kelly in a pinafore organdie and Peter Cotter and his sister Bettine, and her friend Dawn Austin and Gordon Heaslip; and we drank sherry and reluctantly left the fire and went in cars to the Salters' Red Cross dance. It was a good dance, if slightly peculiar, and I came home with the Sawers. Ken Pope was there, "my first date", and he was overcome once at the thought of Lawrie, his brother who died recently in a motorcycle smash, and his arm was a little too tight, but then, it always was.

Saturday 21st June: We take Damascus. Germany invades Russia which pleases the world in general even though Hitler will have endless war supplies if she wins. But it is time we want.

Monday 23rd June: The Great Dumas summoned me today; I crept shudderingly into his office. It occurred to me half way through the ordeal that I had been here before; in a rush of suppressed mirth I remembered sitting on the right side of the desk in this room at midnight, and making Stewart Cockburn a war correspondent. Dumas said He Would Let Me Know. I spent the rest of the day interviewing Women's National Services. Aunty Pol took me home to dinner and I stopped Sibyl from doing any homework, so, after being stocked with chocolates and passion fruit, was sent home.

Tuesday 24th June: Mr Dumas, on being informed, told me that 100 speed was not particularly good, so I went to Chartres Business College this morning and discovered that 80 would have been more honest. Mother and I lunched at Quality Inn and Gordon Heaslip who apparently lives there, asked me to a dance tomorrow night and on my refusing, asked Mother. She blushed slightly, stammered, averted her eyes so I suddenly remembered, "Your Bridge, darling." But later in the afternoon I found her having tea with a young Flight-Lieutenant, Denis Winterbottom, so I refuse to rescue her any more. He reluctantly left her and drove me home - a compliment because of petrol rationing which allows 2 gallons a month.

Wednesday 25th June: Richard's pre-embarkation leave at the end of this week has been curtailed. But he has been made a Pilot Officer - a commissioned man! Funny how I generally forget to record the really important events in this life. There are reports of tremendous German advances. What will Japan do? Germany is urging her to join the Axis against Russia and the Pacific and Australia.

Friday 27th June: I came home from a typing test at Chartres, tied my hair up in a handkerchief, put on the blue painting smock and size seven sandals and trapped Gaby. After bathing him I weeded and raked and got earthy, with the help of Bryan who carted dry leaves like a dryad in Australian May. We wandered heartily across the links at night, watching Gaby break up the shadows across the lawns and feeling the cool dew rise up from the grass, talking of Muscles and Exercise and Manual Labour and the Supremacy of Fitness. At bedtime, Bryan tucked me up with his enormous hands so that I was bound in bed by iron sheets.

Monday 30th June: I arranged flowers, made drink, set the table with the best crystal, silver and smoky wine glasses, dusted, and shelled peas. We could not stop laughing all the way down to the station in the dark and sucked barley sugar to steady our nerves. The train came in, and with it Richard. His last leave before going overseas. We fell into his arms and I struggled against weeping for happiness. We dined on turkey - fatted calf - and talked idly by the fire. Richard is very thin and trying to be older than he is. I think I shall like him better tomorrow.

Tuesday 1st July: Tonight we walked across the park to the films, with Bryan racing ahead and Richard and Mummy holding hands and suddenly kissing each other as though this were the end of the world; the city pink and luminous above the dark trees. We saw the French film "La Bandera" about the French Foreign Legion. By us sat a young Free French sailor in a pom-pom, a striped shirt, dark blue uniform and the Cross of Lorraine. He swam from his ship to Alexandria against Vichy orders; escaped under fire on a raft, fought in the Libyan Campaign and is now on his way to England and General de Gaulle. What Hell these boys get when they are captured.

Wednesday 2nd July: Richard has borrowed Denis Winterbottom's uniform and is now a Flight-Lieutenant, but no one knows the difference. We lunched at Quality Inn with Mother who has to go to Melbourne tomorrow on business. But tonight we splashed about in velvet and cyclamens at the South. Barbara Kelly, Denis, Mother, Bryan, Richard and I were there. We dined and drank Richard's health and Long Life in Rhine Gold; had coffee, cigarettes and talk in the lounge and then we went to the Tuxedo. We had the place almost to ourselves. I wished then so much to hold time, to go on dancing securely with Richard with pleasant people like Den and Barb about us and I suppose that someday we will - again -

Thursday 3rd July: Bryan and I saw Mother off to Melbourne, and I felt incredibly sorry for her, sitting there with a hard faced spinster and a Fijian Chief, while Richard's minutes were so priceless.

Friday 4th July: The Russians have adopted a "burnt earth" policy. If they lose, then Germany won't get a thing out of them. Only the Russians would be so defeatist enough to carry out such an idea. Unfortunately, the wheat crop is still green.

Saturday 5th July: Sibyl came for afternoon tea and Richard and we two walked down to the river to watch Bryan racing, taking snaps as we went. Later I dressed, wearing my velvet frock, the pendant, and the fur cape. We drove to the Regent and during the Interval I met Peter Anderson. Just suddenly, like that. He came over, looking very white and we talked of aimless things, hardly looking at each other, because there were others, watching us. He tried to light a cigarette but his hand shook as though he were drunk. I carried it off far better than he. During the film, I shivered and felt ill, and dancing at the Tux until four, I counted the minutes and was sick. He is not worth this. There is something between us that is so vital and powerful that it deprives us of control.

Sunday 6th July: He is not worth it. The thought of him breaks my health and fills my life with mad despair. Richard left home for St Mark's Embarkation Depot, so I went to dinner at the Brookman's, feeling better. What would I do without them? I came home early and tired and lay in Richard's room, listening to the wireless. I became frightened of myself. The world and everything in it was futile and depressing. I thought I was going mad with melancholia. It is impossible to judge, but I have never come nearer to suicide than last night. I was on the point of ringing up someone like Dr Wigg or Mr Hackworthy, the Minister, when Lillian came home and we sat on the kitchen table and drank hot milk. I remember last night with a terrific shudder, so lonely was the misery. I can only say, "You are 18. Just 18. You should love living at 18. You are 18" over and over again. Joie de Vivre!

Tuesday 8th July: Yesterday I went and consumed passion fruit at the Brookman's, reaching sublime heights at the moment when one picks up a spoon and thrusts it into a wine glass of passion seeds and condensed cream and sugar, mucked up deliciously together. I am becoming a gourmet. We always do the same things at the Brookman's but they never bore me. Mother came back from Melbourne this morning and I am still suffering from the last faint reverberating echoes of Saturday night. I shall never do the things I want to do, because I am tied so firmly to Mummy's apron strings, not by force, but by emotion. Unless I am hard and self-contained and objectionable....

Thursday 10th July: Richard came home to bed after a dental operation and I read a "Saint" novel to Mother by the fire. She said I am more as I used to be, pretty and happy. In spite of Sunday evening, I think she is right. I have been reading my old diaries and I regret that the person I used to be has been suffocated. She was an intellectual child and amused and amusing. She was completely optimistic. She might have been able to write Best Sellers. I can't write anything these days that is not emotional or heavy. Here comes Lillian to read me juicy extracts from her latest writings.

Saturday 12th July: Mother spent the evening at St Mark's with Richard and as we were pointedly not invited, Bryan and I sat by the fire and then went to bed and to sleep. An ear splitting yell from the telephone awoke me and a voice said, "Come to the Tux. It's John Portus." I looked at my watch which pointed to twelve. I remember wondering if it were morning...or midnight. But as it was John Portus, I doused myself with cold water, dressed in ten minutes and was driven off in high spirits by John McFarlane and John P. I have often wondered what people have been doing who turn up at the Tux at one, now I know. We had enormous fun that night, and chugged home in John McFarlane's automobile at four in the morning, yelling part-songs.

Sunday 13th July: Richard told us he was embarking tomorrow for England. It has begun.

Monday 14th July: Mother and I visited St Mark's Embarkation Depot for an hour, and took dim photographs in the rain. We completed any arrangements that were left to be made and, in town, bought dried fruit, books and magazines. The three of us, very subdued, trammed down to the station to see Richard off. We talked brightly to the last minutes, then Richard flung himself into Mummy's arms and held her tight for a long time; then he hugged me and kissed me; shook hands quiveringly with Bryan and ran to his carriage when the whistle blew. A few yards away, Mr Kenneth Milne said to his son Lance, "I'll be seeing you soon; well, so long, old chap"... and walked away. It was admirable, although Lance half wept. We saw Richard sitting by himself, not looking out, with his respirator and helmet beside him, and in a great coat, like a Nazi General's, and a peaked officer's cap -and we walked down the station, trying not to weep. We had booked for the film "Florian", knowing that would be wiser than going home to an empty, cold house, but now that it came to the push, it was agony to us. But it was successful. We grew interested in the film, and half forgot, and the hero survived the Last War. We walked back across the links, with the listless mists swirling between the trees, and white gulls bathing in the floods, and we were consoled of many things.

Tuesday 15th July: The "Situations Vacant" columns always interest me but today it was simply pregnant with possibilities. I applied for the Secretaryship (Executive) of the Housewives' Association, and for the position of governess to a small boy of ten somewhere in the Never-Never. Mr Hackworthy, promised to write me a Reference on condition that I call for it myself and have a talk with him. We sat comfortably in his study by a fire and discussed my rapid progress towards Cynicism, and much, I admit, was solved. And he does not, unlike Mother, think I have a weak character, but that I am a dear little (but remember, very little) girl, half kissing me. So I bounced home joyously - thus does someone else's opinion affect me.

Wednesday 16th July: Mother bought me "Orlando" by Virginia Woolf and I am rapidly consuming it. I eat it up and fall on my knees to a great woman who, while so full of life and loveliness, has killed herself because of wars, and lost illusions which she counts so precious. "I am growing old," she thought, taking her taper, "I am losing my illusions." And so I took "Orlando" with me to bed and savoured phrases of perfection.

Thursday 17th July: I have been asked to the Law Students' Dance. I have a policy not to miss first dates. They sometimes lead to new crowds, and young men are fearfully short these days. There are only consumptives and medical students left. The eldest are married and the youngest are small fry. Sibyl and I sucked aniseed balls all over O'Connell Street and ate twelve passion fruit non-stop. She read me a new play which is amazingly witty.

Friday 18th July: Went to a minor sherry party and dance in one of those box-on-wheels and saw Billy Bray and Philip Hargrave there and sundry dreary females too dreary to name, excepting Anne Ayliffe, who spent most of the dance apparently consuming whisky and soda in the box-on-wheels with Philip. I acted as a stooge for Ros Dumas and wrote up social notes for "The Express and Journal", but everyone else seemed to be doing the same things for other papers. I was most interested in Philip Hargrave, remembering the time when casts of his childish hands were shown in Allan's windows, and the greatest honour was to be led up to him at the Town Hall in an organdie party frock and ask the little boy in the Eton collar for his autograph. He was the only one of us allowed black coffee at supper – "What it is to have been a blinking prodigy", said Billy Bray, which is all it means now.

Saturday 19th July: Arrived very late at the Woodland's Old Scholars Dance. Tommy Simpson was there and of late he has been wandering about with all the kick out of him. However, tonight instead of ignoring me, he even danced with me, but also whisked me off under some dark cloisters and started petting me with kisses. I did my utmost to avert them. I said, "The same old Tommy," and he replied regretfully but with the same old challenge in his eyes, "And the same old Carys!" It was quite fun, this dance, but not as good as the afternoon I spent writing.

Tuesday 22nd July: I am now the first secretary of Both Electrics Ltd, a new firm opened by the inventor of Lord Nuffield's iron lung. Today I was presented with wads of pound notes by Mr Gleeson, the manager, and told to buy everything an office needs. I looked wistfully at the newest type-writers and radiators, but bought instead, paper and brooms and calendars ad infinitum. I don't think I shall like this job very much; it reminds me of Sargood Gardiner and has atrocious hours. Later, I wrote long pages of My Great Australian Novel, all about introspective young men stripping the world of her artificialities, with dear Virginia Woolf well in mind and Simon Templar very much in hand, which is not a good combination, as one's style is apt to be a mixed pie of subtlety and exaggeration.

Thursday 24th July: There is a Health Academy next door, and when Mr Gleeson is dictating a letter, we hear "slap, slap, slap, slap" on some-one's bottom, towels being rubbed over bodies and muscles massaged. It is very discomforting, particularly when a woman through the parti-tion gives loud lectures on Constipation, the curse of our Civilization. We blush and raise our voices.

Friday 25th July: Sibyl gave herself a Surprise Party tonight for her 17th birthday. I trailed round there at eight in walking shoes and savou-ries, with Bryan following after carrying crockery. There were about thirty people, all dressed for hard walking. I went hunting with Kenny Price, Charlie's younger brother. We set off ahead of the others, crossed a park, found a clue, held hands, bought chewing gum at a shop and were given a clue in exchange, drank at a fountain, pelted along to Colonel Light's statue, pursued by eager couples, raced along dark lanes, rang up "Dr Jekyll", found another clue in my powder bowl and hared off to catch a crowded tram ahead of the others. We zoomed through the shopping crowd, urged the driver on, with half Adelaide pelting down Jeffcott Street after us, with the shopping crowd leaning out and persuading them on, tipped a woman out of a telephone booth and tore Wody Blackburn's hand out of a hedge and shared two boxes of chocolates with her. We sank onto sofas, ate enormous quantities of supper and limped round the drawing room to the accompaniment of a gramophone. I was still laugh-ing when I fell asleep.

Sunday 3rd August: Wody Blackburn came to tea. Her father, Colonel Blackburn, took the keys of Damascus by mistake, but will nevertheless go down in History. He was standing outside the walls, talking to some Free Frenchmen, all the British Field Marshalls having grown bored and gone away, when out dashed a Frenchman with a white flag, presented it hastily to Mr Blackburn and waited tremblingly to be struck with thunderbolts. So Colonel Blackburn marched into Damascus, and the papers give a different story.

Wednesday 6th August: Bryan read D.H. Lawrence's "The Snake", and came roaming into the dining room this evening where I was sitting alone by the fire, and asked me to give him some poetry of the same sort. I thought Rupert Brooke might appeal to him, but it did not. Neither did Masefield, I'm glad to say. Edith Sitwell did a little, and a small modern war poem. He likes modern poetry, calling it "different from the old da-da,da-da,-da-da,-da-da stuff." An inevitable reaction from "Drake's Drum"! It is rather thrilling and a little ludicrous to see Bryan sitting by the fire, immersed in Wilfred Owen. After one has been sitting by the fire for a whole evening reading poetry and Virginia Woolf, the room - if it is small - grows very significant and symbolic. One becomes conscious of knives and apple skins, and books of verse, silver candlesticks and almond blossom and sugar bowls completing a very desirable existence..... The Germans claim to have reached the Black Sea.

Sunday 10th August: Mrs Clive Carey took me to the Regent to hear the Prime Minister at a Happy Sunday Afternoon service, in which Adelaide's Deanna Durbins sway their hips and sing "The Daughters of Cadiz" and Mr Menzies delivers an oration before white satin curtains. He looked like a tired grey slug from the second row of the front stalls where we sat among the Swells, displaying our complimentary tickets and regarding rows of ministerial collars through lorgnettes. But his speech was quite fun, particularly as he is in a rotten political position, the Labors wanting to force an election and Japan ready to pounce. We dined on omelettes at the Railway Station and met Clive at the University, where we heard a dress rehearsal of "The Lady from Alfaqueque" - "La Consuela" by two Spanish brothers. It struck me as being rather pointless, but I was told on the programme that only Philistines thought these Spanish works pointless; that, subtly and obscurely, in the lines was life itself. Clive Carey is very much loved in his black broad-brimmed hat, his low beautiful voice and his clear pink features.

Tuesday 12th August: Mama had a bridge party this evening, so I pansied myself up and went in to drink sherry with them, and was told what a big girl I had grown into. Their conversation is alarmingly trite. It seems impossible that after forty years of conscious intelligence, they can only talk about - I've forgotten what. When we play cards after two glasses of sherry, everything we say is hilariously funny and we lie round on the floor and yell with laughter. I suppose when one is forty-five and a grandmother - most of Mother's friends are - one knows one can't hitch up one's velvet frocks, fling one's furs and rings onto the mantelpiece and lie down on the floor, so they don't allow their conversation to reach any entertaining heights. Mother always stands away from her friends when I see her with them - and I don't believe it is an exaggeration of my own mind. Tonight, her hair was very dark among the white heads, with one or two streaks in it, which made her look younger, as though she had lately stepped off the stage in London, wrapped up in light and applause. She wore a wine coloured velvet frock with tight sleeves, and diamonds, and sandals. She was tall and slim, and very poised.

Wednesday 13th August: Miss Hassell, my school teacher, was coming to supper tonight, and the house was filled with cherry blossom and cakes after last night, but her brother came home on final leave, so Sibyl came instead. I was very disappointed because I so often think of her, and I would have had her alone tonight. Sibyl and I sat by the fire in the dining room with the light out. A fleet of planes flew very low over the house and we sprang up out of our chairs, holding each other. The shadows on the walls grew large and spilled over onto the ceiling, and it suddenly occurred to me that we had a right - o uncivilized world! – to expect to be bombed.

Thursday 14th August: I had lunch yesterday with John McFarlane, who is most amusing but stirs nothing in me, until I get him to talk about John Portus who was at Oxford studying Law while I was buying doll's clothes in Piccadilly in London. We were staying then with Mother's family in Wales. Nevertheless, I believe John Portus talks about me a good deal, even to men in camp who don't know me, which, if I didn't want to think wishfully, I should refuse to believe of him. Today I sat in the grass against a white elm tree by the University Bridge, where everything was terribly quiet. Walking away later, I heard a flat sort of splash and read later that Max Harris and four other disliked students had been hurled in by the University, to give vent to their displeasure. It is officially announced that the President of the USA and the Prime Minister of England met in the Atlantic with the heads of their respective Army, Navy and Air Forces, and have drawn up a list of aims.

Friday 15th August: Sibyl had dinner with me and we went to a musical evening at Doctor Duguid's, stopping in town to buy Debussy's Sirens Symphony at a shop in Charles Street owned by a certain little Mr Larcher. There is something definitely odd about Mr Larcher; he twitters or has a deep voice that breaks or has a Hitler moustache or is very shy or is very bold. I really can't say. When Sibyl introduced me, he looked wildly about the room, said "I've met you before, Miss Harding Browne," and on my asking where, replied mystically, "In an office". I naturally asked which one? and he looked at the carpet, up at the lampshade, studied his finger nails and said in a low whisper "Mr Harding Browne's". Then very hastily added that he "didn't want to bring it up". I felt under the circumstances that a deep look of pain should cross my eyes and I should reply brokenly. Instead I laughed and we sat on a couch discussing Voltaire, while Sibyl argued with an acquaintance about Mussorgsky in the music library. Judith Crase and Barby Salter had arranged the Duguid Soirée, which was obvious by the long pauses between each item, the untidiness of the chair covers, the splendid ease of the audience, the queer crowd who arrived, the fine playing and the fact that the people present and the money received didn't balance out. Young men called "Carl" played the violin with lugubrious eyes and Ronda Gehling, whom I can never address without feeling a vague stir of awe as though she was a celebrity already, played a Chopin Nocturne as though she had composed it herself on a verandah in November. Sibyl and I trammed home, knitting like a couple of old maids, and eating peanuts out of a bag.

Saturday 16th August: Virginia Woolf has gone back to the Library after showing me a style I should like to achieve. I should love to have her feeling for words, and her delight in playing with them; I should like to have her subtlety, but also a certain vitality and robustness which she lacks. If I had that, I should die happy in Poet's Corner.

Tuesday 19th August: Nob Good came to dinner and we drove off in the Box on Wheels - as distinct from "Liz" - and saw "Escape" with Robert Taylor, Norma Shearer, and Conrad Veidt. It is another of those Young American Goes to Germany to Save a Friend and Falls in Love with a Victim of Nazi Oppression who Dies against a Background of the Swastika (or Lives against a Background of the Statue of Liberty). In spite of this, I came away with a bewildered feeling that man is capable of altering his life (created by thousands of years of inherited progress) in the space of seven years. Perhaps when I - or someone else - reads this in years to come, they will be amazed that I believed in this figure of horror - a Storm Trooper, when he may be nothing more than a mere man, who dangles his children before a fire in a "Mon Repos". I hope so. There is no other hope, otherwise. Nob and I drank iced coffee in the "Night Owl", and argued about something. Duncan, his brother, is still missing; the body of his navigator was washed up on the coast of France.

Wednesday 20th August: Miss Hassell had supper with me this evening. We sat in arm chairs opposite each other in the firelight, Mother having gone to bed with a cold. She disappointed me a little; from two years experience of the world, she appears to me a little old maidish, narrow and without the illuminating brain that I had imagined. She has very little sense of humour; but on the credit side, she can discuss with me the people who interest and excite me, and she can direct me along sublime paths, having given me already Virginia Woolf and Alice Meynell, who in turn gave me Francis Thompson. Besides this, she has given me a great deal before this, faith in myself and a wild desire to "with rude fingers pick thy branches never sere". I apologise to Milton who didn't write it quite like this. We ate crumpets by the fire and discussed "Orlando".

Thursday 21st August: I was visited by an atom of that tremendous thrill I used to experience on seeing Peter at the National Bank when we were both office boys. John Portus came in and asked me to dinner and a show. I danced on air for half an hour but that is where the resemblance with Peter ends for that went on for days! - and trammed home in ecstasy, thinking how lucky was I above the rest of these women. The Portus home is rather attractive; small and modern and in excellent taste and very near mine. We drove to town and saw the film "Penny Serenade" with the most attractive Cary Grant and Irene Dunne, which was all about Babies. We raced through the rain, holding hands, and drank coffee in "The Cavendish", and agreed on the best way of bringing up our - separate - babies. He is so whimsical and distant, like another Stonewall Jackson, until I feel like a Barbara Fritchie marching ahead. I should like to have him, but I doubt whether I should keep him if such an impossibility occurred. Empty-headed chatter!

Sunday 24th August: I must write to Daddy and tell him I can't accept his invitation to Singapore. He says he can get me a job and a boarding house if I go there, and that I will have hundreds of young Englishmen ready to marry me. Mother is most upset and wants me to write back and say I need not go to Singapore to find a husband. Nevertheless, impossible as the letter is, it thrills me to think how near the world is to me, to think that if I said "Yes" and paid forty pounds, it would be mine.

Tuesday 26th August: I spend most of these lunch hours when working for "Both Electrics", on my back in the Botanical Gardens, reading "The Pastoral Loves of Daphnis and Chloe," a translation from Longus's second century Greek by the delightful George Moore, who seems to me so very modern. Mainly, however, I watch the people around me - little girls chasing ducks, with their legs kicking up behind and their knickers showing; wounded returned soldiers in their blue uniforms and red ties, with mobs of small children jumping over the battered chests of their new fathers; business girls chatting; old men sitting in the sun; gardeners burning blue leaves.

Thursday 28th August: I went to the Public Library at lunchtime and read Walter Pater's essay on Prosper Mérimée. But I found it difficult to settle down. I look up and see "Coventry Patmore"; I glance through him; I look up and see "Bernard Newman"; then "Bertrand Russell". The names recall vast echoes, and I go on from shelf to shelf. I want to put my arms about the whole Library, but only scratch the covers.

Saturday 30th August: After leaving Both's, I ate my lunch at a milk bar and went on through the rain to the Library, where I stayed all afternoon. I left Pater and read Sichel's biography of Lady Hamilton, which seems very fair to me. Then I got a key and went into the Josiah Symon Library with a young librarian, who after putting first editions of Tennyson and Thackeray into my hands, left me there. I sat on the great tables and looked through a fifteenth century volume which had been annotated by a young Elizabethan, underlined, marked, questioned, so that one almost visualized the man drawing idle circles and adorning them with legs as he read. I passed on along the shelves and through the rooms and was rather proud that Oscar Symon, Josiah's son, had instigated this diary. Then I sat for a long time on the window sill, watching the steady grey rain through the window as it brushed the old Government buildings with their broken casement windows. The empty rooms were behind me, filled with thousands of years of experience and frustration, and the rain fell on, and silence went out of the room into the rain.

Monday 1st September: Germany marched into Poland two years ago; in the headings today is the statement "We plan out our third year of war" as though it were a relay race, and this only the preparation. It leads one to suppose that on the 1st September, 1942, I will be writing this same sentence, with the same dulled, hopeless pen. I have only one personal prayer for that date. The Russians have held up the Germans, but I don't hold out any hope in that quarter. Prime Minister, Mr Menzies has resigned and Mr Fadden with the same personnel under him, has taken the Premiership. Menzies will possibly go to England although this is not decided. I regret Mr Menzies, because he became a definite personality to me a few Sundays ago.

Tuesday 2nd September: Sibyl came to dine and we went to the pictures. But Sibyl had a theory. Instead of choosing the best programme, we - she - chose the worst. It turned out to be Cesar Romero and Carole Landis in "Dance Hall" and Tim Holt in "Along the Rio Grande"; and the theory didn't work. The first film was weak and watery - the second film was crude and utterly bereft of taste. Nevertheless, we shrieked with laughter, kept up a continual stream of frightfully witty remarks that appeared to us unsurpassably brilliant at the time and ate peanut roasties. We staggered home, making awful asses of ourselves but uncaring, like a couple of drunks - "angry penguins of the night".

Wednesday 3rd September: Sibyl's Mr Larcher is lending me Voltaire's Dictionary, so I lent him George Moore; he rang me up and said it was "the loveliest thing I've ever read in my life", and invited me somewhere to discuss it with him. I feel in much the same position as with Herbert Adams - nothing more than a demure little Victorian. Is it wise to go out with strange young men whose mothers you don't know? Isn't Mr Larcher reaching the dangerous age? Is it wise? And then I want to walk round the world alone - like Mic Sandford's eternal ladies who imagine that every man has evil intentions.

Saturday 6th September: I warned Sibyl that I was only coming to dinner on condition that she didn't take me to the pictures. So we played games and shouted a great deal, until Aunty Pol came in in her red flannel dressing gown, with her hair down her back, and said how happy she was because we were like the kids we had been at school. But she didn't know how sophisticated were the games we played.

Monday 8th September: We have a cable from Richard at last, reading "Arrived England safely Spending leave with family". Yesterday, John Portus and I wandered up to the Botanical Park and, sitting on the wooden benches under plane trees, listened to the Labor leader, Richards, give a most tolerant and plausible speech. He is the first Labor man I have heard tell his followers not to forget their cause the second they get a job and a full stomach. He said it is better to sacrifice a few shillings to raise the standard of general living. It appealed to me. Elliott Johnston (amid shouts of "Can ya swim?" and "How's the Torrens? Cold?") spoke on the aid to Communism Movement. He always strikes me as being the typical Undergraduate-turned-Socialist, with his dark, square, ugly face, white teeth, crooked smile, sincerity, red ties and dogged manner. It must hurt him to be in love with a girl who plays Polo.

Friday 12th September: A most important buyer from Tasmania, to whom the whole staff has been greasing for the past few days, asked me to the Vaudeville Show at the Majestic. I stammered, blushed, said "This is very unprecedented!" in a demure, Victorian way and finally accepted on being told he was quite safe, as he has a son four years younger than I. I met him at the South and loved the Vaudeville, particularly a most beautiful woman called Lea Sonia, who does a strip tease and turns out to be a man. I still can't believe it. There is a lovely remark of the comedian's, as he gets up from one of the boxes. "I wonder what happens to one's lap when one gets up?" Thinks. "Perhaps it goes behind, under an assumed name." We had supper at Quality Inn and taxied home, sick with chocolates.

Saturday 13th September: I met Bryan on the way home and he donkeyed me on the carrier through the yellow daisies and under gums. At ten o'clock, when sitting by the fire with Bryan, the front door bell rang and Mother was carried in from the Repertory, where she went with Mrs Hooper, for she had fainted in the third act and had been carried out in the arms of a neighbouring Colonel. I made coffee, piled up cushions under her legs, because she is suffering from great loss of blood, bathed her temples in scent and tucked her in, and went to bed and thought how much I loved her. It is definitely change of life.

Thursday 18th September: Some minor official called Harrison, whom no one has heard of before, has had the temerity to ban "Ulysses" by Joyce. Thus can one man withhold a milestone of modern literature from 6,000,000 people. Roosevelt says that America will shoot at sight any raiders near her - anywhere. By this, it means that American ships are now actually guarding our ammunition routes.

Saturday 20th September: The weekend came and kicked Both Electrics into next week. Walking home from work, everything was changed subtly by green grass under oak and olive trees and yellow carpets of daisies, which we used to wear round our heads. I put on my little silk petticoat, Liberty frock and spring coat with the mink lapels, and went to a garden party at Springfield. Louise Matison rescued me from Mother's friends and we drifted round the garden, watching archery and drinking tea on parapets. Then Louise took me to her home and showed me her new nephew, David, who is the son of a University student and a Czechoslovakian refugee. There lay the little Jew in a great sleeping green garden. I have one of those incredible school girl pashes on Louise who is so lovely. She came across the road to the garden party in a brown suit and a wide white shirt, bare legs and her hair caught back by a white band, yet she made me sort of close up and join the nondescript just in my most entrancing mood. It is the only thing I have against her. Auntie Mabel and Uncle Hal took me to an Ignaz Friedman's Chopin concert, during which he played the twenty four preludes. I was entranced and leaving the Town Hall in a burst of thanks, went with Sibyl to the South for supper. It was pleasant going from table to table, chatting to everyone about the concert, and making luncheon dates with Louise. Sibyl and I, inveterate hero worshippers, sat at a table within two yards of Friedman and gaped as the great man dropped his sandwiches into his tea. We leant over to each other and whispered, "What can you expect of the lower classes", about the, perhaps, only really civilized man in the room! He made rather a cute joke. He waved to Louis, the head waiter, and wasn't seen. One of the women at his table said, "I always clap when I want a waiter" and Friedman said, "Ah, but then he might think I want an encore".

Tuesday 23rd September: I am seriously thinking of putting an "Ad" in the paper under Situations Wanted, for a secretarial position at night. But I am at a loss how to frame it, what with all these vaudeville jokes on the boards. The Isolationists are getting angry with Hollywood for producing nothing but propaganda. They say a very few Jewish refugee directors have the power to sway American opinion. This is hotly debated in the Senate. The Russians are following out their burnt-earth policy. That is, if they lose ground, they destroy its value. They burn their own towns to the ground. Only Russians could be so fatalistic. Others would hope - to the last minute.

Sunday 28th September: I am now a secretary of Roofcote Co, at the almost philanthropic salary of two pounds ten a week! It all happened very suddenly and giving notice to Mr Gleeson wasn't nearly such diabolical fun as I had imagined. Ever since the first day I have detested his boorishness. John Portus came for afternoon tea and took me out into the fields. Gaby came dancing with us, leaping high into the air after willy wagtails, doubling back, madly exalting in the wide wet fields. I ran after him, dragging John by the sleeve, scattering the rain in the yellow flowers.

We sat on wooden gates and raced down to the embankment where the small boys were skimming flat stones on the water and girls made love publically, embarrassing us. The sky was hugely blue, bordered by long trailing clouds and the trees were a darker green than the grass. The roofs were very red. We were country squires wandering along the river, with every silver elm a part of us, swishing long sticks into the sour sobs. And yet when he began wondering what life he would choose if he had such a choice, John said he would be a miner's son – if he was free from bitterness. I was amazed at this queer whimsical fellow, who, I believe is a little in love with me. Coming home, we talked to Sibyl and Margo Waterhouse, and I was completely happy. I was pleased that they had seen me with him – "To the J.P." in their History Book by his father, Professor Portus! After tea, Mr Mühlstein sat by the fire in the lounge and sketched me in a large book, while I leant back against a green pillow in the gay rose-covered frock. He is going to draw me, which is thrilling, considering Adelaide is clamouring for paintings by him. He is a good looking man, wonderfully graceful, with lazy, crossed legs, silk socks and bright colouring.

Wednesday 1st October: I interrupted Sibyl's homework, which I have solemnly sworn never to do again, by drifting round and chatting to Graham. Sibyl eventually gave up the ghost, and joined in. We had a general knowledge test by the fire. "Who discovered that the world was round?" "Tell me, in three words, what Philosophy is?" "How many husbands has Kay Francis, the film actress had?" "What were the two most important books in the nineteenth century?" "Who is Lucille Ball, the American comedienne married to?" "How do you find the rectangle of a circle?" Sibyl won.

Friday 3rd October: Gaby always walks as far as the hollow in the first parklands with Mother and me. Then we tell him to go home and he sits unhappily in the daisies till all we can see is a black and yellow mass. He probably smells a few tree trunks and drifts off to play with friends. A dog's life........ Today I departed from Both Electrics. So far my leaving a job has not brought forth a presentation - but that will come. At least Mr Gleeson gave me the money I had had to make up in Petty Cash errors.....I washed my hair, and sewed and lay in bed, reading "The Human Situation" which so far holds the same opinion as I do, that nature is continually waning, so why should man, a part of nature, live peacefully in opposition to her dictates. I wish I didn't always return to such defeatist principles, because I am longing to find something to earnestly believe in. There is something. It is expressed in my new motto - a rather long quotation of Terence's "Nil tam difficile est quin quaerendo investigani possit" (Nothing is so difficult but that it may be found out seeking). This will I drape across the Tree of Knowledge.

Sunday 5th October: Mr Mühlstein arrived with his paints and easel, and adorned in a blue linen apron and carrying a palette, he began to paint me. Meanwhile I was dressed in the blue frock, my hair was loosened about my shoulders, and Mr Mühlstein arranged the bed on the verandah as a platform for the red chair. It looked rather attractive with the sun falling in through the wire, Mother writing letters in a blue frock at the red table, and boxed nasturtiums massed along the wall. Into this scene came John, and sat in a cane chair smoking and watching me quizzically, making personal remarks about my poorest features while Ernst painted and I was tied to one position. Then John got a pencil and pad from Mother and drew a most childish scribble of me, very flabby and indefinite. But Ernst's picture will be magnificent. It awaits the next sitting in my bedroom - rough, but me, nevertheless. Mr Mühlstein stayed to tea, and was easy to entertain because we were informal, letting him wash his hands and brushes under the kitchen sink.

Monday 6th October: Today I became Secretary to The Roofcote Company, which is a contractor of house repairing and painting. The office is small and unimposing, but the boss, of the American name of Alvin U. Webb, is a darling. I knew that from the beginning, but I proved it later in the day by collapsing in his arms. He gently ensconced me in his office, bought me some Aspros, and said "he had a girlie of his own", knowing what ails young women. The Roberts Health Academy revived me by putting me under an artificial sunray and hotting me up. Two days later Mr Webb and his Secretary discussed at length the burning question of Communism. We both discovered that the other had unexpectedly intelligent - or, at least, thirsting brains. He agrees with me about my new motto, that knowledge is the one concrete theory to base one's beliefs on. My school friend, Stevie, came to poke among the concrete-filled shadows. She kept on muttering, "Dear, how can you bear it? It's all so... so local!" Then loudly and cheerfully when Mr Webb came in, "How I do wish I were here!" and then going up the wooden stairs of The Roofcote Company to a Red Cross Meeting.

Thursday 9th October: Tonight Mother took the girls from her Department to the pictures to celebrate her bonus. Of course I went, because I'm generally around when I can get something for nothing. There was a Ministry of Information short called "Words for Battle" in which a succession of English scenes drifted across the screen idly, and Laurence Olivier recited apt poems. I reluctantly conclude that Rudyard Kipling's poem appealed to me most - "When the English began to hate", in a low, sad, fierce, throbbing tone. When England began to hate —

Monday 13th October: Somehow I caught an early bus to Mount Barker Rest Home where Mother is there for a week and had morning tea with her in a room full of dreary old women and a few sententious old men. It is no good looking ungracious, when Mother is showing you off. She tidied my hair and introduced me to the d.o.w. and the s.o.m. and was almost about to lapse into baby talk in her fervour. We ate an enormous dinner in this lovely house and walked in the sun, planning our future and breathing sweet briar, although I kept falling asleep on every log. The hills were carpeted in yellow daisies, like sleeping stars, and the valleys were clear and aglow. In the evening I came back in the great bus, with the lights below, as though London were laid at one's feet. It is a good time to dream.

Tuesday 14th October: The Japanese are beginning to flaunt America - a dangerous proceeding even though she is our white elephant, and has failed us. We are continually being questioned about our promise to help Russia not being fulfilled, but we are told that it would mean another Dunkirk. Our planes are there.

Monday 20th October: The Japanese situation is terribly bad. She and America can't agree. Another American ship has been sunk, and the crew drowned. Ernst came again tonight, so that I could help him with his speech for the Society of Arts. His English grammar is not even in evidence; his talk is two hours long; there is no humour, except a couple of twisted sentences which send him into shouts of laughter, but which won't appeal to his audience after forty four pages of twisted sentences. In spite of all this, it is quite an honour to be able to help a famous Architect write a lecture on "Ancient Greece".

Tuesday 21st October: I hastily note that I typed forty four letters out of a forth-coming two thousand, and pass on to

Wednesday 22nd October: Ernst came again with his papers fluttering under his arm, and Part II is far more interesting. In it, he regards the Acropolis architecturally, through technical eyes, instead of gushing about "its simplicity", its "perfectness", its "lovely cloud effects behind", its "preservation", so that the extravagance of this sort of praise defiles its grace, as my praise does. He showed me why it is perfect, why symmetrical, and gave me two pictures of sculptured women, one by Phidias in the height of Greek genius, and the other later in the time of Venus. I chose the Venus, and he pointed out why Phidias was more wonderful - and there it is, in the expression, in the hair, in the draperies, and in the attitude.

Thursday 23rd October: Bryan is leaving for his ship in a month, in a midshipman's uniform, with all the world before him and - please God - a dearth of mines below him. I envy him a little, because he always knew what he wanted and now he has it. Mother and I are always talking of renting the house when the painters, who are in the throes of wallpapering, painting and white ant men, have finished it, and going off to flats at the beach and in the hills. It is a struggle between the immense peace of one's own little rut, and an interesting life elsewhere. I am constantly changing my mind.

Friday 24th October: I went to the Women's Auxiliary Australian Air Force and they told me I may be called up next month - Daddy, Richard, Bryan and now me. Mother wonders bitterly why she didn't drown us all at birth. Even Aunt Polly thinks the same. I went round there in the evening and she was lying on a sofa in a pinafore and surrounded by cats, entertaining Brice McMichael, Sibyl, a Lecturer in Classics called Ron Corney, and me, like a French authoress, Colette or someone. During the night

I kept waking, thinking indignantly of someone else living in my room, and me being tied for years to camp beds and iron sheds, uniforms, - and no way out. Nevertheless, I mustn't change my mind, without despising such lack of sacrifice.

Monday 27th October: I met Oscar Symon in town this afternoon, with the brim of his hat turned up about his face, the sun gleaming on his glasses and his walking stick trailing along the pavement from his arm. His new "cottage", to my dismay, is a twelve-roomed Victorian house. I told him all he needed was white Adam fireplaces and he added bitterly "or a sculptured wife". Sometimes walking home, when I am just about at the curve of the path overlooking the city, it occurs to me that I should enjoy writing my autobiography. It is a dull life, and a short one, so that it would have to be very honest, libellous because Adelaide is small, critical, and more or less symbolical of an average adolescent. I couldn't do it. I couldn't write frankly of how I live. There are small things which I don't mention ever here; exultant conceit over many things; small natural thoughts which may sound unnatural; reveries which I don't need to record ever to be forgotten.

Wednesday 29th October: It was pretty wonderful walking home tonight, because the sky was a dark grey-blue, with long slants of sunlight across the city, lighting up the windows like electric light and catching on the tops of flag poles. The cows stood knee deep in long feathery grass that is beginning to turn brown, but which looks in long vistas like purple plumes. It is raining now.

Friday 31st October: Today I did what I haven't done for a long time unselfconsciously. I went to Sibyl's for dinner and after, danced and acted, and sang. Aunty Pol sat on the sofa at the end of the room, we cleared the furniture against the walls, Sibyl played swing tunes and I acted the titles. Aunt Polly had to guess. We leapt across imaginary Western fronts, sang drearily into old felt hats, swayed our hips and clicked castanets and rang the dinner bell. It was huge fun. We played at Opera, and danced ballets with our toes stuck out and dug up old songs like "Remember My Forgotten Man" and "Little Brown Jug" and "I've Got a Torch Song". Torch songs, they remind me now of the house maid Ruby's old violet evening frock and Lady Jane Grey's head falling off the piano stool. We walked about the room under umbrellas, and sang "When the Lights of London Shine Again" in the dark accompanied by people crashing into things and mumbled apologies. I came home filthy. It must have been caused by swirling round on my tummy levelling a Bren gun, or salaaming Phyl's photo in the "Song of India" act.

Sunday 2nd November: Out in the garden in a pair of white sand-shoes, green shorts and nothing else. I feel like a miner with my spade and nakedness, digging the weeds and slicing the tops off lilies. It is a very hot day. Mother and Bryan are un-nailing carpets, dragging ward-robes into the lounge and beating rugs on the lawn like peasants. A cold shower, clean silk underclothes, strawberries for lunch. Mummy is sitting on the verandah fanning herself with a hat, her legs out like a Dégas, saying this is the last time she will ever have to do this sort of work because when it has to be done again, she won't be here. I remind her of my Welsh house that I have promised her under Snowdon by Llyn Llydau. I spend the rest of the day at Louise Matison's. "Springfield House" is filled with refugees. There were a great many people there, Dr Matison, Louise and her sister Nora and Nora's fiancé Hans Lawetzky, Victor who is Louise's brother and his wife Liesl and baby David, Dr and Mrs Geschmay and me. We sat in the sun, in soft cool drawing rooms, drank afternoon tea and I listened to my childhood idol, a Maurice Chevalier record in French "Quand on Est Tout Seul", and a lilting thing "Oui Papa". I leant over it as I do at such times, my hands limp, my eyes alight, my mouth open, while my heart was bursting in high heaven. I felt I should suffocate with happiness. The Geschmays arrived before tea; I came downstairs and heard them talking at the foot. I was introduced to them and shook hands with both of them. Mrs Geschmay said, "Oh Hans, we are shaking hands." Dr Geschmay is a very grim-looking creature with steely eyes, bristling moustaches and poor skin. I said, "Perhaps I should have done this", took his face in my hands and kissed him on both cheeks. It marked the beginning of an enraptured friendship. In the evening we sat on low couches, talking. It struck me as odd that the house should be filled with foreign voices, and I, in Adelaide, was the stranger. The talk was thrilling. It left our levels and ascended to heights where internationalism and creative art are common subjects. Here the svelte, sophisticated Louise was another Jewess, and that, although I had known it, struck me as odd. Hans Lawetzky drove me home. He is a typical Jew in appearance: thick glasses, coarse features, fat and dark. I like these people. I defy the White Australia policy.

Monday 3rd November: The Nazis are urging the Japanese to invade Australia, telling them to a man how many are in training, how many have gone overseas, how many ships, aircraft, guns, divisions, ending up with "though this doesn't matter, when there aren't 7,000,000 to guard its flat, accessible shores". It fills me with terror. Who knows? The Nazis are also spending some time on dividing Australia from England by pointing out that we are being asked to make sacrifices out of proportion to our population - and that type of propaganda, it is clever. We lack this cleverness as in every other department. This has been a hot, still, brown, dreary day. As I sit here now, my eyes are burning in my head, train noises are very close, Gaby comes in continually and his mouth is warm and damp. I can hear Bryan moving about in his study, complaining to Mother about the bath heater. The Convent bell across the road is clanging. Sometimes Mother irritates me with her lack of interest in good books, good talk. I know she only pretends to be interested in the things I try and talk about. This happens so often. I was telling her about Paderewski learning to play his first note at twenty one. I began, "Paderewski, you know, who is a compatriot of Dr Matison…" and she broke in "Good heavens!" as though I had finished. Of course I talk too much, I know that, but I miss so very much having no one with whom I can develop my ideas, and see theirs grow. Bryan mentioned it to me himself. If I had married Peter, this is how it would have been. I would never have been happy with Peter, knowing always that mine was a keener mentality, and desiring to educate him.

Tuesday 4th November: Mrs Geschmay told me a most brilliant version of Chamberlain's name by the French at the time of Munich - "J'aime Berlin". The opinion seems rather general that Chamberlain was pro-German in his very hate of Russia. Perhaps. I know I wept with relief when Czechoslovakia was sacrificed - and these friends of mine, they hated. I introduced them to Mother at the "Society of Arts" where Mr

Mühlstein (now called Mr Milston) delivered our talk. I heard Dr Geschmay say to Mother - "Your daughter isn't a product of her times - she creates her times." What greater compliment! Mr Milston was quite interesting, but his voice lacks fire, and he fiddled with his glasses. He rang me up a few days later to say that the Geschmays, and musicians called the Schwabs and he, had looked everywhere for me after to take me to supper - a joint author of the evening. I walked home with Mummy in a new pair of shoes.

Wednesday 5th November: Today, at The Roofcote Company, I had the power of work for the unemployed. We advertised for painters and cleaners and there was a steady stream of husky chaps with flannel pants, knotted belts and red necks. I asked their experience, their names, addresses, told them where to meet, kept them waiting, put on a lot of lipstick. I had a great friendliness for them because they reminded me of the film star Robert Newton with his earthy boots and earthy manner and his jet black, longish hair and his large beady eyes. I still like this job. There is a freedom about it which I didn't find in the other places. It is cool at the back among the trestle tables, the paint and aluminium tins, with the knocking of machines above from Cox Bros, and the tap dripping in the slimy basin. It is quiet and I always feel like singing. It is because I am not afraid of Mr Webb.

Friday 7th November: Bryan woke me this morning at seven o'clock, the hour when I was born, by kissing me, and giving me a pair of white silk gloves. Mother is making me a set of white and pink blossomed silk underclothes and a nightie. Lillian and Aunt Polly gave me handkerchiefs and Sibyl gave me "The White Cliffs" by Alice Duer Miller, the Anglo-American poem which has created so much interest and admiration. A poem becomes a best-seller! Sibyl relented and let me go there for the evening, skipping homework. Graham greeted me by "Who's the lucky man?" I remember years ago that I had made an ill advised statement to the effect that I would be engaged when I was nineteen. The brute remembered too. We listened to Backhaus and Friedman playing Chopin; Brahms' 4th Symphony; read magazines, groaned in artistic delight and had supper.

Saturday 8th November: Richard's long-awaited first English letters arrived, rather in the style (as he himself admits) of Rupert Brooke come home to Grantchester. The Welsh family's letters are rapturous. They worship the ground on which he treads. They seem to represent him as an airman holding a flower between his fingers. They admit they will be furious if he looks at any other woman than an aunt. Aunt May secretly confesses that he is happier at her home than at Aunt Beti's. We are immensely proud.

Sunday 9th November: Mother took me to hear Mr Glyn Jones, the little Welsh minister I met in Hamilton, preach at an afternoon Welsh service. I was rather proud, sitting there among my fellow patriots, hearing about me the lyrical unintelligableness of my own tongue. He is a flirtatious little man, this Mr Jones. He puts his arm about my waist in a most feeling way, whispering to Mother that he could kiss me - easily, and to me that he could run off with Mother - easily.

Wednesday 12th November: The house is a mess. The hall is stripped and hanging with sodden paper; the boards with ancient Kalsomine. Mother's bedroom is beautifully papered and her old brown and black fireplace is white and Adam-like. No more plaster falls from the ceiling. Bryan's room even has his furniture in it, and the Toby Jugs are arranged along a cream shelf.

Friday 14th November: John Portus and I decided tonight not to go to the Tux, but ate asparagus instead at the Athens Café, where we found a great wooden emptiness and a Negro gambler with a white girl. I peered through a door and saw a long room of silent men shuffling cards. We walked back across the park which was huge and cold, with the cold stars above our heads. This is pre-embarkation and John has won his commission.

Saturday 15th November: I went to John's party, which consisted of numerous solicitors, four girls, a piano and much beer. I felt at first very tired, and the sherry spun in my head, but after I adored it. Fred Field was most attached, and Arthur Cocks simply hung like a limpet. John wandered about, smiling gently and distantly while I tried to be nice to Fred and Arthur without looking as though my heart was involved. John

McFarlane insisted on my sitting next to him, glared solemnly into his beer mug and said, "I'd love a sister. I'd give a sister everything I could. But anyone else, I couldn't give them much. That's how it is." I stared helplessly at him in a good deal of embarrassment, so he continued gloomily, "What am I saying? I'm drunk, I think." Three people proposed to me during the course of the evening, all of whom I accepted out of principle. When the rest had departed, John walked home slowly with me and kissed me solemnly four times, saying "I think it's unwise - dangerous - to become wrapped up in a person at these times." I'm in an awful muddle about him.

Sunday 16th November: We finished the portrait today; I was on tenterhooks until Ernst signed it, in case he decided on another sitting or wrecked it in a last effort, which is the main and last danger of painters. He also presented it to us with no allowance of payment, which is splendid of him but puts us under an obligation which we don't want. After tea we walked across the links by the river with Gaby and I told them about the stars, which I learnt from Air Observer John Hereford Portus, R.A.A.F.

Tuesday 18th November: An unpleasant, distressing day. I felt nervy and on edge; the weather was warm and wet; Lillian gave notice which infuriated Mother which infuriated me. Mother has grown rather hard, and the tolerance she possessed seems to be going. Considering that we were about to sack Lillian, it is hardly fair to be angry when she gets another job - and a vastly better one, driving Mrs Dudley Hayward to meetings. Bryan noticed it; he said to me this evening, "Myers has changed Mother. She is harder and more calculating". It has, and I have been no help. I get irritated quickly at the silliest little trivialities like any child narrow enough to think that parents are faultless. The unfair thing is that this one just about is, and I grow angry at the sight of clay. How beastly to talk of my adorable Mother like this. I feel a little ill today, fed up with myself. I am fully aware that I am terribly spoilt, that I am rapidly growing "highbrow" (a worse word than one would think) and I dread the thought of really having to come up against things, because there is nothing much in me to fight back - all of which I explain carefully to my family, who agree but are bored. I should like to get away from me.

Wednesday 19th November: The U.S.A. has set out four conditions for peace and they are these: Japan to keep out of China and Indo-China; Japan to let all Pacific countries have equal rights of development; Japan to give up further aggression; Japan to leave the Axis...... Barbara Kelly and I lunched at John Martin's and she urged me into falling in love - to the marrying point - with John, because she is an inveterate matchmaker of the old school. She does something about it. She made up her mind that night when John said "She fascinates me, she's so attractive" and I said, "I have laid Peter's ghost. I've got a crush on someone else!" The Harveys are arranging a party to the University Swimming dance on Saturday, and we are all invited. I hope nothing happens —.

Thursday 20th November: On Tuesday, Barbara Salter had said to me, "There are so many people who, at school, showed promise of doing so well, but have just sunk back into oblivion," which incensed me, because, even if no one else did, I thought and dreamed of doing - well. So I stirred myself out of this peaceful, aimless rut and wrote an appealing and desperate letter to Mr Morley of "The News". Now every time that Mr Webb is particularly adorable, I feel ashamed.

Friday 21st November: Bryan brushes silently about the halls of the house in long waterproofs reaching to his boots, and capes and sou'-westers attached. "His trousseau" as Mrs Brookman calls it. Sibyl rang and I went to her place after dinner to sit on cushions on the dining room floor and eat cherries and read Shelley. Her exams, with Bryan's, start on Tuesday. There was the most fantastic moon in the sky tonight, thin and luminous and warm and gold, sailing in a perfect arc, like half a wedding ring from the Holy Conception.

Saturday 22nd November: All morning I was afraid something might go wrong, and visualized over my typewriter the dance, our party, our music. "How glorious", said Herries Harvey, "to go back into evening frocks and dance stately dances with civilized people." The night was warm and breathless and filled with stars and a distant sailing moon. Everything, I knew, must be glorious tonight. It was. It was. I wore the new frock with bare shoulders, and scarlet and blue roses strewn over it, scarlet shoes, scarlet beads and a wooden bangle, and my hair was long and soft to my shoulders. I had to look well for my evening to be a success. John called for me in his car and his new uniform, well cut, the thin blue stripe, the epaulettes, and the heavy hat. We were early and strolled about the University, looking at new buildings and the stars. In our party were Herries and Charlie Price, Barbara and Alain, and Margaret and her brother John Walters (on pre-embarkation leave with John), and we two. We danced together, and walked between the cloisters and sat in sweeping skirts on the lawn listening to the music, and in the long yellow light. John Walters suddenly wanted to row on the river, as we leant over the bridge and watched the yellow lights bobbing about on the dark water. After supper we went. John Portus and I were sitting in the car watching the girls in long cotton frocks and the men in blazers and uniforms, and he said, "How civilized this all is; how secure; how real." I asked him if he minded the fact that we would still go on dancing after he had left, and he said he would, a little. On the river, we went in two boats, oars dripping in the dark water, under English trees with filigree branches across the river. I rowed a little while John sat behind me, singing his endless song "My heart stood still". The others were quiet, only talking spasmodically. Charlie's boat drifted past, with the oars across his knees, like an Indian canoe. We rowed a long way up a dark tunnel, hitting each other's boats, and shouting in the pitch dark, until we came out again into the starlight and the overhanging trees. I dwell on it; it was sublime. Barbara and I kept whispering "It has to finish. It must end." I looked at the two Johns, fair and wholesome and young and much-loved, and I hoped they come back with every inch of my being. We moored the boats and swept up across the lawns to dance. John and I didn't drive straight home, but watched the lights and the trains go by, playing at kissing in a gentle, fiddling, and mischievous way. We talked quite seriously and stayed there for a few hours - life and birth and death and men and women. Then he shook himself and said he still didn't believe in working himself up at this stage - though I believe he has. And I? If I had a little more of the physical love for him that I felt for Peter, mingled with the amazement and love I feel for this odd, never endingly astonishing creature, I should be sick at heart at his leaving, As it is, I am wonderfully happy at having someone who is entangled in this senseless chaos, loving me.

Friday 28th November: A burning hot day, even my office was heated and exhausting. I came home and washed my hair, but John rang in the soap suds stage and told me to grab my stuff and go for a swim. I did so, and appeared with lank, dripping hair, and stockingless. He loved me just the same. More, I believe. Mrs Portus, Professor Portus, John and I drove to Grange, bathed, danced along the beach, drank gin cocktails on empty stomachs and came back in dressing gowns. He held my hand, and kissed me quickly on my shiny, salty nose. We had a very late dinner with French wine "made when the Spirit of France was free"; then sang rather badly while the hands flew round quicker than I can ever remember. Instead of walking straight home, we drifted on and through the park, eventually finding a place under a pepper-corn tree (forever belovèd) above the lights. The breeze came and went in tiny, uplifting puffs, but the night was warm and starry, and the grass smelt of hay. He made love to me, called me a "lovely little thing" and made up a very bad poem. But what's the use? I can't write about it. I am falling in love with him.

Monday 1st December: Sibyl came round for a while and we talked miserably of war. The HMAS "Sydney" has disappeared with all hands. Peter Rudall, Allen King and Eric Mayo from Adelaide....... six and a half hundred men went down into the sea. For what reason? I talked for hours over the phone to Barb Kelly and she doubted too, and was extremely bitter. "A great national loss", "we must inaugurate a fund to replace...", "are sure the mothers are fortified in knowing it was a great victory...?" A merchantman sinks a battleship! Oh, my children, never think that there is glamour in war.

Tuesday 2nd December: The Pacific situation is very tense. Japan is reported not to have accepted America's dictum. America is rushing men to key points, sending planes. Singapore men all on guard. "Precaution", America says. ... It came out in bits, reluctantly, that John expects to leave on Friday night. He walked home with me, and was very gentle, and tucked a wisp of hair under my hat, and promised to ring me. I stumbled some of the way home by myself, trying not to cry. I have grown so fond of him, with his chuckle, and brown face and twinkling, sunny eyes. Tomorrow I will ask him for a photograph of him - in case I forget what he looks like.

Wednesday 3rd December: John drove up and took me to the Gresham, telling me then that this was his last free night. I felt wretched about taking him away from his parents, but he said he was glad he didn't have to spend a morbid evening at home. But John Walters there, thought otherwise. He was champing to get back to Reynella and was very quiet, and rather starry-eyed. Alison Harvey was the other person at dinner. Alison and John Walters decide to drive up immediately to Reynella after dinner, so I said good bye to them, to dear John Walters. Meanwhile Professor and Mrs Portus had rung, asking if we couldn't go to the pictures together, so we decided to meet them at the Piccadilly Theatre in North Adelaide. We arrived late. Professor Portus was sitting there with a large trumpet in his ear, holding hands with Mrs Portus, so we sat down beside them and held hands too. It was a screaming programme. Bob Hope and Bing Crosby in "Road to Zanzibar". Bless them all, they made us laugh when, at least two of us, were ready to weep. We drove the family home, then John detoured to take me. I didn't keep him long. He opened the present I bought him, kissed me, held me very close, and said, "I don't exactly know what to say to you, sweetheart." He thanked me for all the fun we had had, and said he would write; then after the war - more, much more, fun. I kissed him and rushed out of the car into my room. But I came back and watched him drive the car back down the hill. And I felt nothing. Nothing at all. This frightened me. It occurred to me what I may have done – sent him off believing that I loved him, and then found out that it was just a mad pre-embarkation infatuation.

Thursday 4th December: Actually, though, I don't think I need fear this, because he is such a reasonable creature that he continually kept the "affair" on a level that could meet emergencies like infatuations. When I asked him for a picture, he said that he purposely hadn't given me one or asked for one – "though Lord knows I've wanted one far more than you have. That little serious one, for instance" – because every time he looked at it, he would think, "God, why aren't I back!" Which, for a person who is reluctant enough at going anyway, is wise, I suppose. So I gave in, but I regret it.

Saturday 6th December: President Roosevelt has sent a last minute letter of appeal to the Japanese Emperor over the heads of the Cabinet - an unprecedented thing.

Sunday 7th December: As Lillian is gone, we are now batching, which is not bad at all. The house is so clean and fresh, after the workmen have gone, and the kitchen so sunny and bright, that it is a pleasure, like a bride in a brand new home in a brand new life. Sibyl lunched here, with Bryan in his uniform and shining gold buttons, and Mother with her hair tied up in a scarf, and enveloped in a filthy smock. She is revelling in owning her own house once again. Sibyl said it is such a relief to come here and find people smiling and gracious, leaving her own house (which use to be Mecca to everyone under 21 at one time) where her mother is bitter, and her grandmother nagging and Graham casual and tactless. He is going into an A.I.F. camp tomorrow. We went to Church for the purpose of showing Bryan's uniform off because, said Bryan, "a church is made for such an occasion, with rows and rows of people there for the express idea of looking at me." He certainly got his money's worth. The whole Church prayed for him and wished him luck, and gripped his hand, and dear old women came up and said "To think you were on my Cradle roll!" Bryan stood it miserably, then swore that he would never go back within the next six months at least, as they obviously expected him to be going off to the Mediterranean to sink battleships. I came in and announced that Great Britain had declared war on Finland, Rumania and Hungary. "Good Lord", said Sibyl, "now listen to this bit. It goes high in the octaves, and discordant here, like Debussy...." She's right. What does it matter? We go on playing Chopin.

Monday 8th December: But something happened this morning that does matter. Japan bombed American bases in the Pacific. The fire has spread to the Pacific, and the whole globe is on fire. From Iceland to Tasmania, from America to Japan. Does the planet hang in the stratosphere, and do flames leap up from it? I spent the morning listening into street radios and buying up special editions. During the afternoon I sat with my head in my arms, while waves of sleep assailed me. They come in long, irregular swirls, and meaningless pictures begin to appear in one's mind, while noises grow huge and distinct. I felt what a waste of life this was; what a useless passing of good years. I wonder if I shan't join the W.A.A.A.F.s who have called me up recently, instead of waiting for my promised land, because now my small ambitions become immensely small.

Tuesday 9th December: Bryan catches his boat tonight, but we all lunched together at Quality Inn, where my friends looked with surprise on this new brother, better looking even than the first, in his strange uniform. Officers of the Merchant Marine are scarce. There was a conscription meeting at the Town Hall, and we went. It was fiercely patriotic, and we all shouted "Rule Britannia" and "There'll always be an England" and "Land of Hope and Glory", while veterans from the Relief of Gordon, simply dripping medals, whipped out flags and kissed them, and everyone pledged their every penny and every drop of blood, and paid two shillings and became a member of the Service League. In the panic, I did too.

Wednesday 10th December: Sibyl was coming "to play" after dinner, but rang and asked me to go there. I broke a moral point and went, although we are now in the same position regarding lonely mothers. We have decided to take it in turns. So I went, rather under the impression that I was conferring a favour, and talked to Aunt Polly while Sibyl played cards and typed. I told her how worried I was about leaving Mother by herself, and she - of all people in this world! – said "If Sibyl wanted to do something for the war, I certainly wouldn't make a song about it." I was simply blazing, and could hardly bear to be in the same room. I wanted to tell her of the bitter, depressed attitude she took about with her, and how she had changed the whole carefree atmosphere of a once happy home, and I did tell her how gay Mother was and how generous in sacrifice she had been. I am amazed to see how a small thing like that could so upset me. It spoiled the whole evening and I came home early.

Friday 12th December: I went to see the Portuses. Professor and Mrs Portus were playing an earnest game of Chinese Checkers in the sun room, so I lay on the lounge and looked at the forbidden photos of John, which are wonderfully good. Professor Portus initiated me into the secrets behind the war news and eulogized on President Roosevelt as other men laud Napoleon. He believes firmly that Roosevelt intended the Japanese to declare war; it certainly is a known fact that he was working during his whole third term to bring America into the war. And now he has done so with a phenomena - a united United States. They were both very pleased to see me, because things are a bit empty for them just now. Some Australian new war measures are introduced: no petrol for pleasure, huge forces sent to Darwin, air raid precautions and blackouts, no window lighting at night or late shopping, no weekly races or night sports etc. etc.

Sunday 14th December: Yesterday Mother showed a Bank Manager about the house, who is wanting to rent. Today, we went house hunting at Glenelg, but returned utterly and irreconcilably depressed. Even the better Guest Homes were musty and dusty and smelt rather like lavatories; aspidistras sat mangily on speckled cane tables, naked women hung from the walls in pathetic imitation of Phidias, and plaster shepherds played on Arcadian pipes. Even the bulk of the proprietors were drunk. We loathed everything by the time we sat down to an unappetising but fabulously expensive meal at the Pier Hotel. We took turns about with the people we dined with - first course, Lady Bruce and maid; second course, John Horner and wife. At nine o'clock we began house hunting in the City. This vagueness depresses me. What is to happen to us? How closely one is bound to the family. How blessed is the family, and how mortal the breaking up.

Monday 15th December: We have eventually decided upon a room at Miss Hayward's, North Terrace. It is a big room, with a fire place, a bay window in a tower looking over lawns and trees and statues and people waiting for trams, and a high wooden balcony, rather Alpine in aspect. We went on to inspect some frocks which were being shown at the South, and we drifted home very late to find a distracted Bryan who flung himself into our arms, and fought with his tears. He hates the sea, and wandered about the house revelling in its cleanliness. We took him to the pictures to brighten him up. It is great to have Bryan home again.

Tuesday 16th December: Louise and Nora Matison and I lunched at John Martin's; I really am very fond of both of them. Nora has just announced her engagement to Hans Lawetzky. David Walters is missing, the brother of John and Margo Walters. It is a casualty I dreaded more than most. On the day he left Margo lay in the Botanical Gardens and wept. On the day he left I met John Portus. Bryan went tonight, drooping and rebellious.

Wednesday 17th December: I write so detailed an account of my life to Richard that I am bored when I come to repeating it ----- Today, I had a W.A.A.A.F. medical examination. I filled in numerous questions asking if I had fits or if my parents suffered mentally, whereupon I continued waiting in pants and brassieres with others in the same position while a troop of airmen marched through the room. When they had gone, the nurse said, "Don't worry; they aren't interested." The door opened and the airmen marched back again. I was there the whole day. We were driven down to Keswick and x-rayed. The outcome was that I was passed medically but failed technically, my typing being too slow. However, the eye-doctor said, "If your mothers realized what their little darlings were about to go through, you wouldn't be here." He marked my mentality as Average. I decided then to try again in a month's time, but later I decided that, having joined the noble band of the Volunteered, I may comfortably return to my rut and Mr Webb.

Friday 19th December: Sibyl came to a scrappy meal, wild with excitement at passing the Leaving Honours, which is rather brilliant as she did absolutely no work. She now says she could easily have gained four credits if I hadn't stopped her from working. We set off for the Brookman's to gloat over Graham, who is now in the A.I.F. and said that Sibyl's pass would have to be a blinkin' miracle. A militiaman followed us, pinched Sibyl's behind and put his arm about my waist. Sibyl began her favourite phrase - "You dirty Choco." "Hey, I've bin fighting for you for two years." "Where's your colour patch." "I cin prove it, see?" He grew so obstreperous that I kicked him with huge enjoyment in the shins; he staggered across to Sibyl who slapped his face (this is a brutal story) and his anger rose beyond bounds. We were petrified by this time, until Sib said, "If you don't go away, I shall scream." Whereupon, we stood in the middle of the road and yelled at the moon. The militiaman said "Gawd" and fled, before he had time to show us his Volunteered Badge. Even then...Childers Street rushed to the gates.

Saturday 20th December: The gods were good to me today. The phone went at work and a man's voice asked to speak to me. I said, "Hallo, who's speaking?" "John." "John who?" "Why, John PORTUS." I nearly collapsed. I had a strange sensation that he had returned from the dead, from the hot shadows of Malaya, from that distance which makes ordinary people heroic and desirable. John Portus is an adorable creature, and I am deeply glad that he is back, a thing I have to thank the little yellow men for. We sat in his car tonight by the old Creveen School Park until four in the morning, making love in a way that made me decide that John's head-over-heart policy may be going by the board. He actually said that he would like to be married, so that one wouldn't have to sit about in cars and get mixed up in legs and bother about getting to bed. You could converge the lot. John is an industrial socialist and a believer in class fraternity. We are of the same opinions. The next day, I was dreadfully tired and quiet and I apologized for being so, and he laughed and asked me if I surely weren't unhappy every time I didn't shine a specified number of times. He is right. It doesn't matter with John. He has gone to Port Pirie.

Wednesday 24th December: Alain and Alison, Barb, Don Mackie from Sydney who is in the Air Force with Alain, and I had dinner at the Quality Inn; John was to come but he can't leave Port Pirie. We went to the Regent, which is cool and comfortable, and saw "Footsteps in the Dark", with Errol Flynn, and after bought cool drinks and ice creams and sat on the parapet looking over the City, eating and talking. The City was very quiet and dark, in a semi-blackout, and the stars were extremely low over it. Alain said something about us having changed, that before we would never have been satisfied with idly listening to a Christmas ticking in, and when it came, to wonder naturally about next Christmas. What? When? Oh! Why? I felt lonely and quiet without John. I can't help wondering about next year.

Thursday 25th December: An odd Christmas Day. The culmination, so far, of this war on our lives. Richard is in England, bombing. Bryan is at sea; no Silver Lake, no cars. It was too hot to go outside the door, although I should like to have gone to church, so we lay all day naked on our beds, reading. Mother gave me a camera. Sibyl gave me two volumes of "I, Claudius" by Robert Graves and Mr Milston gave me Anatole France's "At the Sign of the Reine Pédauque" and "The Revolt of the Angels". The only time I was cool was when I had a shower. We had tea at the South, a cold Christmas dinner, and went to see "Little Nellie Kelly", a musical comedy with Judy Garland. After the pictures, as we were coming down the stairs, there was a shout, a rush of air and I was immediately besieged by a lot of sunburnt people in yellow shirts and carrying bathers. Mr Milston, Dr and Mrs Geschmay and the Schwabs. They rushed off again, talking very fast.

Friday 26th December: I awoke feeling that I couldn't bear another day of this heat. We drift about, hardly speaking, without energy, without even combing our hair, washing or dressing. During the afternoon, though, I pulled myself together, and staggered out into the glare, shrieking like a parachutist falling through the shaft. At Glenelg, I met Nob Good, who is stationed there to register militia conscripts and we fled in his new car "The Red Devil" and rattled away in it to Brighton, as he has no leave. Half way along the road, there was a sudden deafening clap of thunder which rolled from one end of the sky to the other, and a peculiar swishing sound. Towards us came a huge block of rain, not downwards but sideways, and chased us madly onwards. It won, submerged and blinded and deafened us. Then it passed on, leaving a hot steaming day, but a suspicion of a breeze. I had longed so much for a swim that we had one on a beach, already bone dry and a mesh of barbed wire and machine gun nests. We drove to Glenelg and visited Luna Park, putting pennies in the slot for fortunes and fighting with the crowd to get on the Merry-go-round. It was a Merry-go-round from Paris, painted in plush, gilted, smooth and brassy, with that peculiarly grating, romantic music. Oh, a perfectly splendid Merry-go-round. Later, we lay on the beach, watching the moon on the water, and the peaceful, terrible Pacific. That night I went to bed and slept during the black out, hearing dimly the banshee wail and the church bells, and seeing the impudent moon in a dark world, and then I heard nothing more.

Sunday 28th December: Hong Kong has fallen through lack of water, the Japs having bombed the reservoirs. Singapore is having spasmodic raids. I sit here, determined to bring this diary up to date, even though Mother rattles brooms down the hall and packs china in Lillian's room. I am glad to finish this tome; it has been an excellent confessional, and a note book for a few good phrases, but a long, interminable bore. But the habit is deep rooted. I have bought another. Meanwhile, I have become angry with John, whom I have missed deeply this week, carrying on excessive arguments with him in which he is inevitably ousted. For one thing he has brought on this sickness again; and for another he never considers me in the least about leave, just turning up with the cold blooded assurance that the little woman will always be there. I refuse to be taken for granted. I wish he would turn up —

Wednesday 31st December: Alain Harvey, Barb, Don Mackie and I went on the river in the evening, but although the moon was tremendously potent and the stars lay in sprays about the sky, and although the basket willows held lover's boats, and we ate crystallised fruits in the bow, I liked it, and that was all. I was a little jealous of Barbara holding Alain's hand and the way they looked at each other and smiled, and then laughed. I sat in the bow and stirred up the water so that it sprayed through my fingers, and thought of John, and was jealous of Barbara. I thought how thrilling - how it touched every aspect of one's life - to be loved by someone, and forgot that he has never told me that he loves me. I wonder often about that. I am always wondering.

Mrs Eirliw Harding Browne with her three children, Bryan, Richard and Carys, c1931 (Rembrandt Studios, Adelaide).

Mr Clifford Harding Browne (Van Dyk Studios, Adelaide).

(Top) The Kerrs at 169 Barton terrace were neighbours of the Brookmans; (lower) Miss Phillipson's school next door to the Brookmans, 1925. Donald (Sam) Kerr is standing with Phyllis Brookman on the far right.

Sibyl and Carys at the Adelaide Zoo.

HARRY LONGSON has depicted Richard Harding-Browne as the baby of South Australian broadcasting. So he is, in terms of years, but the experience that lies at the back of Richard's work is more than usually falls to the lot of a young man of his age.

Richard is the youngest announcer heard from 5AD and its associate stations in the "Advertiser" network, and is on the air as often as his older colleagues.

He is yet another of the many people in radio who graduated to the microphone from the stage. The theatre interested him at an early age, and at St. Peter's College, where there is a strong dramatic society, he soon found himself taking an active interest in the many productions staged there. From school, it was an easy step to Adelaide's many - branched amateur theatre, and he has played many parts in local shows.

Hies fine work in the name part in Young Woodley last year will be remembered by all who saw that play, and now he has an even more important role to handle.

He is playing what is practically the leading role in Journey's End, the great war play, which will open at the Theatre Royal on Saturday, and which has already earned the praise of experienced theatre men who have seen the play in rehearsal.

At 5AD, Richard is often heard at the microphone, his deep and resonant voice making him an ideal announcer. His stage experience has helped him to score successes in many radio plays and feature productions.

St Mark's College, Adelaide 1940, detail shows (top left) Sam Kerr, (top right) David Law Smith; (Second Row) Willy Kerr, Geoffrey Dutton and Peter Rudall.

(Top) Richard, Mic Sandford and Carys at Glenelg, January 1940; (Lower)
Richard, Bryan, Carys and their mother in the garden, 1940

Bryan, Eirliw, Carys and Richard at home.

Carys in a frock she made, 1940.

Graham Brookman on motorbike with Peter Gilbert, 1940

Peter Anderson and Carys, November 10 1940, a week before Peter went to Military Camp.

Peter Anderson in the A.I.F. with David Law Smith (standing right) and Jack Fuller (sitting).

Carys, a portrait by Dickinson-Monteith, December 1940.

Bryan, Carys and Sibyl at Silver Lake.

Sam Kerr in uniform, June 7 1942 (Kerr papers, Barr Smith Library, University of Adelaide).

(Top) First photo John Portus gave Carys;
(Lower) Carys and John married on February 19 1944

1942

Friday 2nd January 1942: An incredibly frightful day. I said "Goodbye" to Gaby and his nose was damp and he wriggled unhappily; but he has a glorious life ahead at Silver Lake in the Hills. But he was still there when I returned from work in the evening, so we went through it all again. Mr Wickes, our house painter, drove me, with our worldly goods, to 217 North Terrace, and we spent the rest of the night carting trunks and desk drawers up and down dark stairs. Wickes looked about the room, then remarked, "Oh, well, you'll get used to it. It's astonishing what you can get used to—", and left me standing speechless among the chaos. Where to start? What to do? Where to put? Eventually I left my lumpy bed and lay on the balcony, but had the sensation of being hung over a roaring volcano. Leaning over the side, I saw Sam's brother, Willy Kerr cranking Petroff, and was about to call out when it occurred to me that the sight of me standing in mid-air in a diaphanous nightie would be unsettling to a proclaimed Agnostic. At last I fell asleep and dreamed of Shapes.

Saturday 3rd January: When I returned "home", I found Mother gone but the room in a state of well being and cheerfulness. I even received a telephone call from friends and went with them to Sue Yeatman's, where we examined Sue's trousseau, and drank tomato juice in a dark room while Sue paraded her silly hats in a pair of shorts. At seven, we bused to the beach and swam in the twilight in a roughening sea, ducking and splashing and bouncing and jumping, and embracing the coolness of the sea about us. Then we lay on the beach, eating chips and rolls and coconut ice and sucking ginger beer through straws, while a great heavy moon rose up behind us, and we talked about Sue's new life with Lewin at "Cloverdale" in the South East, of girls we knew at school, of frocks and the Fall of Manila.

Sunday 4th January: I wrote to John, which I find very satisfying, although with Peter it was a most inadequate means of expression! We dined at the Hotel Adelaide and partook of black coffee and cream on strawberry coloured chairs. There is a certain amount of gracious living in this venture. Take today. I read "I, Claudius" by Robert Graves, on the lounge overlooking North Terrace, which is very lovely with a sun and cool breezes, eating plums. Then in a dirndl and sandals, I slopped across to the magazine room in the Public Library and read "Punch" in that self conscious atmosphere. Later, we walked to the Botanical Gardens for tea, from whence we were chased by furious gardeners through the Director's residence after the gong had sounded. Thence to Church to hear Mr Lewis, whose voice and manner are so clever that I have my doubts as to who confers the favour on whom - God on Mr Lewis or Mr Lewis on God. In the ensuing Battle of the Mosquitoes, they won and left me a corpse under my own sheet.

Wednesday 7th January: We spent a glorious lunch hour sitting in our window with sandwiches, milk and reading batches of letters in the sun. Richard wrote, and Bryan, and England - all but John. Richard sent photographs from Oxford by a Hungarian woman, which are very effective. He, by the way, is patrolling over the North Sea. After dining at the "Adelaide", during which time I eat extravagantly from consommé through garfish to capon and end up inevitably, with strawberries; I, who am bored by food, have become a gourmet and a gourmand.

Thursday 8th January: As I was hanging out some clothes in a side garden in the dark, I inadvertently met a small, fair headed girl called Marie Ottaway who lives here. She is almost melancholic with boredom, and has chosen me out to be "friends with". I am rather wary of getting to know people too well when you live in the same tenement. It may lead to friendly heads being pushed round doors and hearty voices saying, "Can I come in for a bit. You busy?" We hover exclusively over our hard won privacy, and live in splendid hermitage. Even now there is a lonely old maid next door who asks Mother in to have Quick Ones. We had the worst dust storm in history; the sky was red; the tops of buildings were invisible. The damage was enormous. My eyes and hair are thick with it.

Friday 9th January: Today at the Salters, with Judith Crase, Sibyl, Barb and her sister Lizzie Salter, we lay on cane lounges on the lawn and then moved in to listen to Chopin's piano pieces, and some Bach choral works. We discussed Adelaide's inferiority complex, and decided, like the French Salons in the eighteenth century, to revive art in Adelaide. First meeting, Wednesday.

Saturday 10th January: Richard writes that all our lives we are forced to amble, and side step, by irremediable forces, which is hopelessly, helplessly true.

Sunday 11th January: We waited for the only tram that could take us for lunch, but it caught us unawares, slipping slyly round an unexpected corner, so we had to ring our hosts and they sent their son in a car. You have no conception of what this means. We had to drive to a friend's office to pick up a ruler as an excuse, in case we were stopped and questioned for using a car.

Tuesday 13th January: Richard is 21 today. But instead of being given one key to one house, he seems to have been entrusted with many keys and the safety of Many Houses. Sibyl had dinner with me at the Adelaide. We wandered down Frome Road, weaving histories about its decayed old buildings, and went triumphantly up and down the Torrens on "Pop Eye", a carnival acquisition despised by John in his rowing moments. Later we lay on the couch on the balcony, clinking ice and eating plums and engrossed in the Downfall of our friends - what Sammy Kerr would term, the "decadence of their mental integrity." Oh, vanity!

Wednesday 14th January: We are being pushed back towards Singapore, where a decisive battleground is being prepared. Hong Kong, of course, has fallen, and Wavell has been made Commander-in-Chief of the Allied Forces in the Pacific. The whole situation is frightful.....

Friday 16th January: News has just been circulated that the A.I.F. are at last in action in Malaya. I was once sorry that Richard wasn't to spend a peaceful boredom there!

Saturday 17th January: John rang early this morning on his one-day leave and we made vague arrangements, and he came round at one o'clock to take me to the Gresham Hotel. My ridiculous white flowered hat wasn't much of a success, I fear, because he asked me to take it off! The lunch wasn't much of a success either, because I wasn't in an eating or talking mood, but when we came back to my room, flung off hats and gloves and hindrances, I feel magnificent. I made a horrible faux pas: John said, "Which of these beds is yours?" And I, brushing my hair absently, replied, "This one is mine and that one is yours." Silence. Then he suddenly shouted with laughter and caught me in his arms! We wandered about the Botanical Gardens, discussed politics in the Rose Garden, films in the Wisteria Arbour and Tom by the water lilies. Then along the river on the quieter side till we passed the Morphett Street Bridge and sat in the rushes, watching the swans on that quite large sheet of water. A few kisses, holding hands, a few pointless stories, and John saying that he thought the difference of nine years between us was too great to take me as seriously as he was. I said, "No." We walked home and parted.

Sunday 18th January: newspaper cutting from "The Advertiser" pinned in Carys's diary:

Pilot-Officer Richard Harding Browne, eldest son of Mrs. C Harding Browne, of North terrace, city, has been reported missing after air operations on January 15. He was 21 years of age on January 13, and was educated at Queen's and St. Peter's Colleges. He was employed at 5 AD at the time of his enlistment. Pilot-Officer Harding Browne was interested in the amateur theatre and appeared in "Journey's End."

PO R. Harding Browne

This foul, blasted, god-damned, bloody, useless war – My darling Richard – In the morning, I walked through the intense heat to the Brookman's, and in search of Mrs Radcliffe, the char, whom I didn't find, and arrived tired and late for lunch. We lay on the sofa listening to Chopin's Scherzos and playing cards and writing crazy skits on Etiquette Books. We had tea with Graham and Ruthie Finlayson, laughing and shouting, and then went again in search of Mrs Radcliffe, finding her in some forgotten alley. Coming home, we danced along the pavement, and licked ice creams, and I came home late, in the dark. Mummy was in bed, but the Telegram had come, Richard missing in air operations two days after his 21st birthday. The thing refused to penetrate me. Then it did. I lay and sobbed, and howled on my knees. Mother had sat all day by herself, waiting for me, while I danced crazy dances. I pulled down all the photos she had put up of him, and we had quite a fight in the dark. I couldn't bear them. What's it for? He did nothing for the war but throw away his life, and bits of ours.

Monday 19th January: I had no idea how to treat Mother, to be firm and hard, or to let her weep uncontrollably. I can be perfectly reasonable; I can't grasp it yet. I somehow (and I feel Mother can't) believe there is hope over the North Sea. Only the thought of a world without Richard means anything. And, as Mother said, "What a drab, pointless world." – I came calmly to work and tried to write some letters, but broke down. I sobbed until my eyes stung and I was quite dried up, then I rang Sibyl but didn't get very far. She came in to see me, had tea with me, and was most cheering. No one knows yet, except through us, but I went with Sibyl to the "Advertiser" and informed the Casualty Department. It was cold-blooded and logical; it was a part of the newspaper I had been warned about. Mummy and I dined at the Botanical Gardens Hotel (where Daddy used to take his lady-friends) and read that Clark Gable's wife Carole Lombard had died in a plane crash, and went for a wet, sodden walk under plane avenues like German forests. I read Voltaire to Mother until she fell asleep.

Tuesday 20th January: It was a tremendous relief, somehow, to have John to write to. I wrote pages of invective and misery, but tore it up and simply notified him. The Casualty List is in the paper today; the room is full of carnations and I have left Mother there. Her friends are wonderful, realizing that she has had more than her measure of unhappiness. To lose an eldest son.....Oh, this cloud, this war, this nightmare.... It is years ago since Richard rang us from 5AD and told us there was war, and "Hathaway", the Sandford's country cottage where we were staying, was filled with daffodils. A washerwoman wrote, saying, "He was just like my own boy; a fine gentleman in every respect." A blind girl said he used to come back from walks in the hills to their mutual boarding house, and tell her about the trees, the ferns and the peeling bark; other people passed the time of day with her. We were taken, a wasted and red-eyed Mother, and me, to dinner at Elder Kiosk, where we ate grills in view of the river afloat with swans. The bunches of letters are hard to read, and come from people who have only been seconds and minutes in Richard's life.

Wednesday 21st January: Nevertheless, the more we think about it and the further that first desolation recedes, we are convinced there is hope. There have been many miraculous returns in this war, and Richard would hardly be satisfied to pass out of this world with anything less than a V.C. or the Order of the Bath. John wrote a splendid letter, pointing out that if Richard has been killed, I have more to remember of my brother than sisters whose brothers live forever; pride, splendour, odd, stray moments of confidence, an intellectual fellowship, however self-conscious, friendship. Bryan rang from Whyalla: the Captain saw the notice in the Lists and told him, our letter not having arrived. They never grew very close together, although they admire each other enormously. I went out tonight to see "This England", and felt rather gala with a box of chocolates and a yellow coat. Who should know that beforehand the most awful realization of all had swept me just before I left? Lois Lapthorne was there, whose brother Hugh crashed .... It was a fine picture, starring Emlyn Williams and John Clements, about an English village who throughout the generations had withstood invasion, and now withstands again.

January 22nd January: Our miseries are minute in the awful chaos of the world. The A.I.F. are being pushed back towards Singapore which is useless as a sea base already. The Japanese swarm in Malaya, the Philippines, China (where repulses are successful) and New Guinea is heavily bombed by aircraft carriers. Australia is demanding a larger voice in the Pacific, and has critics and followers in London. Churchill's reception in England after Washington is not good, the press are demanding new ministers, explanations. America seems to be idle. We are told to expect raids any day. Perhaps I am wise to keep a diary; I wonder what will go into these pages...? Our mail is colossal: from directors, friends who knew him for a few weeks in 1933 or as a child in a little tweed coat. Sibyl came to dinner with us, with her hair curled high in a first perm and holding her head even straighter than usual in case of disarranging it. She remembered triumphantly my first perm standing like straw about my head and I lying distractedly weeping on my bed. Mother was unhappy today, and when Sibyl and I were sitting on the grass by the river, I wept by myself and she didn't say anything.

Friday 23rd January: Today was filled with odd moods which I have never experienced before, and which I think infected Mother. It grew on me all day that the importance of our lives is overrated, that there isn't really the faintest interest in life and death. It consequently made me feel reckless. I suddenly wanted to marry John desperately, whether it would be a mistake or not. This was all caused by hearing the B.B.C. warn Australia that convoys were approaching us from Japan, and that Rabaul in New Guinea had been overcome (Tommy Simpson is among the vanished militia there). They also announced that all capital cities were fully prepared for raids, which horrified me, knowing that only a few trenches had been dug in Victoria Square and a few buildings possessed buckets of sand and a borrowed spade. Outside couples were walking arm-in-arm along North Terrace. Mummy suddenly told me to get John to marry me... A Christian friend, Jean Clarkson came and we had a fierce argument over cups of tea about the existence of Good Influences, being God. Then a methylated spirits addict went mad next door, and I lay in bed contemplating this miserable world.

Saturday 24th January: In the cold morning light, life took on its usual perspective. Richard grew all important, I was worried about Bryan on the coast, and John who will be hurled against the Japs, and I enlisted for Air Raid Precautions (A.R.P.) services. I lost that strange, desperate, despairing feeling and grew quite happy with my own troubles. Mother is staying the weekend at the Wyllie's and I with the Brookman's, so I took my hat box there, put on my green shorts and listened to the gramophone with Sibyl while the rain beat onto the windows outside. Graham is utterly disillusioned about getting into action; he joined the A.I.F. who are digging gun positions here, while the "chocolate soldiers" are fighting the Japanese in New Guinea. The big Libyan campaign isn't the success everyone anticipated, and casualty lists will be enormous from Malaya.

Sunday 25th January: Sibyl is a restless creature. I find myself tracking about the house and garden with her; she plays a few pieces on the piano; picks a few flowers, puts on a few records, and insists on playing innumerable guessing games, while my fingers itch to open my book. We went through some dusty old trunks in the potting shed, and found excellent books of her grandfather, Sir George Brookman, and old photos of family coaches and homes and properties. Sibyl hasn't the faintest interest in her forebears, while I was eagerly peering into the dusty past. Anne Ayliffe came round for a while, looking her usual crazy self in blue clogs, green trousers, a blue yachting jumper and a turban. We went to evening service at Christ Church whose congregation is negligible and whose choir has been depleted to one solitary little boy. I prayed and wept and believed in God for ten minutes.

Monday 26th January: At Sibyl's, Bizz Brookman came to dinner from munitions where she is a typist, and we had an interesting discussion about nothing during the evening. Outside the world is blacked out, and Bowden below shows only a very few stars. Bryan, by the way, passed all his subjects in the Intermediate. Sibyl and I lay in bed until past midnight analysing our friends' characters with interest, a stimulating and harmless occupation.

Tuesday 27th January: I am back at my little inky desk in the office simply champing to go out and buy Sue Yeatman a present, as she will be married tonight. I sit and write to John and then stop and think of him, with my chair tilted and my hands clasped behind my head. Sibyl told me last night that I am an egoist – introspective, not complacent. That I suppose, is some consolation, as I could hardly be more discontented with myself. Apparently I "stood Barb up" over lunch so forced her to go with me to Sue's wedding as a sign of forgiveness, and we arrived just as Reverend Irwin pronounced them man and wife and Edward Walter Godfrey hurled organ notes to the arched ceiling. Barb and I sat in a bath of emotion, and then went into the vestry to find Edward, whose ears have grown out of all proportion. He drove us to our room, where we sat in the dark owing to fused wires, and ate chocolates, talking till quite late. We drank milk in town and dispersed.

Wednesday 28th January: Yesterday I posted a muddled, moody letter to John, which is rather ridiculous. I hope he understands it. It was written over a series of unhappy nights. Churchill has given Australia a vote in the War Cabinet and in the Pacific Cabinet. We have drowned many Japanese in the Straits of Macassar; Churchill refuses to go on without a vote of confidence from the Commons. In all, though, the position is better – or is it that the news of Richard is receding day by day? I dined with the Salters, where we sat round a tremendous table and discussed Angaston snobberies, a town where they use to live.

Friday 30th January: Lizzie Salter and I lunched together, and I found, as ever, that wearing my floral hat made me so staid and stiff-necked and self-conscious that it was only when I took it off that the conversation leapt to life and interest. We didn't get terribly far with the Soirée (loathsome title) and spent most of our time pulling writer Beverley Nichols to pieces, he to whom I have returned wrathfully and bitterly and ashamedly to see what other of the ideals he planted on me he is railing at now. Pacifism has gone, but any sensible creature would agree to that. He still believes in God. I take off my hat to him, he is more constant than his erstwhile silly, susceptible little disciple.

Saturday 31st January: I slept all morning at my desk, yet subconsciously fought against what I consciously wanted, in case someone came in and found me slumbering peacefully. So during the afternoon, although we were expected at the Truscott's, Mother and I slept in semi-darkness, whipped out of bed, flung some garments into a case and trammed to Victoria Avenue. It is a splendid home, of high ceilings, cream carved woodwork and clean cream paper, gilt chamois, chandeliers, eighteenth century china clocks and French Empire furniture, ponds filled with purple lilies and water spraying from dolphins' mouths. Everything one touches and drinks from is exquisite, and Mr Truscott sits at table and drops his "hs". I wonder sometimes if I have anything to do with it, but Mother really has nothing much to talk about. She has no new ideas, is filled with platitudes and – she told me Daddy always squashed her, and I know Richard did, and I do. It depresses me hatefully. We went to the pictures to see "The Trial of Mary Dugan" and a Maisie picture, both good in spite of the fact that a small boy sat behind me with his pants torn open, displaying all – which sickened me.

Sunday 1st February: We have withdrawn from Malaya across the Strait of Johore to Singapore, and blown up the Causeway, awaiting Japanese bombs. All our forces are trapped in that small island, with naval docks useless, waiting to be smashed to pieces by Japanese aircraft. Yet we dress in silk frocks and wander arm in arm with friends about well-kept gardens, taking photographs and playing with babies in little white baskets. I called in to see Barb Kelly who was hammering away on the piano at "Jesu, Joy of Man's Desiring" without any accents, and we drifted along the avenues, dark and leafy with plane trees, with trunks "like a mouse's skin". I wrote a pencil letter to John sitting on the stairs while the rest slept. After tea, Mother and I packed our stray garments back into the case and came home. Our room looked drab and colourless, and the girls next door shouted and struggled with their "boyfriends". I hated it all when I fell asleep.

Tuesday 3rd February: A fifteen page letter arrived from Bryan, which is indescribably loveable. It is delicious and unselfconscious and naïve and adorable. Barbara Kelly followed me back to the office after lunch at Elder Gardens and I suddenly felt depressed and burst into tears; it was all very ridiculous. Richard was on the air last night in a new radio serial "Yes, What?" which has considerably shaken us, although 5AD says we can remove it from the air any time. His voice brings his whole personality back too clearly. Miss Hassell came to supper and we had a long talk on the balcony. The whole evening was rather a success, although I had so much to say and said it all, that I benefited not the slightest from her visit.

Wednesday 4th February: It was Mother's turn to give up today and I found her writing letters in floods of tears on my return. John wrote me a letter a few days ago on his religious ideas, which was clever and at least mildly personal, but I am tiring of this distant policy to the extent that at the moment I feel I am tiring of him. Perhaps I'll marry a Frenchman even yet. I tore myself away from Mother and went to dine at the Brookman's, having climbed the darkened stairs to Miss Ward's where Sibyl is now, and seen her typing under that dusty eye. We picked armfuls of rose buds in the sunny garden – the evenings are long this summer – and spent a usual evening, Sibyl and Gray(Graham) playing cards with Beethoven bellowing in the small sitting room, and Aunt Polly and I reading. But outside the blackout is dense. Bowden is a shallow valley filled with black shadows, reflecting a few stars. The blue trams pass through street after street without a light, and cars are hurled out of the darkness, with only narrow slits to guide them.

Thursday 5th February: I am sitting at the inky, narrow desk, while Mr Webb is discussing munition wages for himself. A telegram came from Aunty May and Uncle Louis in Wales, consoling us….My brain is filled with figures, and the world feels stuffy because of it. Wages are crowding in my head; unfortunately not in my purse. Although I was growing chronically tired – I think "chronic" is such a good word – I had to stay up while Mother entertained Mr Mühlstein and Mrs Horner, a disability of a one-roomed existence. They roared at each other, didn't see and show the slightest interest in the other's views, and talked their heads off. They screamed, railed, yelled, bawled, and accused each other's countries of rank cowardice. I trod on Ernst's foot and went out to wash my hair. It was rotten arguing. No one gained anything from it – And all the time the Island of Singapore looks across the Straits of Johore at the massing Japanese troops and no one can guess what endless more years of war their defeat will mean.

Monday 9th February: Bryan came stumbling down the stairs with his white cap and self-conscious smile, and he and I went off to eat crayfish salad together for lunch. He doesn't feel there is much hope for Richard. I feel this more and more. He came back later with the deck boy, a scarlet young man who doesn't know where to look, but I turned any glamour on him that I had at my disposal, to please Bryan. He is doubly precious now. After dining at Quality Inn, we went to "The Tree of Liberty", a very poor picture with Cary Grant and Martha Scott. We ate peaches and drank milk in our room, whereupon Bryan retired to the balcony to sleep above the trams. The Japanese have landed on Singapore and are driving our troops backwards. Sweeping new changes about wages, profits and idleness have been introduced. There is an attempt to nationalize industry here, but the critics are angry that the Labor Government have waited until the wages are almost at inflation levels before pegging them. America is scornful at our losses, and our prestige over Singapore is nil. This is a dangerous state of affairs. The loss of Singapore would leave us no jumping off place for an ultimate attack on Japan, especially as Burma is in a bad way.

Thursday 12th February: I must have mentioned that Bruce Cowell crashed up, now Harry Wesley-Smith's young brother has gone too. Half my friends have died in air craft accidents. There was a blackout last night in strict earnestness, but I rushed home before it, nailed up our cardboard and lay down to sleep in a stifling room. The Japanese claim to have captured the City at Singapore and are demanding surrender. The Germans are supposed to be massing for a Spring Offensive in Russia, now that the Russians are slackening around Leningrad. The Vichy Government has offered Germany more bases, one in Madeira or Madagascar, I think. This will seriously endanger Australia. The French must be rotten to the core.

Friday 13th February: There were three letters from Richard today, regretting the waste of time his inactivity was. He ended "But it won't be for long." How bored he would be in a prison camp, particularly as this war must go on now for countless years. The letter has brought back very clearly that exciting, loveable person who but for the disgrace of a few incompetents, would now be living and squabbling and loving in this incomparably lovely world, this adored Australia. Oh, my God! Oh why? Questions without answers. I read Max Beerbohm's essays at the Public Library, and an American "Theatre Art", but all the time I felt that I was stealing something of Richard's, while I sat there in smug comfort with he - God knows where? There was a telegram from John announcing his arrival that night.

Saturday 14th February: Tonight John and I were going to the Tux with friends after a party, but we decided to walk to his home instead. We went into the side sun room and he lifted me onto a sofa and lay down beside me. He was awfully adorable, and when I told him not to snore, he said he wasn't, only purring. He said he would like to marry me after the war when we could live together normally with children and a home. But certain things worried him; our ages mainly. He knew I was old for my age, but in some ways I unconsciously showed how young I was. He said he was older than I thought – an old twenty eight. Then I told him plainly that I too was very muddled, that sometimes I loved him and sometimes I didn't think I did. We stayed until two thirty, and when he asked if I thought it was safe to go to sleep, I said I couldn't imagine not being safe if he was asleep. I told him not to. There were no taxis so we walked home, John telling me legal stories and holding my hand. It was a thrilling and lovely night.

Sunday 15th February: I slept the sleep of the deeply contented until about eleven when I partook of breakfast, remarked on Love to Mother and ventured out to lunch. When we came home John was ensconced in the only armchair, and we decided to go down to the sea. Which we did. We put on bathers and shorts and wandered along the beach to a less crowded part. We dug ourselves in and went to sleep, carrying on an inarticulate and monosyllabic conversation. When we were sufficiently dazed we leapt into a cold sea and swam fiercely until it grew warm and invigorating. Later we walked to the end of the jetty and had tea in a rather gusty place. You held your lettuce about a foot away and it flew into your mouth. The seagulls hovered rather perilously near. Coming home in the tram we discussed the deb parties we had been to, and when he mentioned some names, I refrained from saying they were elderly prefects when I first tottered into Creveen School as a little girl. I knew it was a man's war when I got into bed and John took a second class seat to Port Pirie for a four hour journey till midnight. Singapore has fallen.

Monday 16th February: A sad thing happened today. The Bulletin sent Richard a cheque and copyright papers in return for his story "First Solo". He may never know that his literary career has begun. But I looked at the official cheque and wept for him, with joy and regret and pride and promise. That's another thing he must come back for. There are always things.....new frocks and bits of news and amusing letters and reviews of books. The Australian Government is bringing in "sweeping" measures to mobilize the whole country's wealth and labour. They announce a "virtual dictatorship" – which we are demanding, and proclaim The Battle of Australia Has Begun. The Liberals are still trying to get a National Government, which is necessary in times of war. There is deep disappointment in Churchill in England. We are continually told that there is no defeatism in the Allied Group, but the Netherlands East Indies are saying scornfully that they fight their battles alone now, because they know then where they stand.

Thursday 19th February: Last night I dreamed that Mic Sandford came back blinded, bitter and old and sad. In the paper today, John Goodfellow is in the "Killed" list. I remember trying to break Peter's heart by flirting with him at the Lisle Johnson's sherry party. Peter talked to another girl, and broke mine! Sir George Murray is dead. That might make Mr Reed a Judge. Mrs Webb has just rung through to say that bombs are being dropped on Darwin. It has begun. And at home there is a letter from Richard written two weeks before he crashed, reviling me for the little effort I make in this war, for my letters of parties and films. Why does he always use me as a butt? He makes me turn on him, even now, when I love him so unutterably. I'm weeping now as I write. This is a day of news. Sibyl dined with us and told us that Tony Young, a master four years ago at St Peter's College, whom I have just written to, is in the Sydney Criminal Courts for homosexuality. "The Truth" in a beastly article mentions him and an Adelaide name. Sibyl mentioned other names that are being rumoured, Mic Sandford, Pirie Bush with his young manager, John Hammill at "Quality Inn". It doesn't shock nor disgust me. I can't imagine it, that is all. But it fills me with a dull disillusionment as though the world and my friends were dirty. And I feared for

Richard's name, because I remember how they loved each other. Mother told me then that in a talk with him about how his friendship with Tony might be misconstrued, he was upset and sickened and angry. She also said later when I was laughing about Mic's name being dragged in, that she had heard rumours before of him – but by filthy minded people like Marjorie Horner, dangerous people. Oh, it's all mad, crazy. The night is full of people whispering foul things.

Saturday 21st February: Winter has made a mistake, and sleet has got mixed up with sunshine, and frost with flowers. I walked in it this afternoon. The leafy trees in Frome Road looked bare, and wet mists along the river banks painted the lawns a vivid green. Driving mists of rain swept against my face. I sat on the balcony watching people below on the wet pavements, their coats flapping. Mother and I dined at Elder Park, and as our conversation lately has been somewhat intimate, and my voice at all times is apt to be penetrating, I suddenly found myself next to a table occupied by two convulsed women. I had merely remarked (wistfully) would it have mattered much if I had spent the night with John. So I thought desperately of something very innocent and announced loudly to Mother, "There are fairies at the bottom of my garden." But I packed up myself when I turned to see the effect.

Sunday 22nd February: Java is raided and invaded and she calls for help. Rangoon is in peril and her fall is expected. The Burmese battle is grave, and we retreat. Tremendous naval battle around Bali. Apparent victory to us, but with losses. We had afternoon tea at the Harley Hoopers, sitting round a table and arguing fiercely and delightfully. We examined their notorious dugout which is a miniature mine; steps leading into the earth, sloping down to a cabin lit by electric light sixteen feet underground; down further to another room. Then onto the Brookman's to dinner, where nothing very much happened except that I heard there the Japanese warning to expect a raid on the 28th February.

Monday 23rd February: I suppose this Tokis warning is part of a nerve war, but it is dangerous and discomforting. I find myself wondering more and more how I will take a raid. The thought of it fills me with terror. Panic. It is a beastly world. Courage, in spite of speeches and propaganda, is something I don't think of with relation to Richard and John and Alain and – Yet Richard flew over Germany in a bit of silk and ply-wood, and dropped bombs and was followed by enemy planes – was everywhere surrounded by death and people wishing him death. Anne Warden and I lunched together with a peculiar creature called "Ormsby", who knew Peter at the time of our Romance and kept enquiring after him in a shrill voice, while Anne kept kicking him under the table. My first evacuation officer's meeting was tonight at Madge Church, our area (8) comprising Hutt Street, Wakefield Street, South Terrace and Carrington Street. There are about twenty of us, and it is a job which demands common sense, courage, leadership and discretion. The registering will be amusing; asking elderly women their ages, symptoms and occupations.

Tuesday 24th February: There's a bit of romance in war after all. Adelaide (and Australia) is filled with American army and air force men in khaki uniforms and little cook's caps; they stand about and admire this lil' being and the ankles that go by – and often stop. Lunching with Margo Walters, she told me that Hollywood actors Lewtenant James Stewart and Private Wayne Morris are in Darwin. In other circumstances they would have had Australia at their feet, now they are phantom troops, as the Americans are rather thrilling secrets. Sibyl yesterday had an inoculation for typhoid and small pox in case of invasion, so I went there to dinner to cheer her up. After dinner we walked about Bowden and discussed poetry. Sibyl has an amazingly retentive memory and the ability to argue cleverly on subjects she knows nothing about, a quality I possessed, but possess no longer.

Wednesday 25th February: The "theme" running through my life in the last week was the absence of a letter from John. Three mails a day mean three disappointments. Still, it has come, but instead of abject apologies for proposing one week and forgetting to write the next, he tells me the joys (ephemeral) of milking a cow. Death by slow strangulation, perhaps……..Today at work I read Shelley's "Adonais" aloud to the tins and the long shadows on the ceiling from the street outside, and to a picture of Hitler slipping "on your elbow grease". It's impossible to get to sleep early in a tenement like ours. At ten o'clock there was a distant splashing sound which slowly grew to a dull roar. I rushed out and discovered the bathrooms flooded, water pouring down the back stairs and sogging heavily through the ceiling onto the ground floor. Miss Bungey had pulled the plug out of a full bath, when the pipes were choked, even though notices were hung blatantly about the room. She stood accusing everyone of a frame up, and waving a broom helplessly in the passage, while we seeped around in bathers and shower caps. I heard 11.30 strike.

Friday 27th February: Mother caught the Melbourne Express on a buying trip for Myers, and I ached to go with her and stay in Collins Street where there are summer mists about the plane trees, and to meet all Melbourne's delicious people. I was just there about a year from now. This time last year I was waiting for a letter - After I had seen her away at the station I came back to my room, and tried to sleep. I kept waking. I have no idea if John is coming down this weekend, or if I should make other arrangements. As though it matters one jot as the headlines are at present. "Allies Attack Japanese Invasion Bases In Java. Australians There." "Enemy Gathers Strength, During Lull, For Rangoon Attack." "General Gordon Bennett, A.I.F. Commander In Malaya, Escapes." (This is viewed with mixed feelings. Should a captain leave his ship, however valuable he may be? I think "Yes.") "Evacuees Arrive From Darwin After Nightmare Journey."

Tuesday 3rd March: Richard's story is in the Bulletin, with headings quite an inch high. How madly thrilled he would be. He's reached Mecca. It was still ninety degrees at midnight. I retired early after a meeting at Madge Church, during which we practiced registering evacuees, with us playing harassed mothers. But we will be needed badly soon because Java is falling. We next. I had just fallen asleep surrounded by mosquito sprays, incense burners, iced water, fruit and burning pillows, when I awoke to find a dark huge figure standing over me, and I with nothing on. For a horrible moment I thought it was John, but it was Bryan. Mother will be most disappointed about not seeing him, as she lives for his leaves.

Wednesday 4th March: Bryan and I breakfasted and then he went down to the Port to receive a month's pay - £1. I receive £10. We arranged to meet for lunch but he turned up at North Terrace half an hour late and

I had already had some. He is very depressed, to the extent of looking as though he were on the verge of tears. He informs me he is blue for no reason, but I believe he is homesick for Mother, and still angry at the unfairness of a cadet's lot. It worries me. What's one more worry after all.... Sibyl took me out to afternoon tea, and we brought back drinks for Mr Webb, who has won her heart as he has mine. Bryan and I dined at Quality Inn; he doesn't eat much, but drinks quantities of milk. We argued a bit about pictures but I guiltily won – of course – and we saw "Bluebeard's 8th Wife", which was most amusing and delightfully pre-war; and "The Trail of the Lonesome Pine" of which we couldn't hear a whisper so poor was the recording. But the scenery was good and the acting showed us the plot. We rang Mother and went to bed. There's a big moon behind streaks of black clouds.

Thursday 5th March: After breakfast Bryan left, still too quiet and sad looking, although he left me broke, with long distance calls unpaid and Sibyl's meals to pay for in the future. I hope he comes home soon again so that Mother and I can make him happy. Mr Webb let me go at half past four, and as I passed through Gawler Place the Siren went: Mr Hooper rushed out of Red Cross House and dragged me inside. When a raid comes, people will simply look up and smile self-consciously, think-ing it's a practice. I wrote a long, rather nice letter to John, and then ate eggs at the Kiosk in Elder Gardens.

Friday 6th March: Paris has been raided by our planes and over a thousand killed in German factories. The kid gloves are off. But will this foster hate? We are only sorry for the French; our tolerance has amazed me. Everywhere the public are demanding an offensive spirit – hurl all we have into the battle and turn the tide, give it 'em. Jim White, Peter's Geelong friend, has died of Dingo Disease at Darwin. It was Peter who got Jim to enlist in the Puckapunyal crowd.

Saturday 7th March: I was sitting on the floor cleaning my shoes when John burst in, said he was back for a week on pre-embarkation leave, that he was taking Biddy Dean out tonight, but could I go with him tomor-row. I haughtily told him to ring me and I'd see "if I could make it." He withdrew in an enormous hurry and left me flabbergasted. I looked in the mirror and was promptly sick. I continued to be vaguely ill all afternoon although Sibyl cheered me up enormously and I realized there was nothing extraordinary in taking a silly little ass to the films, when she had entertained him at Mount Gambier. Nevertheless, it hurt my pride. It is Saturday, after all, and it is his last leave, and the Japs are frighteningly near. So I said "Dammit" and forgot about John and Biddy. Instead, I went with Sibyl to see Robert Newton in a film at the Majestic, having a passionate affair with a Tamara, and ending up as a corpse. He was very sweet with raven hair and a curling mouth, but didn't attempt to act.

Sunday 8th March: I met John at the station and we entrained in comfort to Blackwood, while I was informed of a bachelor's party last night at which I was not asked. I wondered wistfully if the Boys had missed me... We passed a country house "The Spinney" and sat on top of a windy hill, talking, with my head on his knee. Then we came down to Blackwood and dined. I had very little to eat. We sat in the empty lounge talking again, and then on through the windy, dark, cold night to the station waiting room, and John went to sleep with his head on my lap, among the prams and "Ladies W.C."s. At ten, he came into my room to have some tea and made love to me, with the small lamp on. He was feeling very guilty about being there; so I said, "Actually it's really a sitting room." "Yes", said John, "but we are not sitting." I was very in love with him but didn't mind when he said he wasn't ready to get married yet. We talked about marriage and lots of things pertaining to ourselves. After a bit he grew very excited, and left in hurry at midnight, announcing "I must arise from the cloying pleasures of the bed" – which was rather exaggerated (hastily added in case of future reference). In spite of being secretly sick in a darkened railway station without being seen, it was a good day.

Monday 9th March: John came down to the office and asked me out next Wednesday to my utter fury, because although I had decided to go to bed early tonight, I wanted the pleasure of being asked – And tomorrow! What on earth has come over him? He loves me tremblingly one night, and lets my love peter out for the next two... I had a chat with Dr Wigg and received a recipe. Mother arrived on the late express. Wonderful having her back.

Tuesday 10th March: The news these days is so horrible that I have given up reading, and listening to it instalment by instalment over the air. It can't end under less than ten years. Java has fallen. Australians captured there with Brigadier Blackburn at their head. Rangoon is reported captured. Who next? India or Australia? There is no Dutch aircraft left intact, so thoroughly have the Allies been beaten in Java.

Wednesday 11th March: John pays his little visits down to the cellar, and makes me brew cups of tea while he reads the evening paper and utters scornful sounds about my typewriting. He comes every day. This night I swallowed a capsule given to me for nausea from Dr Wigg. Feeling like a dope fiend, I went off to dine with John at the Gresham in a new pink Martin Stillschweig wool frock. The capsule didn't exactly enlarge my appetite but it sent me on to the pictures in excellent spirits. Afterwards, we had supper at the Quality Inn but I had taken too much dope and, muttering something about "giving Pirie Bush a message from Gordon Heaslip", rushed Pirie off down subterranean passages to where I could be sick. Pirie stood sympathetically in the lavatory. We came straight home because there was nowhere to "sit and dream", so I went to bed frustrated.

Thursday 12th March: Last night I realized what it was like to be homeless. We drifted about thinking vainly of places to sit, but it was drizzling slightly and Mother slept in the only room we knew. So we kissed and said goodnight…. Australia is a land of excitement. The Americans slouch about the streets laden with water bottles and hip revolvers as though they don't quite know what to expect; Dutch and Javanese rabble troops have crossed here in battered, lop-sided planes or unarmed boats over which the Japanese pilots have leant from their planes, waved and dropped their bombs: their stories are unreal, of families left to be raped and murdered. Our own men are coming, back in droves, ringing up, saying "Darling, I'm home" as though it were Armistice and not their last stand.

Friday 13th March: John came down for his little chat, snooped around the back and came back and said, "I was a fool to leave law" - I forewent my principle and put on the clothes I know John likes – the silk floral frock and bunny wool jumper - and dined tonight at the Portuses. Professor Portus, Mrs Portus and John and I politely chatted in deep armchairs, and I wedded Professor Portus with his ecclesiastical ring, and John was interested to know if the engagement and wedding ring was the same finger! Then John took me off to his room and we looked at his Oxford and European pictures, as he was when he was my age, very earnest and sweet – John on a bicycle in Wales with other undergraduates; John in Hamburg with two black-shirts; and ironically enough, John standing by a German Air Raid Precaution sign which said "Warning from bombs from the sky". He pulled me down beside him on the bed, but my nerves were on edge and I couldn't stop shivering. He stroked me gently like a kitten – the gentlest person I know, and said he was sorry if he had been difficult lately and not made this week very happy for me. We walked home clutching hands fiercely with the stars asleep through the branches of trees as we passed. We kissed goodbye and I said, "What a bloody war." He said, "Goodnight, sweetness."

Saturday 14th March: I didn't try and weep this time. I know that I love him, and his going before meant nothing to this. This morning there have been a stream of interesting men wanting jobs, some refugees from Darwin, a lame man who looks like a Duke, and a returned man who has been through Greece, Libya, Crete and Darwin. Yet when he told me his pals were marrying Jewish girls for £400 in exchange for their nationality and I asked if it was business or if they lived with them, he blushed like a girl and the warrior backed away and muttered "that what I mean to say is, yer don't get much chance in camp." I walked to the Blackburn's with my case as I was going to stay with Sibyl. However, Sibyl suddenly had a date so I stayed with Wody instead. Brigadier Blackburn is fighting in the hills about Bandoeng and his troops can hang on until their ammunition runs out. The Dutch here say they have a fighting chance. Wody and I talked about books until we slept, but I should have liked Sibyl to unburden my heart to. John has gone.

Sunday 15th March: We breakfasted in the sleep out, eating fruit and fig jam on our beds, and then spent a most peaceful day bathing George, the Sealyham Terrier, swinging on the swing, taking snaps of people eating linseed cake on the front lawn, reading French magazines – "Marie Claire", hitting balls around the court in our bare feet and shouting at each other in Grade II French and looking with awe on the V.C. and the flag of Damascus, which was handed over to my host at the gates. We also drank countless cups of tea and coffee with a succeeding group of visitors – General Allen and his aides, who arrived in scarlet staff bands to tell Mrs Blackburn the latest news from Java, but as military secrets were discussed we departed and sent tea out to the military driver. Then three Dutch captains in green uniforms and leggings came to dine, and we taught them Australian slang and flirted with them.

Monday 16th March: It's a grey day, charged with losing battles and floating cities plunging down into a green sea. A little alien called Johann Greussing has just come to the office and asked for a job, but it must be within city limits and it must be something harmless. He has dark eyes and shabby clothes and doesn't look dangerous. Tonight Mother and I are going to the pictures with Mühlstein who was a lieutenant of the Axis last war and has just been made a sergeant in this, - on our side. Sibyl dined with us first and we discussed the art of making love, quoting examples from our overcrowded lives, but her life is just beginning to take on glamour and glitter as mine sinks into oblivion.

Tuesday 17th March: During the present few days, I have been overwhelmingly depressed. I think I shall splash my moods across this page and then turn over a new leaf. Everywhere our boys are coming back. The girls who are engaged are rushing wedding frocks together. A woman at dinner caught her breath suddenly as though she had a heart attack and flung herself into her husband's arms as he came into the room. My friends are playing fast and loose with the American and Dutch. Mary Brock is about to get married; Jock Britten Jones is also. Louise Matison has married Neil Ligertwood in Melbourne. Excitement, madness, the streets a mass of men. Men everywhere. But no Richard. No John. No Bryan. The Holy Trinity, Three-in-One, who matter are not here in all this adventure. This slow job makes me restless with boredom, and at night it is the same. I seem to have lost touch with people, and can't meet new ones. Sibyl is having a grand time; I am not. The mood is wearing off. There are thousands like us whose boys are not coming back – 17,000 in Singapore alone. In war it is useless making exceptions of yourself.

Thursday 19th March: General MacArthur of the Philippines has been given command of the Australian area. America takes over Australia in all branches. We are saved. Everyone is exhilarated by the news of MacArthur's arrival here across enemy country. The general idea is to sit back and say "Thank the Lord, the Americans will get us out, pull us through. Thank God for Uncle Sam."

Monday 23rd March: The Japanese are pushing on to Port Moresby, but are being hindered severely by our planes. I met Jo Simpson, Tommy Simpson's sister, who insisted that I write to him, which I have done. He is at Moresby, thinking wistfully that all his women have deserted him.

Tuesday 24th March: A letter arrived from John, and the address is England. I am dejected, because I distrust her shores: and his number is almost identical with Richard's. We received a letter from an officer in Richard's squadron, who said that he left with great excitement on his first raid and the weather turned bad suddenly: no more has been heard of any of them. There is a good deal of hope in this news – a forced landing seems the best possibility. I had lunch with Stevie, who won't join the W.A.A.A.F.s because "boys don't like them. Too masculine." I don't much care for Stevie. Mother went out, so I had dinner alone at the Adelaide, while all around were gay parties and soldiers drinking champagne. I wandered back along North Terrace and bumped into a boy who was at school with Richard, and spent most of the evening listening to him saying how badly he wanted to get into the Air Force, but how the boss wouldn't let him go, and how his mother's heart was breaking at the thought – until I felt a bit sick and went home. Thank God we don't have to make excuses for Richard, or I to myself for John. I wrote to him up in my room, with the lamp on, all the way to England.

Wednesday 25th March: I spent the day translating Verlaine, and then had my hair combed, put on my seersucker evening frock with the flowery earrings and ate a pasty with Mother at the Ritz, while shouting across tables of leering youths in uniform at Mr Clive Bonython. Met Barb Kelly and trammed with others I knew to the Norwood Town Hall which was taken for a troop dance. There were my stately friends bounding about the floor with hardy men of the battlefields. The blackout made the room hot, and everyone perspired and bumped and laughed and drank diluted raspberry drink. There were many too many soldiers – a regular state of affairs – but I whirled them around, and walked with them out into the cool streets and listened to their stories. All of them were grand chaps, loving every bit of fun, sophisticated and unsophisticated, that they can get. And I met Donald Bernard Godfried Parser, Dutch officer of the Fleet air arm, or rather I pinched him from Diane Basse who refused to speak to me after we had spent three quarters of the evening together, dancing, walking, drinking in cafés off high stools, telling each other our life stories, making dates and exchanging telephone numbers. He is like a young Robert Newton in a naval white uniform, and I like him tremendously. I came home in triumph, feet blackened.

Thursday 26th March: Don is the son of the Consul-General of Holland, where his father was Albanian representative; he lived all his life there except the last few years which he spent in New York, which he loves, although he talks of "our Queen." He was twenty one two days ago and is stationed at Parafield. We are going to the Tux and dinner on Saturday night. Sibyl came to see me in the office and we walked home to her place, where we talked and chewed. Now that I have Donald "Piper Cub pilot" it isn't quite a bore hearing all about her Cam and Peter. Every time she attempts to outdo any compliments I may have had, I kind of murmur, "John! I wish he were back" as a nasty way of pointing out that a man in hand is worth two in in the bush. Which, on my part, is faintly exaggerated. We received an official letter from the Air Ministry about Richard, saying he was much loved by all and that he was a splendid pilot, having landed a bomber safely with an exploded engine from 4,000 feet; that this was his first raid and the objective was an aerodrome in Holland. The weather grew bad soon after they left and nothing has been heard of any of them since.

Friday 27th March: Mother and I spent an hour dragging about town looking for a hotel in which to eat, but being jostled and stared after by soldiers in the filthy streets which are unlike our nice, clean Adelaide. The gutters are blocked and the mess outside hotels is nauseating. At least we got into the Savoy in the Arcade and waited an hour and a half –

until eight – for omelettes and asparagus. At tables about us were Javanese airmen in R.A.A.F. uniform, keeping much to themselves, polite,
attractive and quiet. Their table manners give them away - Don rang as
he promised and I went to sleep filled with Lillianesque excitement. Two
parcels of our letters to Richard have been returned.

Saturday 28th March: Don called in his white uniform and was presented to Mother, bowing over her hand and clicking his heels together
and murmuring "Donald Parser" into her eyes. We dined at the Gresham,
then onto "Out of the Fog" at the Regent, a depressing but well-acted film,
during which I was surrounded by a long arm which knew exactly what
to do. Before going on to the Tux, we sauntered down to the river, with
the Dutch fleet airman cap on my head and holding hands. We sat on the
edge of the river watching a big heavy moon on the water and he asked
me if I would go back to Rio de Janeiro to live with him, if he cabled,
muttered sweet Dutch nothings, and said I was his ideal girl and how
could I bear to have everything right about me, etc. etc. We couldn't get
into the Tux in spite of a booked table, so we drank Port on the Richmond
balcony, while I let him make love to me.

Sunday 29th March: Don and I trained up to Mount Lofty, standing
on the "observation" platform at the back, watching the rails melt away
from us and the gums slide by. The sky grew grey and overcast and soon it
rained, but we walked about the rear hills for a while, and sat in the gully
under a tree while we took grey snaps which won't come out. We arrived
in town soaked through, in the dark, so he changed at the Richmond
and I at home and then we went to Sibyl's with some sandwiches. Don
talked a tremendous lot and grew merrier and merrier as we drank tea and
discussed the "Yaps doin Yava". Sibyl broke my heart by saying she much
preferred Cam and then he took Bizz Brookman and me home, very flir-
tatiously, so that I almost agreed with Sibyl.

Monday 30th March: It drizzled all day, in a damp grey way that I
rather like; it suited my mood when a telegram was phoned through to me
from Bryan, wishing us well from an overseas port. I went to break the
news to Mother, which stunned her, the port having been censored and
we concluding he was posted to convoy duty. I came back to the office

and wept until my eyes ached. Then Bryan walked in. He knew nothing about the telegram, having taxied from his ship at Pirie for a few days, through special favour of the Captain. Oh, the contentment, the peace of will and spirit, the kindness of the gods, the Relief….. Don rang from his tailor's. He is getting a P/O's R.A.A.F. uniform for winter, asking me to have a cocktail with him at five. He was simply adorable today, quieter and steadier. He had on a khaki flying suit (the warmest thing he has) and he produced four records for me of the doubtful music I don't care much for, but I adored him for it. He walked to the hotel with Bryan and Mother and me and then had to go back to Parafield.

Tuesday 31st March: Today I was keen to play my records on a non-existent gramophone. One of the records is "Please Take a Letter Miss Brown"! I went home to Molesworth Street to pick up my gramophone and my spirit was heavy within me. Knick-knacks and rugs and masses of furniture and "baubles" cluttered the rooms. The back garden had withered to a few vegetables and a trench. So I visited Mrs Portus who even at this late hour looks cool and tidy. We talked more about John than usual and the whole of his personality grew clear and strong in his own home. Then I had dinner with Bryan and Mama at the Black Bull Hotel. A soldier accosted me on the way home, so Bryan fought him until he was dragged ignominiously away by Mother.

Wednesday 1st April: Godfried (Don's new name) listened to our records, and looked through the albums, taking numerous ones of me, leaving staring blanks; then we two dined at the Richmond, and staggered happily up to the Repertory Theatre. We saw "Ladies in Retirement", which was extremely well acted, and an odd play, a little in the style of "Night Must Fall." But because Godfried came from New York and was sitting beside me, I felt it was amateurish, and he couldn't understand it anyway, so he gave up concentrating and played with my hand. Darkness. Whispers. "S-sh. What will people think? Lord, there's Miss Knott!" "May I put my arm around you?" "No. S-sh." etc. Diane Basse was there with her mother, and every time I guiltily looked across at that mass of white fur, I caught her eye….We took a rug and went and sat by the river with a white moon splashed across it, and around us. Filigree branches of poplars and willows. Lovemaking. Mother angry when I came back.

Thursday 2nd April: Damn, blast this bloody diary: a week of it. It's growing more unimaginative and banal. Gone is Oscar's advice, gone is the Woolfian subtlety, gone are the ghastly "epigrams" (Beverley Nichols' variety), and I find nothing else in life except that I dined in a crowded hotel with Bryan and Mother and then went to " The Shepherd of the Hills" with them, a picture of even such dumb, inarticulate illiterates as I am. I also got engaged....I met Godfried for a few minutes in the Richmond lounge, and he gave me a fearfully expensive little Marcasite brooch. Then he told me he wanted me to wear a ring for him – a Dutch engagement ring – and after pointing out that it was just a "fraternity ring-nothing else", we rushed down to a little jeweller's shop, and they served us sympathetically. I came back to a room filled with red roses from him, and Sibyl and Mother told me I was a silly little fool.

Saturday 4th April: Tonight we were going to the Tux, so I came down the stairs to meet Godfried dripping with velvet and furs and red roses with dew in their leaves. At the Tux door we met Sibyl, looking glorious, with Cam (at last!) but there wasn't much chance of getting in, so we went to a champagne party at the Richmond. Later we went on to the Blue Grotto. There was so much champagne that Godfried brushed his teeth with it that night. We danced, watched disgusting exhibitions of female decadence, and met people, and Godfried and I drifted back along North Terrace at three.

Sunday 5th April: I slept all morning; then Godfried, Mother and I caught a train to Aldgate after lunch, where we were met by Mr Caldwell in a CAR. The infinite pleasure of driving silently along a hill's road, with the sun on damp gums. Then Gaby....He came up to us, sniffed carefully, then went crazy. He hurled himself at us, whined ecstatically and pattered about after us, implanting soft black kisses. He knew! Oh, glory halle-lujah, he knew! We boated on Silver Lake, while I lay back in the canoe smoking a stubby cigarette and hoping Mother wouldn't call out from the shore, telling me not to pretend I'm grown up. We walked along the up road, eating blackberries and breaking off blue tips from the gum trees. It grew dark and we ate fried eggs and tomatoes in a little room filled with walrus-moustached young men and antimacassars, overlooking the lake. Later we danced in the hall with young campers. In the blue train going home, we talked French, and everyone loves Dutch soldiers.

Tuesday 7th April: I went home to dinner with Sibyl, growing steadily more helpless in the tram as we read a letter Godfried had written me in horrible English. Margo Waterhouse was there, and was rather entertaining all evening. We bragged about our respective "goings-on", but I am still careful never to mention John, whom, in spite of all this, I miss extremely. He's entirely opposite to Godfried, a peaceful haven. When I write to him, I have nothing to say, as I can't mention my extravagant life to someone who is fighting for it – something I learned from Richard.

Wednesday 8th April: There have been some big naval disasters lately – the Hermes, the Cornwall, the Dorsetshire. Most of the crews are safe - but this has become a minor point in this hard, monotonous war in which one's sensibilities are not affected by mass murder, and rape, and bestiality. R.A.A.F. and American planes have been bombing enemy occupied territory in the North, and the Japs have advanced in Burma, taking the oil fields. Since MacArthur's flight, the Philippines battle has gone against the Americans, and Bataan Peninsula, famous for its courageous retention, has fallen into Jap hands. But all this still seems so far distant. I lie in my green bed reading Flaubert, with the reading lamp on and the gum leaves reflected up onto the ceiling, and the curtains drawn, while the world snarls and licks its wounds, and little brave people die.

Thursday 9th April: It was such a lovely day until I walked into a music shop and met Caroline Campbell. I happened to ask her what she is doing now and she told me she was a cadet reporter at "The News". She got the job two weeks ago, and is younger and far less experienced than I. She said her father knew Mr Morley well.....Oh Lord, what a filthy business. I too know Mr Morley. I came home and wept with despair, bitterness, exasperation, disappointment and jealousy, and the least of these was jealousy.

Friday 10th April: Since the "Campbell Affair", this job has become intolerable. I rang Mr Dumas but he is in Melbourne. I came home to find Godfried waiting for me – A.W.L. (absent without leave). We sat in

Miss Ottaway's room, and talked and snogged, I'm afraid. I got heartily sick of it, and of him, and went to bed irritated with him and myself. That is bound to happen.

Sunday 12th April: After lunch Godfried and a Dutch friend called for me and we trammed to the Blackburns for tennis. Patar is six foot four inches, is slim and strong and brown, and has the faintest streak of Javanese blood in him. His father is in command of Holland's last destroyer. It was grand strolling arm in arm with these two attractive creatures into Brigadier Blackburn's admiring family. We played tennis in bare feet with Mary Yates and Wody, who both fell madly in love with Patar, following him with adoring looks and sitting next to him. We had a peaceful tea around a polished table, while the two boys broke off at times and laughed and talked in Dutch, and we shuffled uneasily. They talked Java strategy to Mrs Blackburn, while I half slept on the sofa next to Godfried in the dimly lighted room. Patar had seen Brigadier Blackburn with British Field Marshall Archibald Wavell. I dragged them off decently early, and in the tram the people nudged each other and listened to everything we said.

Monday 13th April: Although I felt shivery with fatigue, Mary Yates and I went to the Richmond with Patar and Godfried, dined well, felt happy and went upstairs and kissed everyone and turned up to the pictures in time to see the tail end of the programme! We tramped loudly up to my room – Mother away – and made tea, drank sherry, blasted on the radio, danced, threw pillows about, leapt over beds and under them and on them, and were all highly amused until 12.30, without feeling cheap. Patar kissed me without Godfried getting sulky which I liked better – as he didn't kiss Yates! They tried to stay the night, saying I could trust two surely, but I at last said goodnight, and Patar kissed me firmly goodbye, while Godfried waited. Then he said this was really the last time they had official leave before leaving for America, and I suddenly felt sentimental, and we parted heroically.

Tuesday 14th April: But today, a wreck, a miserable, nervy, sleepy wreck. A few minutes before the train bearing all the Dutchmen away, left, Godfried rang to say a last goodbye. He tried to think of anything to say, but couldn't. "Well, goodbye…Write to me…..Here it is….Well the time…" There was a huge bunch of gladioli in my room, wrapped in pink ribbon. These things are sad.

Wednesday 15th April: Life, instead of falling back into a tomblike silence, has suddenly taken an unexpectedly dramatic turn. I saw Mr Dumas, who shook his head and sent me protesting to the Commercial Department, who turned out to be handsome and courteous, who arranged for me to see Mr Chapman of 5AD, who is on the point of giving me a position in the Programme Department. This is delicious. Mother is going to Melbourne to buy, this weekend, so I reminded her of a promise to take me. Which she is doing. Mr Webb has someone temporarily, but I hope she will be permanent. We are leaving on Saturday night. This is glorious. My magic city….at Easter time. We have had a good old suburban row with the landlady, and are on the point of taking over a Colonel's apartments at "The Olives" at Brougham Place, North Adelaide. Thank God, clean bathrooms.

Thursday 16th April: Owing to a modest little list of achievements, I forgot to mention that last night I distributed Householders' instructions for the Evacuation Section, all around Hurtle Square and Halifax Street, guided by a torch and Mr Glover. An old man came to his door: I explained my call: he said, "Thank the Lord, now I can evacuate the old woman." At another door, I found poor old Mrs Crafter, who recounted all her woes, which I admit are depressing…At another, they said in a dim scared way, "Go 'way, Go 'way. There's just bin a death in this 'ouse." I went. I dined at the Brookman's, reading a book, while Sibyl grew bitter and sarcastic at Cam over the phone. He is continually jilting her. "You are sure you don't mind?" "Oh NO!" says Sibyl, full of irony. "That's good", says Cam. Home in this thick frightening blackout.

Friday 17th April: We have received the last letters from Richard – for a long time. They were written on his birthday, two days before he was lost, and are vital, young, and very living. About a party in his honour in the Mess: he was going to get drunk for the first time to see what it was like. I hope he adored it. His last line was "Mother precious, don't be too lonely." Just before I left the office, I told Mr Webb there was a likelihood of my getting a job at 5AD, and so I wouldn't be coming back. Walking back along North Terrace, the sun was everywhere, and the tops of the plane trees were bronze, and the whole aspect of my life was fine and free, with veins of content throughout it. In spite of this, I have a bad cold. But what is this when I can see again the Rubbos, and the Copenhagen mermaid gazing out into the garden.

Saturday 18th April: How many other times have I experienced this exhilarating sensation of sweeping up the old office for another gi rl, of putting clean blotters and filling ink wells, and going out with my arms full of vases, glasses, tea towels, and jugs, the Petty Cash balanced for the last time. Mr Webb was very kind, saying he had felt for some time that I was wasted there. As an inefficient secretary, I don't agree, but I shall be excited doing something at last into which I can fling something a little intellectual. Mr Chapman gave me a position at £2.5.0 in the Records Department, with the not far prospect of rises and more interesting jobs, and told me to stay in Melbourne as long as I liked. Richard makes sacrifices, gives up his adored work, and who knows, his life, while I being a woman, come like a vampire into his kingdom. I recognize and sicken at the unfairness. Furious packing, washing, mending, ironing. Melbourne! It was a hellish trip, sitting up in the train, leaning against Mother with pins and needles in one's lower limbs, watching the luminous darkness flare by. White morning and soot in your eyes and hair, and eating breakfast in the buffet car with a young man with false teeth.

Sunday 19th April: Melbourne slides into view. The red soil of Bacchus Marsh first and then the wooden houses and brick kilns of Sunshine, and then the factories, and then the spires and skyscrapers lying in the sunshine. We taxied to the Esplanade Hotel, St Kilda, left our luggage in the hall and walked along the Pier. George Formby was singing and grey ships lay in convoy about the harbour, casting grey shadows upon the misty sea. Girls in slacks everywhere, and old men sketching for 9d., and Jews in bright flannels, and American doughboys lounging over the railings. We paid £10.0.0 for a room with a bathroom, but the water refused to go on, the walls were salt damp, the curtains torn, the blankets filthy. We were miserable. Mother had a row with the Manageress, who said we had to stay now we had paid. I went down and grovelled in the dust. We left with the £10.0.0 for a good room at the Oriental Hotel, where we got in with a bit of luck. There was a Red Cross dance for Service Men in the ballroom, so I went and met a Melbourne girl called Sheila Wallach. I danced with a dumb American called James (Jeem) Robey Warbee from Noo Jersey. He played ball, I gathered, had a scholarship to Duke College, was still at school at 21 (playing ball) and was impossible to understand. We sat on the stairs outside my room and chewed gum. The Americans are everywhere, in corduroy jackets, waterproofs, camel hair and khaki, and we fawn and grease to them. It is disgusting. We stand up to "The Stars and Stripes" but forget to play "God Save the King," are told to hold out the hand of fellowship to our Saviours. This England...this emerald isle....We are forgetting the stern little people who laughed at Coventry, and won the Battle of Britain. We ate a colossal breakfast and sallied forth down the shady streets, feeling drab among the Melbourne women in their smart suits. This began a series of purchases which have lasted the whole week. Mother went off to buy for Myers, and I to shop and get my bearings. The sun was out, and the plane trees were losing their bronze leaves. We dined in the evening at "Henry's" and then saw "49th Parallel", an English propaganda film with Leslie Howard and Laurence Olivier.

Tuesday 21st April: I met Sheila Wallach at the Athenaeum and we lunched together, while outside the clouds gathered, and the streets were wet and shining. I said to myself, "I shall go and see the Harold Herbert Exhibition, then the Connell collection in the glass section of the Art Gallery, then perhaps home to write letters," but I said, "First I shall just go and see how long 'Jamaica Inn' with Robert Newton will be on for." I stayed of course. I sat in the theatre among the sparse crowd, hugging myself and breathing deeply in my soul, while the adored was hung, drawn and quartered by the worst looking cut throats to come out of Denham. Even then, he was attractive. Guiltily, but immensely contented, I came home through the torrential streets, and we caught three trams in wrong directions to get to the Crows, eventually landing some miles out. We did get there to a cold chicken, feet wet and shoulders soaked, two hours late, and the Crows forgot to ask us to dry ourselves. They are dears, but that great admiration I had for them has gone a good deal, because I feel they can't care very much for people outside their family.

Wednesday 22nd April: Today I met Peg Espie from Adelaide and we saw "Blossoms in the Dust" with Greer Garson, Walter Pidgeon and hundreds of babies crawling about in night gowns. It was quite sweet, about Edna Gladney who brought in acts against the using of "illegitimate" on marriage and passport certificates, and was very sentimental, as all pictures about children are. Peg (who has lost about six lovers in air crashes) and I wept copiously and bitterly. She is at the Invergowrie Hostel at Hawthorn learning how to be a good housewife, but after the deaths of Bruce Cowell, David Tucker, John Goodfellow, Peter Ingoldby and so on, she doubts the wisdom of it…. She's a funny, freckled, vivacious, rather attractive person whom Richard liked. I have tried to ring Mary Fitzpatrick but she's always out, having just got engaged to a writer invalided at her hospital. Ellen Rubbo told me. There's another Rubbo now called Anna. I retired to bed to read Mérimée's "Carmen" and eat candied fruit.

Thursday 23rd April: So far I have bought a tailored brown tweed skirt, a cherry twin set of brushed wool, brown suede shoes with bows, a cherry wool frock and a brown sports coat from Nobles. This is flawless, very severe, with fiercely straight shoulders, and every line and stitch accurate. When I talk to Charles and Louis, I talk to geniuses. Meanwhile, I go shopping with Mother, and buy masses of frocks for Myers in quaint old buildings, have lunch every day in arty little cafés, and sometimes wander in the parks, as the gardeners burn brown leaves.

Friday 24th April: As you see, the whole week has gone in shopping, films and lunches, and I remember that I must find somewhere to live for the next few weeks, or go home. Mother is going on to Sydney. The Princess Mary Club is full, so I take a room at the Y.W.C.A. for 24 shillings a week! It is central, safe and cheap. It is a little different from this Hotel. Next week I want to leave the centres, and go out into the parks and gardens and zoos. The week after, I want to go to the Dandenongs. Boy, what a life! The fruit stalls are full of corn on the cob, mushrooms, raspberries, strawberries, chestnuts…The sun is out again, but the streets are wet. This is a little London. Looking like a Vogue model (when I didn't see a mirror) I went out to see Peg at Invergowrie. It is a big, untidy, rambling, pretty place on top of a hill and filled with unaccountably plain girls in odd clothes. We sat on a window seat and talked about Adelaide and her people. I met Mother at the Berriman's – Jeanne ravishing and engaged to George – and we dined at Johan Quist's.

Saturday 25th April: Today is Anzac Day when Richard used to broadcast at the Dawn Service, saying in his fine voice how splendid was those men's sacrifices, and then making them himself. I shall be glad when the day is over. But the tops of the trees outside this window are swaying in the street, and the green trams go by, and the people pass. There is a cool, shady sun on every leaf. Mama and I slung our coats over our shoulders and marched with the crowd into the sun, across the bridge where the ferries ply, along the river where the flowers grow, and into the gardens where white swans drift on the lakes and trees grow out of lawns until you feel it is all yours, these parks and shadows and lovers and the warmth on your back. Very tired, we saw "Fantasia", the Disney-Stokowski experiment – the interpretation of music by laymen in pictures, meaningless, pictorial and progressive.

Sunday 26th April: Last night, the music the Philadelphia Orchestra played was Bach, Tchaikovsky, Dukas, Mussorgsky, Beethoven, Schubert, Ponchielli, and "The Rite of Spring". It was an exciting experience, to be taken, as I imagine lovemaking is, in small doses. All the brain and subtlety and imagination, time, art and skill that goes into its conception is admired by we little people and forgotten in our sleep that night. Mother and I walked down Collins Street to Spencer Street Station, booked on the "Spirit of Progress" for her trip to Sydney, and darned, packed and read. After afternoon tea in the lounge, watching two American soldiers go crazy over an attempt to get a barman to make a correct gin cocktail, we taxied to the station, and I left the angel in her grand entourage ("Nice", says Mama, "to think that Myers is paying") and came back to my funny little clean room in the Y.W.C.A.. So once again I have the City keys given me, and a longing homesickness mingled with excitement.

Monday 27th April: I walked along the river through the early morning, with a book in my hand, and the grass was shining with dew, and sitting on a bench, I saw the lovely city lying across the water, spires and skyscrapers together. Little barges went backwards and forwards under the bridges, and an old man came by with a spike, picking up the dead leaves and burning them in blue smoke. An American doughboy, without socks, a wash or shave, came and sat down beside me, and told me he was a coal miner in Wes' Virginia. He had escaped from camp to sit in the sun, because he didn't want to mess around kitchens. And why should he today? Come sit in the sun with me. Sheila Wallach and her mother took me to Menzies for lunch, and amazed me with their hard, social talk.

Tuesday 28th April: Fortunately I had left today entirely for myself, so I lay in bed, foregoing breakfast. At about ten I dragged myself up to have a wash, but on coming down the passage Room No 5 kept going away from me, although the other numbers fled by in a progressive blur. I got the door open and the bed came up and hit me. God, I felt awful. The Matron came in and found me absolutely panicky. I had started. She gave me hot water bottles, bread, milk and aspirins and I fell asleep, exhausted. Later I dressed, ate some lunch at three o'clock and walked to the Galleries. I couldn't stand reading for the evening in that sitting room, filled with old women talking about their boys who had been killed, so I went in my jumper and skirt to Johann Strauss's "Nightbirds", sung by the Gilbert and Sulllivan Company and produced by Clive Carey, whom I went backstage to see. It was quite amusing, but – like the story – uninspired. Thea Philips was enormous in purple satin and her husband was a wisp of a little boy. During the intervals, I retired unromantically into my book.

Wednesday 29th April: Once more to the Galleries to roam about among the Connell Collection, to touch the wood lingeringly, to look into the peeling mirrors, and the old glass. I went out to the Berriman's, and shopped in tinned food with Jeanne, eating out of them and lazily washing up, and then going to St Kilda and walking along the jetty, with the wind coming across Port Phillip, and old men fishing on the empty steps, watching the grey convoys coming in. After dinner, I arranged to stay the night and Jeanne and I went to a suburban theatre to see "Skylark" in which Claudette Colbert played the ridiculous role of a woman who thought her husband didn't love her because he wouldn't give up his adored job to please her. She didn't deserve the men in her life, Ray Milland and Brian Aherne.

Thursday 30th April: Jeanne rushed off to her job at the Navy department, her fiancée George Harris being in Singapore, and I had a quiet breakfast with Maudie, and then left for town, forever carrying my book which is gripping me, although I think the hero, while affirming on every page that he is an ordinary fellow, only makes the story possible through his hypersensitiveness. I sat in the writing room, scribbling those poverty stricken letters to John which I hope will cease after I get a letter from him, while a storm crashed up through the sky, shaking my nerves and the building. I saw it come across the Shrine, blotting everything with mists and a rainbow – the Almighty made a mistake – and then, with the world hemmed in, crack and scream and sizzle in the air above it. It stopped suddenly; the sun came out, the trees caught the sun. I walked in Fitzroy Gardens down the avenues of wet, gold leaves, whose trees stood stupidly naked. Later I talked books over coffee at Menzies.

Friday 1st May: Mother came through in the train today from Sydney, bringing with her an ice blue cotton shirt with a peaked collar, and a pale pink ensemble with a jacket bound in midnight blue and covered with fuchsias. Lovely. Lovely. But I want three boys who can't, to see me in them. We discussed our mutual lives within the last week, and rushed off to Myers with Mother to see directors – little Jewish men who chucked me under the chin and called me "little girlie". We had afternoon tea at Russell Collins with Maudie Berriman, then shopped. I would have liked to have the darling to myself but Maudie stayed on to dinner. The day was a continual rush back and forth through the streets, but eventually the train to Adelaide drew out and Mother went to her berth with a pregnant young woman as companion. We two who were left only hoped nothing would happen on the trip over. Still, Hollywood actor Paul Lukas was born on the Continental.....

Saturday 2nd May: I had my hair set at the Oriental, and then went to the Quamby Club to lunch with Mrs Britten Jones and Peg, whom I bumped into yesterday in Collins Street. They tried to persuade me to stay in a flat with Peg and do munitions. Unfortunately....I feel rather ashamed at going back to a non-military job. Here, the conductors are girls, as are the drivers of trucks and military cycles, and of official cars: as well as the usual branches. After the charming Club, I drifted about an empty Melbourne and at 4.30 decided to see "Our Wife" in the late afternoon session. It was particularly poor. I went to bed, wondering why I felt so odd, and on realizing that I had had no dinner, rose and ate an incredible mixed grill, passion fruit drink and bananas and cream. Back in my little white room high up in the sky, I leant out of the wide window, breathed in the cold clear air and sang at the top of my voice to the music that drifted up from a dance hall far below. Little black specks under the lamp posts looked up and waved.

Sunday 3rd May: The Rubbos! Laden with bronze chrysanthemums and chocolates, I set out through the rain to see them at their flat at Ivanhoe. There was Syd, darker and more attractive than I had imagined, with a yellow tie and a few more grey hairs. The Adelaide University had offered him – at 29 – the Professorship of Bacteriology, but he wanted to finish his medical course and go to the war, and how can a Professor muck about as a student? I fell in love with him again, as everyone must. I fell in love with Ellen too, in her blue slacks and surrounded by her paintings which the Sydney Gallery are buying up. And Michael and Anna. We took snaps in the garden and ate spaghetti and looked at old photographs and sketch books. I left regretfully, burning with unrequited love. On to the Wallachs, in their colossal, dark, comfortable barracks of a house in Toorak, smelling of leather and wood. I lost my way after dinner and found myself in a library where old Mr Wallach, a little lonely German, sat in a leather chair under a lamp. I closed the door behind me and we looked happily at books: first edition, signed copies, facsimiles. His hands shook with excitement at having someone interested in his treasures at last. For hours I forgot to go back.

Monday 4th May: I dragged my bag down to the station and came up here to Sassafras and Sherbrooke Lodge. I have a cold wooden bedroom, but the lounge is covered in chintz and chrysanthemums, and chestnuts fill the fireplace where the great logs burn, and music plays in the next room. I found a book by an American, Olive Saxton, called "Heavens

Above!" and snickered into that until lunch, after which I set out to Belgrave through the best fern gorges of Australia, under tall slim white gums with brown bark twisting in flakes, like harsh veils about them. The road was empty, and everywhere the water sang. The ferns flung their green heads high in the gulleys and I flung mine up also, and sang at the top of my voice in the valleys. After six or seven miles I arrived and bought some chocolates, discussed life with a bored young shoemaker who had left England to see the world and had ended up in a Dandenong village, and swung back in the cool dark twilight. In the evening I finished my book by a great log fire.

Tuesday 5th May: I have sat all morning writing in this room with a fire, while outside the great windows the sky is bleak and moody, but the valley far below is full of a slanting sun. I shall walk in the forest today. So I went, and lo! The forest was beautiful and closed in on me. The tall trees speared the sky, and fell across the path, and occasional patches of blue sky opened through the branches. At the other side of the forest one looked over a blue plain hundreds of miles wide to the sea. Cottages hung despairingly on the sides of the Dandenongs, with their windows wide open with admiration like huge eyes drinking in the beauty. I did a bit of shopping in Ferny Creek and then plunged into the forest again. The sky grew dark overhead but I couldn't hurry. Halfway through it came, those harsh sadistic drops, and I arrived home panicky and soaked. So I read "Rain" by Somerset Maugham, sitting near the fire. Only this was evil rain...

Wednesday 6th May: Oh, cold bleak dark day.....icy feet and a draught between one's shoulders, and sloshing paths and hopeless skies. But keen air in one's throat and through one's veins. I found two pages in eulogy of Robert Newton, in an old deserted magazine here, and went out for my walk holding him happily in my bag. It rained but I didn't care. I had a chat with a petrified kangaroo; and picked up chestnuts and tore them brutally out of their green husks. I played ping pong with an intellectual fireman, and moved my things into a cold room across a veritable lake of a yard, for an embarrassed honeymoon couple to begin marital life in my double bed. The crowd here consists entirely of old maids and honeymooners. It hurts to have to belong, inevitably, to the first group. So I'm feeling a little homesick tonight in a comfortably mournful way: Mummy, Richard, Bryan, John, home, Gaby.....Oh God grant my six wishes.

Thursday 7th May: I went out into the forest to kiss it goodbye, running down the paths as though into the heart of a cabbage, darker, quieter, full of whispers and mocking birds. I flung my arms around it and kissed the long strips of bark. This lovely forest – Still no kind man helped me with the heavy case, so I reviled them all and staggered into the Y.W.C.A. Then I rang up everybody I had seen in Melbourne, missed a beat over Sydney Dattilo Rubbo, and then went out in my best coat to dine alone and see the play "The Man Who Came to Dinner". It was priceless, a long Broadway hit by Hart and Kaufman, starring Edwin Styles. It is about a pampered and insupportable playwright who breaks his leg in a Middle West household, and turns it into chaos. It is filled with skits of people including Alexander Woollcott, Noel Coward and Harpo Marx, who say outrageous things. Gosh, how lovely this has all been, and how lucky I am.

Friday 8th May: So I packed and cleared out, discovering as I did that Godfried's brooch had disappeared. So the morning was wasted in searching vainly and miserably for it all over Melbourne streets. Then I did what I had meant to do once I arrived, spent the whole day in the Museum and library breathing on cases where the Connell glass is kept, looking for Rubbo and Newton in the Gallery and reading up people in "Who's Who", and chuckling to think that John got in under "1 s." – issue of Professor Portus. I stuffed an Elizabeth Collins pineapple salad into me and departed through the night in the Express. I went to bed early in warm clean sheets, hugging a hot water bottle, and my last words were "Boy oh boy oh boy" like any other Cinderella. During the night I discovered that all this talk of the Romance of Roughing It is tosh. And I thought of the Second Class.

Saturday 9th May: It was good to be home and to see Mother and hear Sibyl's voice on the phone again. I shopped in the morning, visited Mr Webb and was grateful that I didn't have to go down there again on Monday. There were letters from Bryan and Tommy Simpson but neither

John nor Godfrey. I gave Mrs Portus a ring but apart from a cable on the way some weeks ago she hasn't heard and doesn't expect to. After dinner Sibyl and I went to Friedman's concert, the last which I am just over in time for. The Mendelssohn was good, and a Chopin Sonata. Otherwise the programme was poor and somehow untidy. He looked a little older, a little square grey man. An American said on the way out, "Gee, I didn't think Australia could put on such a good show"…We drank coffee at Judy's and then back to my uncomfy bed.

Sunday 10th May: Mother's Day! This couldn't have been a particularly happy day for this Mother. She must have remembered the Sundays when we all went to Church with her, wearing white Michaelmas daisies and ate the chocolates we gave her. Now her eldest son may be blown to bits on a shore that hates him, her baby is a sailor along coasts that are notoriously spawning ugly breeds of yellow submarines, and her daughter – God forgive her – forgot it was Mother's Day and arranged to dine with the Brookman's. Even when she found out, she went. The whole idea was to meet Captain Cam Robertson, who has been giving Sibyl an extremely good and romantic time, and this was the only opportunity, as he is passing through from Syria. He is an attractive devil, one of those casual spoilt creatures who, because of their charm, makes you love and hate them at the same time. So Sibyl tells me and so I believe. We swung hymns round the piano, enacted operas and raced arm in arm though the cold to my tram.

Monday 11th May: A new job. It was rather wonderful walking up the Advertiser steps in spite of not belonging to the editorial department. One can pretend till the first floor, and then it isn't necessary to pretend because everything in my own department is intriguing enough. I seem to have a tremendous lot of work to get through, and haven't worked so hard in all my life as this day. But I loved it. There is music all about you and song titles that make you sing the tunes. There are people all about you, girls who call you "Carys" and men who call you "dear", and if you think of something you can tell them, and make jokes with them, and not be lonely and introspective and look dismally round at empty roof tar tins and think "It's begun at this. What next?" I staggered out in the rain to Mother at six o'clock, not minding very much, and was injected for typhoid at Dr Wigg's. There was a case in our house. I'll bet there are germs in every bit of filth throughout it.

Tuesday 12th May: Mr Chapman told me that it would take me at least three months to get to know the run of the Programme Department, but with supreme conceit it occurs to me that I understand it today. I take in the day programme, take out the former evening records and check them, file them. Then I take in the afternoon programme, and log the evening records, taking them in with the next early morning discs. This involves dragging a truck about and dating packets with a rubber stamp. Thus all records pass through my hands last before entering the studio so that I am in a wretched position in regard to faults. Mother and I went to see "Andy Hardy's Secretary" with Mickey Rooney, an absolute born entertainer, but not a great actor. He is extraordinary plain and abnormally short, yet he can put it across, somehow….And "Dr Kildare's Crisis", probably the last film Dr Kildare star Lew Ayres will make, as he is in a Conscientious Objector's prison in Oregon. Feeling must run high in the U.S.A. because his films are banned and his studio denounces him.

Wednesday 13th May: Well, here goes ----

Thursday 14th May: Still going -----

Friday 15th May: Private Harmon J Denton came to chat to Mother - they discuss everything, I'm told - so Barb Kelly had dinner with me and we saw such an awful Australian film that I shall skip it thankfully. I told Harmon to introduce me to a nice U.S. American because I'm rather tired of things at the moment.

Sunday 17th May: I went to the Matison's to visit Nora Matison, and loved it. I always do. I walked along the top of a hill with Doctor Matison and stumbled about in a maze of words in order to condemn Capitalists. Being one, he was more able to uphold them than for me to condemn.

Tuesday 19th May: Met Americans, Herman W Riedeburg and Bob Winker Worden, at the Gresham. They came and asked if they could drink coffee with us, as they were crying out for loneliness. Had just arrived. Attractive chaps and we arranged a party for Saturday night, under Mother's approving glance. Herman is going to be too keen, I can tell. Pity, because I wanted Bob. ----

Wednesday 20th May: Barb Kelly came to dinner and we talked and listened to Godfried's records in the lamplight. Alain has disappointed her wildly and I doubt if things will be the same again. Still, he has left for overseas. His family influenced him out of an engagement which was to be settled next day.

Thursday 21st May: Someday I shall cry out for a day in May when I was nineteen. And here it is, forgotten a week later.

Friday 22nd May: Spent all day ringing up people to come tomorrow but all the pretty girls were going out. Finally got Diana Waterhouse who was a bit startled at the invitation. So I darned and swore at the wretched room we live in, and Miss Bungey came in for some tea and tried to lead me astray with a book of Norman Lindsay.

Saturday 23rd May: The usual mad haste, swirl of records, creak of trolleys and scrape of condensed violins. But I left, with a prayer that the weekend programmes wouldn't fail me. Faults are charged up in the Blue Book, a performance in which great pleasure is taken. At the Gresham, looking my utmost best, Herman told me Bob couldn't come, but a Dick Goodridge was there instead. I was inwardly furious until I saw him, a young boy, perfect complexion, quiet, well mannered, a Yale man. Yet looking nineteen, he has a family of three. How superficial we all must be to a homesick father whose son is two months old. Mother was dining with her private so we couldn't mix! After dinner, we left for the Tux, with Di who looked very attractive in uniform. The usual wait outside the Tux, and the shuffling about the ballroom. The place was full of ugly American officers, all of whom I seemed to meet, including a footballer from the "Redskins". Dick was rather sweet and intellectual, and I sort of doubled up with mirth over Herman's witticisms. An egoistic captain came over to bore us. He talked in a wet voice about "I" until we nearly screamed. Eggs and bacon at the Night Owl, Di home in a taxi, a vague kiss from Herman, and sleep.

Sunday 24th May: It's so long since I opened this disgusting diary that I have almost remembered the days before when I was free of it. But five years grows into a habit. Momma and I went crashing about getting dressed in awful haste, she for Harmon and I for Herman. He called for me with a "nosegay" of pink carnations and autumn leaves, which half compensated for the disappointment of hearing that Dick was leaving at two for camp. I realize that only one girl is important to him, and two children, child as he looks himself. We couldn't get into the South but the Gresham took us as usual to her bosom. Mother was there with Harmon; they are walking about the hills today. Herman and I had afternoon tea in this room, and looked at snaps cozily. He is a sweet person with a soft, shy smile and a grand sense of humour. I hope he doesn't fall in love with me.

Monday 25th May: Sibyl and I lunched with Ann Barritt at the Cavendish, where we slouched in our speckled cane chairs eating the Special. A poor lonely devil of an American came hesitantly to our table and asked us if we would recommend something for him on the menu: it was a poor but pathetic opening. We said "Omelettes" and dismissed him. He went back to his table snubbed, leaving us virtuous but rather mean. Sibyl, who has been left high and dry by Cam over the weekend, had quite a lot of things to say about people generally who Pick Up Strange Young Men and Go Out With Them. There are times when she is a dreadful hypocrite. Mother and I were inoculated again for the third time and beat our way through the rain to "The Olives" to inspect our new home. We were shown a rather charming place and I accepted on the spot before Mama could think it over.

Tuesday 26th May: How glad I shall be to leave this dump. They are putting beds in the halls and in the kitchen, and screaming babies and wretched fat women litter the stairs. Whenever a bath goes out of order, it stays so, so that if one has a bath it's a stroke of providence - because the water is cold. We have a largish room at Brougham Place with a green carpet, chintz chairs and shot silk covers on the beds. The walls and halls and people are clean there, too.

Thursday 28th May: Tony Osborn and I discussed Yanks and Aussies over lunch at the Arcadia, where Mr Reed caught a spy a few days ago with Mr Arnold Moulden, another lawyer. They hid behind pillars and telephoned in breathy whispers to the police. I met Herman at the South but we couldn't get a table again, so I showed him "Quality Inn" and then we went – at last – to "How Green Was My Valley", the Welsh story by Richard Llewellyn. It was grand and glorious. The little boy, Huw, sees his green valley grow smoky, and the mines keep but kill his people, the birth of organized labour in unions, the English schoolmaster, the male choruses, the bluebell woods and the trucks under the mines, the Welsh accent, the Welsh chapel and the deacons in front, damning the sinner. The valleys were green....Sitting next to Herman, I was proud to belong to these people, however superficially. He gave me chocolates, and a lamp to guard me from the Yanks. The rape and murder of three women in Melbourne have been traced to one, so it isn't so hollow.

Friday 29th May: After work, Nob Good, looking splendid in his lieutenant's uniform, took me to dinner at the Gresham. He went to wash after "Lizzie" trouble so I wandered in in my new fur hat and John's friends, Fred Field and John McFarlane and others rose up and welcomed me. Before Mother's startled eyes, I was pushed into a chair, presented with a tumbler of sauterne and drawn into the dinner amid shouts and guffaws. Until I saw Nobby, hovering unhappily at the door....We went on to "When Ladies Meet" and he bought me a big fancy box of chocolates. I was already in a good mood: I had a presentable lieutenant with whom I am always at ease, a beribboned chocolate box, a new fur hat, and a good film straight from Broadway. We drank coffee at the Athens Café among Yankee privates.

Saturday 30th May: I fell asleep to the normal sound of a night-out-with-Nob, of fierce cranks, of wheezing brakes, of panicky rattles as the engine catches and of wild laughter in the hinges as the Red Devil finally makes it down North Terrace. I took shorthand in an armchair in No 2 studio, while a U.S.A. private dictated on the arm and twelve stood around helping. It is for a show we are recording as a good will gesture to the States. It takes a certain amount of good will to listen to it. I came home to a great flurry of packing, bottles stacked in wastepaper baskets and electrical gear in boot boxes, so I joined the chaos with my own things and after fell asleep on the balcony of North Terrace for the last time. The rain swept by me in sheets, but ceased in time for Mr Wickes to take us to "The Olives". Ye Gods, nothing would fit. We had far too much stuff. We yelled at each other. Mama went off with Harmon and I had dinner, coming back soothed with mushrooms and coffee to fight the good fight. By ten everything was fixed, so I fell asleep in my pretty bed of shot blue and purple silk. It's a charming room.

Sunday 31st May: They bought us coffee and honeyed toast to bed, after which we arose and I washed until my fingers were spongey. At lunch Mother recognized Miss K... at our table as a former foe whom she had had occasion to call "dishonorable" so things were a little subdued. We walked to the lookout on Montefiore Hill in the bright sunshine, watching the lathering clouds hang over this city. Then I had to go and meet from Melbourne, Stewart Wallach, Sheila's brother, whom I had promised to befriend and who this weekend is staying with the Conrads. We took him for a walk about the river and the University, and when I happened to see Mr Reed, I asked to be allowed to shake hands with a Hero. The Conrads then took us for a Drive. This is an Event. We went through St Peter's College and about the foothills, blue and still in the sun.

Monday 1st June: At our table sit Mrs Lewis, grey, attractive, exclusive – "nice people, I mean... people like us...", Miss K..., youngish, sleek, manageress of a corset department, completely self-contained and probably a little bitter because of it, and John Ambrose, a medical student, lays down the law because he's the only man, and consequently feels his opinion is valued. A boring young man. Harmon called with a U.S. Army Engineer from Arkansas called Burl Courtney, who is tremendously keen on clothes, designing, advertising and commercial art. Also most attractive and possessing a Southern accent. We all walked into the pictures in the frosty night, and Burl and I ran like children holding hands. Then home under the bare dripping branches, and a cold dead moon quite bumpy around the edge. A mist thick through the parks and no lights on the river.

Tuesday 2nd June: This is our room: white walls and an ornamented ceiling, green wall-to-wall carpet and green rugs, beds like couches covered in shot blue and purple corded silk, green curtains and chair chintzes splashed with purple delphiniums, Milston's portrait over a white marble fireplace, brown cedar furniture, the leather chair and tapestry fire screen, a riot of blue and green cushions, sherry glasses, books, cigarettes to hand, a wireless and, momentarily, a vase of waratahs. It is here I sit, with a red radiator at my feet, writing to John those hard unreal, rather unhappy letters, and to Bryan repentant, adoring, frivolous pages of possessiveness. Mama has gone to the Harley Hoopers to be nursed out of a bad cold, and Sibyl, who was to have come, has put me off: we had a cold row over the phone, she apologised, we crawled out of it and rang off friendly but annoyed. The news is good over the radio: Rommel has broken our siege of him but is withdrawing, thousands of planes swept over Germany over the weekend, three submarines were captured in Sydney Harbour.

Wednesday 3rd June: One or two trivialities depressed me and spoiled the day. First the girls began a craze for planchette and asked it questions; it answered sensibly so I asked: "When will Richard return?" It stuck. I asked, "Does John love me?" It answered "Q a c q y d". I asked, "When will I get married?" It answered "Perhaps". I asked, "When will I get a letter from John?" It answered "October". I loathe it. Then Bill Heathersay, a friend of Bryan's at the Advertiser, gave me a letter from him discussing girls, and told me he was quite girl crazy when with them. Also that the sailors had taken him to a brothel and he had walked out in disgust, once his curiosity had been satisfied. This he never mentioned to us, nor his natural interest in women. It somehow shocked and scared me needlessly, this sudden realization that he isn't a child anymore. He must by now know more of life from these foul men than I know from all my books. Foul? No, not that. It is time he knew these things exist, and he has the character to withstand them. But I have lost something because he has.

Thursday 4th June: As far as I can see, the best thing we can do for Bryan is to arrange parties for him on his leave of nice kids like Judith Conrad before he considers them too tame. Because the only women he can meet would be thoroughly undesirable, and he has had no experience at all to cope with them. I am taking all this far too seriously. I know nothing of boys in puberty. 5AD was an absolute gaming den today, with announcers leaning over peanut jars and asking if their wives are faithful, and Mr Jakes with the Continuity poring over mystic circles. Until

Mr Chapman summoned everyone to No 2 studio and waved the Blue Book at us, saying it was "not good enough" and that we were making "far more blues than 5DN in her worst moments". He warned us, praised us, condemned us, forgave us, but we returned conscience stricken. The depressing coincidence is that it all began two and a half weeks ago when I arrived. Yet all the other public departments are involved. Maurice Chevalier, once the idol of Paris and movie fans and me, now today urges collaboration with the Axis! Death of a hero.

Friday 5th June: Am sick of this diary business so have decided to take the leap and compromise. I hope it will just be a blank soon. As a good send off, I've announced that I've clean forgotten what I did today – so it will have the honor of being the first unrecorded day of my life for five years. God bless the fifth. A letter came from John. I nearly cried for delight, even though it was a pretty cool, usual-sort-of letter.

Saturday 6th June: Went to the pictures with Herman who made a nuisance of himself by holding my hand in the dark when he knew quite well I loathed it. It made me madder to think he probably took my rebuffs as coyness. Even so, he gave me an enormous box of Whitman's U.S. chocolates, and I'm a mean little beggar to give nothing in return. But I loathe prostitution.

Sunday 7th June: Mother, Harmon, Burl Courtney – a very handsome U.S. private whom he introduced me to, and I went to the Sandford's cottage, cooked chops, bought cream, fruit, rolls, etc., ate it by the fire, then sat in the dark and told ghost stories. Back in the train. Glorious, glorious day. Dead tired.

Monday 8th June: Went to a Regimental Dance with Burl. U.S. band, flags, anthems, partners, dances, food. Rather fun, but Americans are disappointing creatures. All so plain. All but Burl. Poured with rain and had to walk home. Sat in the dark by the radiator and drank sherry. Nice platonic friendship.

Tuesday 9th June: It seems rather a waste to ruin a nice clean diary by all this drivel, but it's a habit I can't entirely abandon. Letter from Godfried, Yankee Clipper, "Say, kid, still crazy about you...." Very thrilled.

Thursday 11th June: Sydney has been shelled and two submarines sunk inside the Harbour. Very worried about Bryan. Merchant ships being sunk off the coast about Newcastle. The Japanese audacity is amazing.

Sunday 14th June: Yesterday with Burl, saw "Kipps" at Parkside and I loved it. Settings and costumes by Cecil Beaton. Not an American film. Today took Burl to the Matison's, lovely place, Louise gorgeous and sweet. Talked. Burl a success.

Monday 15th June: Holiday. A loving cable from Godfried anxious because I haven't written. My 1d postage obviously not a success! Matisons rushed me away in an old red jumper and powderless – to Spruhan Kennedy's, awful stables converted into an awful home, his wife Vera just as affected and neurotic and petite. Then dinner at the Matison's, where I discussed clothes with Louise feeling like a bumpkin in my old stockings. Home in a tram in old coat of Louise's, pockets full of oranges and money for fares.

Wednesday 17th June: Yesterday Burl and a friend, Chester Wolfgram, took Hannalene Stillschweig of Sydney's "Continental Modes" and me to "Sally", the Jerome Kern musical comedy at the Royal. Not terribly good but I adored it. Bryan's letters are full of dodging enemy submarines and of biscuit tins full of tobacco and sweets to last him months on a raft in the sea. God bless him. I'm going to force a party on him when he gets home attended by tawny-headed babies. Hannalene allowed me to buy a blue tailored linen suit for £2.10.0 with coupons. I couldn't resist it.

Thursday 18th June: Mr Chapman always walks in while I am talking or singing or not working. This worries me. I work quite hard but he never seems to see that. I love the job, but we are overstaffed. Visited Sibyl and discussed books self-consciously because in Melbourne we wrote and swore to be more unworldly in our talk. But it always gets back to Yanks.

Friday 19th June: Cable from Godfried, full of rash sentiment. Very expensive.

Saturday 20th June: War situation appalling. Russians receding. Sebastopol almost lost. Tobruk surrounded. Thousands of our men killed or prisoners. Bardia gone. Big drives by Germans to retake Russia. Move for new front in Europe. Massing of American and Canadian troops in England. And a bread strike here!

Sunday 21st June: Burl Courtney and Chester Wolfgram of America went up with me to the Osborn's; saw over winery, had magnificent dinner, drank three glasses of sherry, two of hock, one of Burgundy, two of Sauterne, three of Port, one of Mulberry Liqueur. Very content. Very cold. Good, pleasant lazy day. Message from Sibyl "Come round quickly. Cam's back and you must help me to vamp him away." I went and found her in the bath. Talked and came home. Tobruk has fallen. Seems to be all up with Libya. Bad leadership blamed but the boys say Lieutenant-General Ritchie is as good as Rommel.

Monday 22nd June: Letter from Herman. They come intermittently and compare me to the Southern Cross and discuss the weather.

Tuesday 23rd June: Affectionate letter from John, telling me a letter of mine was worn out with his reading it so much. A snap of him. At last!

Wednesday 24th June: Quiet evening writing to Godfried and Herman. Waste of time corresponding with lovesick youths. Getting as hard as nails.

Friday 26th June to Thursday 2nd July: Blank!!

Friday 3rd July: Coldest day I ever did remember. We are holding up the enemy in Libya. Is it a flash in the pan? Sebastopol has fallen. A ruined shell. Saw University plays with the Blackburns. All rather mediocre. The best part was the Interval when I met Maxie Harris and we went for a walk eating peanuts and holding hands to everyone's disapproval. He excites me rather. He has just published a new book called "Dramas from the sky".

Saturday 4th July: American Independence Day: Flags flying. March of the Yanks and the Aussies with Colours and mechanics, which we watched from 5AD above a crowded city. Sun and rain intermittently. Watched American "football" on the Adelaide Oval, under umbrella with Herman. Padded men and Yanks eating peanuts and four military bands swinging it. Bought Max's new book. It looks rather good.

Sunday 5th July: Took Herman to the Conservatorium concert where Nora Matison played Mozart. Apart from this, rather uninspired. Had dinner here, and went to first picture show for troops on Sunday nights.

Huge crowd. The film was "The Feminine Touch" with Don Ameche and Rosalind Russell. Quite good. Bored with Herman for no reason, as he is grand fun.

Monday 6th July: Arrived at 5AD to find a book of Max's from him. Shall give the other to Burl who seems struck on him for no reason I can see as he is very obscure. Wrote and thanked him. Get a kick out of this, as the Sammy days are the ones I regret most in my life for their illusions and young hopes and new orders.

Tuesday 7th July: Quiz session, and then home to write a letter on my knees sitting up in bed for John to read six months ahead. I miss him. I miss him. An invitation from Max.

Wednesday 8th July: I went out with Max tonight. We read lots of poetry he is editing for "Angry Penguins III" at Judy's Coffee Shoppe. One that Sam sent is one he wrote for me. Told Max who was most impressed. I didn't admit I never understood them. Had gloriously ghastly food at Chinese restaurants and saw "Fantasia" which I adored the second time.

Thursday 9th July: Burl took me to "Tom, Dick and Harry" with Ginger Rogers, Burgess Meredith, George Murphy, and it was very good, but I was so tired and irritable that I was ashamed of myself. Came home and wept for no reason. But I swore then that in the morning I would write and tell John I loved him hopelessly and would wait forever. I didn't.

Friday 10th July: I was so tired that I reached a numb state. Bed. Bed. Bed. Was just getting into it when Herman arrived. We fought for half an hour when I gave in and went to see the best concert I've ever seen given by U.S. troops at the Tivoli. Grand fun. But weary....bed at last.

Saturday 11th July: Headache. Pain. Stinging eyes. Sick. Greasy hair. Mental vacuity. "Women's Weekly" took a picture of Mama and me in this state. Bed all afternoon. Saw Mama off to Melbourne, and Don Sawers going off to officer's camp for two months. Burl rang to say he was leaving almost at once for battle station, which relieves me. I was going out with him, having refused Herman. So Stewart Wallach, Judith and Beverley Conrad and I went to the Piccadilly, and saw "There's Magic in Music" with Alan Jones, and supped at Conrad's. Pleasant, dull evening, just what I needed. No Yanks.

Sunday 12th July: Lovely day. Washed my hair. Max called after lunch. Saw Conservatorium Concert with him and Bruce Williams of the eccentric hair, a lecturer in economics. Good concert with Ronda Gehling and Spruhan Kennedy. Back to Bruce's for coffee. Awful little den with washing on cord across the room. Dirty dishes. Books everywhere. Burnt but delectable coffee. Listened to Bach.

Monday 13th July: New office boy. Fun being alone for a change. Wrote all evening and rang Mrs Portus. Have never been so near giving up this diary as tonight. It will come....... Two more towns fall in Russia, on main railway route to Moscow, near Kharkov. Very, very grave. Eighth Army still holding in Libya and Egypt. A.I.F. back in the fight.

Tuesday 14th July 1942: newspaper cutting from "The Advertiser" pinned in Carys's diary:

L/Sgt. M. Brookman

L/Sgt. Michael Brookman, elder son of Mr. and Mrs. George Brookman of Barton terrace, North Adelaide, was killed in action on July 14. Educated at St. Peter's College, he attended the University of Adelaide, where he took his law degree, and was admitted to the Bar at the end of 1938.

Tuesday 15th December 1942: newspaper cutting from "The Advertiser" pinned in Carys's diary:

DIED ON ACTIVE SERVICE

... ∴ illness on
... tiful memories treasured
GRIFFIN.—A tribute to the m
te, Jim Griffin, killed in action
Guinea, Nov. 30, brother of Jack .
Guinea). His duty nobly done.—Ever 1
membered by the Parry family, Nairne
   HARPER.—A tribute to the memory of
Booth, died of wounds Dec. 4, in New
Guinea.—Ever remembered by Vina.
   HILL.—In loving memory of Cliff,
killed in action Nov. 29, New Guinea.—
Ever remembered by Chic and Thelma
Hancock.
   KERR.—On Dec. 15, Flying Officer
Donald Beviss Kerr, eldest son of Marjorie and the late Donald Kerr, L.LD.,
on active service.
   SLATER.—On Dec. 16, at Militar'
Hosp. (result accident), A.C.1 Sydney '
B. (R.A.A.F.), son K. and S. Slater, N'
manville, aged 20 yrs., beloved bro'
Jean, Thelma, Dulcie, Kath Go
best. Sadly missed.
   SLATER.—On Dec.
Hosp. (result acci'
B. (R.A.A.F.), '
membered by '
law, Jean a'

EPILOGUE

Carys finished writing her diary on July 13th 1942. In November of that year, Carys joined the Australian Army Medical Women's Service and nursed at the Northfield Army Hospital. In a speech at the Queen Adelaide Club in 1987, Carys spoke of this experience. "We were the first of the clumsy, heavily dressed, newly named AAMWS privates, cleaners of latrines and luggers of hot boxes. We settled down to endless months of what in the final analysis of war is to most people - a waiting game, waiting for life to return to normal, and for memory of love to return to us. Well, that was how it was for me. We all lived comfortably in tents. We had swinging kerosene lamps, and the lights blew out and the tents blew down. We wore gum boots and raincoats to the long, unenclosed ablution blocks, where we showered. Later, we moved from the tents into long iron sheds, where we hurdled the iron beds. We all had pictures of young men beside our grey blanketed beds. All around were empty paddocks up to the hills and down to the sea, apart from a mental hospital, a reformatory and a prison, and a brothel. We marched, we served in our own mess, and we wheeled heavy hot boxes full of food about and served breakfasts, lunches and dinners to the men, like early Meals on Wheels. We made beds with mitered corners. There were certain units that we especially loved to look after, because they had had a difficult war, like the Second Tenth and the Second Seventh. We dreamt of our day off. We cleaned out the sisters' huts. We boiled crockery in the Infectious Wards. I remember when everyone was asleep, except for that endless quiet coughing, walking in the dark towards the next building, a long low place surrounded by high barbed wire, and watching the Japanese prisoners inside, sitting on the ground, rocking themselves, in the middle of the night, ashamed perhaps that they were ever prisoners. It's odd to think that they were once there in the suburbs of Holden Hill, so exotic and grieving, in what would now be someone's petunia beds. We woke in the dark to bugle calls and began work at seven thirty, some distance away, across fields, with no roads. We spent most of our evenings, washing (no machines), starching (no Fabulon), and ironing (no steam irons) our uniforms. My own love affair with a long, absent airman flying in England, was kept going by those tiny, shiny microfilmed letters or cables, until one day, his parents - he was an only child - rang to say he was posted as "missing". "Missing" meant died. I went to see them in their desolation. Thereafter, continued in the wards, in a sort of black hole. Two days later, I was passing through the mess, when the flighty little girl who looked after the switchboard, yelled out, "There is a message for you. Sorry! Something about John turning up?"

On the 1/8/43, John Portus had been shot down in his Sunderland aircraft by a German U-boat in the Bay of Biscay, and half of his crew perished. He was rescued unconscious from the sea. He completed his "tour" of 800 flying hours and returned to Australia in January 1944, having been awarded a Distinguished Flying Cross. He landed in Sydney, and twenty eight days later, married Carys in Adelaide, on February 19th. They were both to find deep happiness in a long marriage. Their first year of marriage was difficult. John, immediately after their marriage, was treated for an anxiety state for several months. His father helped his return to normal life, by encouraging him to coach the University Rugby Team, a sport which John loved. Later in that year, John was appointed an Assistant Conciliation Commissioner in Adelaide. Then in 1947, he became a Conciliation Commissioner until his retirement in 1978. John and Carys had five children, Richard, Philip, Ann, Martin and Matthew. When Matthew was four, Carys went to the South Australian Institute of Technology, gained a Diploma in Social Work and became a social worker. She continued to write short stories throughout her life and wrote many wonderful letters to her children, many of which still survive to this day.

Bryan Harding Browne, from 8/12/41, was an apprentice with the Australasian United Steam Navigation Company for twenty months. His ship the "Mungara" took on coal and coke in Newcastle and offloaded it mainly in Melbourne. The "Mungara" also visited Port Pirie, Whyalla, Port Kembla, Wallaroo and Albany where it sometimes picked up and unloaded iron ore and limestone as well. Bryan lived in a world of dust, and on his watch kept lookout on a cold windswept bridge, for periscopes and mines. From July 1942, because of danger of attack, the "Mungara" often travelled in convoy. In August 1943 Bryan joined the "Nellore", a ship belonging to the Eastern and Australian Steamship Company. The "Nellore" ran between Australia and India and the round trip from Australia back to Australia took approximately three months. On the 29/6/44, the "Nellore" was torpedoed by a Japanese submarine in the Indian Ocean, and Bryan aged 19, was lost overboard.

When Singapore fell on the 15/2/42, Carys's father, Flight-Lieutenant Clifford Harding Browne went via Java to India, where he was stationed with the R.A.F. in Bombay for over two years. He met there with Bryan on two occasions before Bryan's death, when Bryan was on the "Nellore" travelling from Australia to India and back.

Eirliw Harding Browne was still working at Myers after the War. She had developed rheumatoid arthritis towards the end of the War which slowly disabled her. She did two buying trips for Myers in England in 1947 and in 1958. She lived with John and Carys shortly after they were married until five years before her death in 1972, when she had lived in a succession of nursing homes.

Sibyl Brookman, after she had finished her course at Miss Ward's Training College for Young Business Girls, went to the Penfield Munitions Factory at Salisbury as a stenographer. She'd go to the Cheer-Up Hut several times a week, early in the morning, to cook breakfast for the troops. Her father George Brookman died in February 1943. In June 1944, she married George Mayo, who had fought alongside her brother Michael as a gunner in the 2/7th Field Regiment. They had four children.

Peter Anderson was discharged from the Army on the 7/1/46. He had spent half his Operational Service in the Northern Territory and the other half in New Guinea. During this time, he suffered illness, pneumonia twice and dengue fever. He married in May 1947 and had two children.

Barbara Kelly completed her Diploma in Social Studies in November 1942 and then trained and worked as an almoner in Melbourne. Alain Harvey, Flying officer in the R.A.F., was killed in a flying battle on the 24/5/43 in Germany. In April 1944, Barbara married Michael Tipping and had three children. Both Sibyl and Barb remained close friends with Carys for the rest of their lives.

Lillian Hamilton married in October 1942 and had two children. She was a maid in Carys's home from February 1939 to December 1941. She was born in Fremantle, Western Australia. Her mother died in childbirth when she was nine. Lillian was a prolific writer of letters, children's stories and poems published from 1926 to 34 in The Sunday Times and The Daily News (Perth, W.A.). Lillian came to South Australia in 1938 to meet her brother Keith, a foster son, whom she had not seen for sixteen years. Private Eric Keith Stagbouer, aged 21, of the 2/48 Australian Infantry Battalion was killed 26/10/42 in the Second Battle of El Alamein.

David "Nob" Good not only lost his older brother Squadron-Leader Duncan Good D.F.C. in the War but also his younger brother. Christopher Good, a Warrant-Officer with the R.A.A.F. was killed in an air crash in the Philippines on 13/11/45.

Thomas (Tom) Freer MacGregor-King was in the Militia with Stewart Cockburn. They were members of the 27th South Australian Scottish Regiment. Tom MacGregor-King left for overseas in 1941 and joined the R.A.F. He was killed in a flying battle 6/5/42.

Robert (Bob) Cotton, studying Law at the University in 1940, died in New Guinea of illness while serving as a Sergeant in the Australian Army on the 4/8/42.

Richard "Dick" Agnew Wills, a friend of Peter Anderson, born in Adelaide and working at the Valley Worsted Mills in Geelong, enlisted in the R.A.A.F. in Melbourne 12/10/40, was awarded the Distinguished Flying Cross May 1944, and was killed in a flying battle on the French Coast 18/7/44.

Paul Pfeiffer, poet, and tutor in English literature at St Mark's College in 1940, had six poems published in the first edition of "Angry Penguins". He joined the R.A.A.F. and died in Scotland on 3/1/45 when his Sunderland flying boat crashed after taking off in poor weather.

OTHER VOICES

RICHARD

Richard Harding Browne's last entry in his diary (January 15th 1942):

Last night we went out for our first operation over enemy territory. As a first op it was successful, but as a bombing trip it was not a success. We left at 5.45pm after having difficulty with starting the engines. As we stooged across the North Sea darkness began to close in, and when eventually we reached Holland it was a black, clear night. It was an unusual twinge I had when out of the dark a searchlight shot its beam into the sky, and then a cone of 15 but they weren't after us. We couldn't pin point ourselves and though we circled and searched for an hour we were unable to find anything on which to guide ourselves. There was no opposition and I felt a little foolish doing evasive action and no one taking any notice of me. After an hour we came home still with our bombs - most disappointing, but they didn't mind when we arrived home. One of the others failed to drop his bombs, but he made the mistake of jettisoning his bombs for safety in the North Sea. I eventually got to bed at midnight after a three hour trip. My flying was poor, and I kept course erratically. We were all of us calm and unexcited as if it were just a cross-country. We had no opposition and all of us were almost keen to have experience of it. One couldn't help having a slight emptiness in the pit of the stomach, always expecting a sudden burst of flak or a night fighter. It was a good first operation, and what we were trying to do was beat up an aerodrome called Soesterberg, just south of the Zuyder Zee.

COMMONWEALTH OF AUSTRALIA

TELEPHONES
XXXXXX LA.5271.
MXT 550

TELEGRAPHIC ADDRESS :
"AIRFORCE MELBOURNE"

IN REPLY QUOTE RAAF.163/24/209(17A).

DEPARTMENT OF AIR

MELBOURNE, SC.1.

85623   AUG 15 1942

Dear Madam,

I have to acknowledge receipt of your letter dated the
22nd July, 1942, with reference to your son, Pilot Officer Richard
Harding Browne.

I greatly regret to inform you that nothing has been heard
of your son's aircraft or the members of his crew since the operations
of the 15th January, 1942.

A cable recently received in this Department from Overseas
Headquarters, London, states that the only additional news available
is that the Blenheim aircraft which was piloted by your son, was detailed
to attack Soesterberk Aerodrome, Holland. The weather was good when the
aircraft took off from its base in the United Kingdom shortly after 6 p.m.
(English time), but it deteriorated rapidly as the evening advanced. No
message was received from the aircraft after the take-off, and I regret to
say that enquiries have disclosed no indication as to the circumstances
in which your son was lost.

I desire to assure you that should any further information be
received in this Department, it will be conveyed to you immediately.

Yours faithfully,

M.C.Langslow

(M. C. Langslow)
S E C R E T A R Y.

Mrs. E. Harding Browne,
130 Molesworth Street,
NORTH ADELAIDE. S.A.

BRYAN

Bryan Harding Browne's last letter home:

26th May 1944

Dear Mother and Carys,

We have only a couple of days to go, before we reach Colombo, after about a fortnight at sea, and I won't be sorry. My time at sea now is just one long round of study, keeping my watch on the bridge and occasionally sleeping. I think the only thing that keeps me happy enough to stop from hurling myself over the side to merciful oblivion is the thought that I only have one more trip to do after this.

My last letter written just before we sailed was hardly worth sending, it was written in such a hurry but I think it's something to get even an envelope to break up the gaps between letters.

We have quite a big crowd of passengers on the ship and a couple of days ago, we got together 6 gun crews teams with 6 men in each and had a competition with 45 bottles of beer for the winners. The result was a bit unexpected, a crowd of submarine chaps travelling as passengers won, the regular gunners of the ship came last (although I must say they had bad luck) the ships number one crew (which I am in) the one that goes straight to the gun in action came third, and the ships number two crew that takes our places as we get killed, came second, still there wasn't much difference between the first three as the marks were 75, 74, and 72 out of a 100. Of course the beer was shared by all hands, so don't worry about your little son going thirsty, I was able to get blind drunk just the same as the winning crew.

Well it seems terrible to be finishing so soon after I start but not much of interest happens at sea these days, so I will finish up wishing you all the love in the world, and the best to John.

Bryan

P. S. I forgot to tell you about my smoking. I gave it up on the 1st of May and I didn't start again until the 17th. I got over the first desires alright, it was fairly hard but I managed it and then I thought the rest was just plain sailing, but believe me it wasn't, I gradually started getting depressed, irritable and a very 'run down' feeling, until I thought I might jump over the side in one of my fits of depression, and as I knew you wouldn't like that I started again. Still 17 days wasn't bad, was it? I started feeling better from the first cigarette I had and haven't looked back since. The Purser who gave it up at the same time (he was going to give it up permanently) said it had the same affect on him, and he also started again.

Dear Mrs. Harding-Browne,

Received your letter this morning and feel
that I must reply immediately, for I can in some measure understand just how anxious you must feel for any news of Bryan.

I was two years in the ---- and knew Bryan
very well indeed; I cannot give you any definite account as to
his actual fate, but I will tell you all that I possibly can.

When the ship was hit Bryan was asleep in
bed and was in no way injured by the explosions. He went immediately to his Boat Station and when the order to Abandon was
given, in the absence of the Captain he took charge of the launch-
ing of his lifeboat. About an hour and a half after the first
explosions our boat bumped into his in the darkness and we had a
few minutes together, during which time we naturally asked each
other the names of the personnel of the respective boats, and whether there were any injured. Bryan assured us that they had no
injured aboard. He also asked whether we knew where the Captain
was, as he should have got into his boat. At that time we imagined
that he had gone off in some other boat, and were about to discuss
going back to the ship to see if he was still on board, when the
submarines surfaced. Realising that if we were seen we would probably be taken prisoner, we broke company so that it would lessen
the risk of being seen, and in any case if we were seen they would
only find the one boat instead of two.

His boat and ours then pulled away in opposite
directions, and as we drifted into the darkness that is the last
anyone saw of that boat. (Starboard 1.)

After the ship sank the submarines remained
on the surface for many hours searching apparently for survivors.
One boat was intercepted and the European occupants were taken
aboard the sub. This boat was not the one that Bryan was in.

During the next month the wreckage and a large
expanse of ocean was constantly searched by many aircraft both by
night and day. It seems rather strange that during this time
the boat was never seen, especially as the planes had located every
other boat, and then we were never more than fifty miles apart and
all heading in the same direction. For the first week the weather
was quite normal, and a lifeboat could have ridden it our very easily,
so that would rule out any fears of the coat capsizing. In any
case, beside Bryan there were many R.A.N. Officers in that boat who
were travelling back as passengers, and we all felt sure that if anyone would make land it would be that boat.

Just what the ultimate fate of that boat was,
I do not know, but Mrs. Harding-Browne they <u>could</u> have been intercepted and taken prisoner.   Therefore before abandoning hope al-
together, If I were you I would make enquiries from the Red Cross,
although before receiving any answer from them you must be prepared
to wait many months.

Bryan was a fine lad with every prospect of
becoming a very capable Officer.   He was well-liked aboard, especially for his quiet and unassuming manner.   We feel his loss
very deeply and I would convey to you my profound sympathy in your
present anxious and worrying period.

I do sincerely hope that your enquiries will
bear some success.

Sincerely your's

(Signed) NEVILLE WARD.

TELEGRAPHIC AND CABLE ADDRESS
" NALDHAM "

BOX NO. 546 B, G.P.O.
PHONE B 7511 (8 LINES)

THE EASTERN AND AUSTRALIAN STEAMSHIP CO. LTD.
(INCORPORATED IN ENGLAND)
MACDONALD, HAMILTON & CO., MANAGING AGENTS
UNION HOUSE, 247 GEORGE STREET
SYDNEY

8th February, 1945. 194

Dear Mrs. Harding Browne,

    I had purposely refrained from communicating with you, since the tragic loss of the "Nellore", until I was able to interview the last of the known survivors and so satisfy myself of the facts concerning the missing lifeboat on which your son, Bryan, was last seen.

    All survivors are agreed that it was the lifeboat, of which Apprentice Harding Browne had charge, which returned to the sinking vessel to pick up Captain Colvin, the Second Officer and the Gunners.   This lifeboat unfortunately cannot be accounted for but there appears to be a unanimous feeling amongst the survivors that the occupants of this boat may have been taken prisoners by the raiding submarine and every hope is therefore entertained for their safety.

    In these long months of waiting for information I can only say that I share with you my heartfelt feelings for the safety of your son and the hope that in the near future we shall be able to rejoice in news of his well being.

    With my sympathetic regards,

Yours sincerely,

Mrs. B.E. Harding Browne,
  130 Molesworth Street,
    NORTH ADELAIDE.   S.A.

203

JOHN

John Portus writes in his diary, of the incident on August 1st 1943, when he was shot down in his flying boat and two South Australian men, Captain Kenneth Gregson "Bob" Fry and Sergeant Bert Lydeamore died:

"Took off at 10am on A/S Musketry. High wind blowing and very rough and unpleasant with winds to 40 knots - Ordered to square search certain area for U/B 1½hours after patrol began. Did hour of Square search then on leg of °45 sighted 5 sloops of Escort. Force and Catalina flying hid them. They looked as though had something and so turned to starboard to approach - Just then Bob Budd sighted a sub. We turned quickly to attack - Sub was on course of 300 and as came down to attack hit at about 300 yards by shell fire. Hear it hitting hard like stones on a tin fence - dropped perfect stick of 6 across conning tower 3 each side then petrol everywhere as starboard main tank holed then ditching signal got into Mae West and crash position - no time to get out of position and undid astro hatch. Hit 3 times and on 3rd hit starboard wing broke off outside starboard inner - Before could do anything on settling A/C full of water and went down. Then something happened and everything above clear and floated to top and after grabbing round at various bits of wreckage found the starboard wing and found to my surprise Petterson, Haslem and Cook standing on this but not in Mae Wests - As had Mae West on stayed where I was clinging to wreckage - Saw Liberator fly overhead. Kicked off shoes and managed to blow up Mae West. Remember ship alongside with lots of people, being sick but nothing more - Ditched at 1642 according to ship and ships finished picking us up at 1735 - Leading Seaman Goff dived overboard and rescued me. I evidently wouldn't leave hold of wreck - Given oxygen and came to in about ½ hour but had difficulty in breathing til sick about 2½ hours later - After that began to feel better and better, bags of minor cuts. Others rescued were Jack Haslem, Petterson, Cook, Ron Welfare, Don Conacher - Others didn't come to the surface were Bob Fry, Bob Budd, Max Curtis, Tubby Fryer, Bert Lydea-more and new navigator Arthur Welch. Only 6 picked up from the sub."

Flying -Officer P.Petterson speaks too of this incident in the newspaper "Recorder" (Port Pirie) on 14/4/44:

"After we had been hit and had attacked the sub, the aircraft began to go into a dive and got out of control. The two pilots were killed and the captain wounded in the stomach. Petrol was flowing everywhere, for we had been hit badly in the fuel tanks. The captain called us into crash position, but owing to the petrol on the floor some of us were unable to make it. When we hit the water I was standing near Bert Lydeamore. I was blown through the astro dome and landed clear of the wreckage. We were in the water about 45 minutes. When we were picked up by the ship we were told that we were very lucky to be alive, because when we hit the sea two depth charges went off."

Flight-Sgt P. E. Cook also speaks of this incident:

"The last time I saw Bert he was handing out Mae Wests to the other blokes. There was not really a chance to do anything, for the plane sank almost as soon as it hit the sea."

MICHAEL

Colin McArthur was with Michael Brookman on the day he was killed and speaks of the incident:

"I trained with Michael Brookman at Woodside Military Camp in the Adelaide Hills. We both joined early in 1940. I lived with Michael for two years. We went to fight in Palestine first, then Syria, then Egypt and then to Bug Bug in 1941, and then to El Alamein. Michael Brookman died on July 14th 1942 at El Alamein. This was not the major battle of El Alamein which was on the 23rd October 1942 but the battle prior to it. Michael had been off duty for a few days with dysentery. I was manning the gun in his place. On the 14th July, Michael returned to duty and took over from me. He was the Gun Sergeant. We were both in the 9th Division of the 2/7th Australian Field Regiment. Michael was given orders to send ammunition away as they were being pressed by the Italians and Germans outside of Alexandria in Egypt. We had to fire off all the ammunition and then retreat. We were number one gun. There were four guns. We finished firing off all the ammunition and as there was no radio, Michael asked me to run over and report to the Command Post that we had finished the task. There was lots of noise because of dive bombing and also from enemy shelling. Running back, I saw Michael's gun blown up only ten metres in front of me. I had to put the parts of Michael and two others killed onto a truck, which took them away to be buried.

Then later, I had to dig them up and re-inter them. Michael is buried at El Alamein. South Australians Pat Mahoney and Cecil Scull were also killed and Murray Pendle and Sid Mewett were severely wounded."

(Interview with Ann Barson on December 7th 2007)

Later, when he returned to Adelaide, Colin brought Mrs Brookman the badge he took from Michael's hat.

SAM

St 9367

COMMONWEALTH OF AUSTRALIA

Casualty Section,
DEPARTMENT OF AIR
Merton Hall,

TELEPHONES
~~NXXXXXX~~ LA.5871

TELEGRAPHIC ADDRESS:
"AIRFORCE MELBOURNE"

MELBOURNE. ~~SCx~~. Anderson Street,
South Yarra.
S.E.1.

IN REPLY QUOTE RAAF.163/40/64(19A)

JAN 21 1943

Dear Madam,

33892

        Further information has now been received from your
son's Squadron concerning the circumstances in which your son,
Flying Officer Donald Beviss Kerr, lost his life.

        According to the information now available, the
aircraft of which your son was a member of the crew was
engaged on the 15th December, 1942, with other aircraft
of the Squadron, in dropping supplies to forward troops
near Soputa, approximately five miles from Buna. The aircraft
took off at irregular intervals as soon as they were loaded,
and returned for fresh supplies. Your son's aircraft, which
had made three trips during the morning, left Port Moresby
with its fourth load at 2.25 p.m., and proceeded to Soputa
in company with another aircraft of the Squadron.

        According to the report of the pilot of the
accompanying aircraft, they reached Soputa at 3.15 p.m.
and your son's aircraft went ahead to drop its first load
on the Strip. The other pilot followed about a thousand
yards behind, and saw the nose of your son's aircraft come
up sharply as it turned away to the left of the Strip. The
aircraft, which was flying at a height of one hundred feet,
climbed a further hundred feet. Its nose then dropped
suddenly, and it dived into some trees. The other pilot
circled the spot, and saw the wreckage of the aircraft
beneath the jungle foliage. Troops were running to the
scene of the crash. This pilot states that he did not
himself encounter any anti-aircraft fire.

        The report of the crash was confirmed as a result
of enquiries made through Army Headquarters, which disclosed
that the wrecked aircraft had been located a mile and a half
north of the dropping ground. All the members of the crew
lost their lives, with the exception of the rear gunner,
Flight Sergeant L.C. Callaghan, who was taken to an army

............/2.

dressing station and later transferred to Port Moresby.
According to a statement made by this member, there was
a burst of gun fire below the aircraft as it was turning
away from the Strip, and he heard the pilot call out that
he was hit. He felt the aircraft go into a dive, but does
not remember anything further.

Your son was buried with his comrades by members
of the Army, close to the scene of the crash. Particulars
as to the exact location of the graves have been forwarded
to the Directorate of Graves Registration, and arrangements
will be made as soon as practicable to have the bodies
removed to a permanent War Cemetery.

May I again express the profound sympathy of this
Department in the loss of your gallant son, who sacrificed
his life in the service of his country.

Yours faithfully,

(M.C. Langslow)
S E C R E T A R Y.

Mrs. M.J. Kerr,
2 Herbert Street,
MEDINDIE.   S.A.

NOTES

The Countess of Bective, an Australian, accompanied her husband the Earl of Bective to Adelaide when he became aide-de-camp to the Governor in 1940. During that year she was very industrious at raising money for the War Effort. She even appeared on screen at all city picture theatres, to urge Australian women and children to buy war saving certificates. However, she was fined in January 1941 for running a lottery to raise money for the Red Cross, as it breached the S.A. Lottery and Gaming Act.

Arthur Seaforth Blackburn (1892-1960), received the Victoria Cross in 1916 for bravery at Pozières in France. In June 1941 as the senior Allied officer present, he accepted the surrender of Damascus, and after the campaign was a member of the Allied Control Commission for Syria. In February 1942 he landed in Java with a small group of Australians where he assisted the Dutch against the Japanese. After three weeks of resistance, he was forced to surrender and was a prisoner until September 1945.

Sir John Lavington Bonython (1875-1960), was Lord Mayor of Adelaide 1927-30, worked with his father Sir Langdon Bonython on "The Advertiser" for several years, and in 1941 listed as a director of Adelaide Newspapers Ltd. He was a very public-spirited man associated with many South Australian institutions and charities.

Sir George Brookman (1850-1927), Sibyl's grandfather, a prominent businessman and politician, who had financial success in the goldfields in Western Australia. He donated funds to the building of the South Australian School of Mines and Industries.

Pirie Bush (1892-1965), born in New Zealand, professional actor in Australia (1912-32), proprietor of the Quality Inn in 1940.

Clive Carey (1883-1968), an opera director and teacher of singing. Came from England to Adelaide in 1924 as Director of Singing at the Elder Conservatorium. In 1929 he married Doris Mabel Johnson from Adelaide. He returns to England in 1945, where he was appointed Director of Opera at Sadler's Wells.

Stewart Cockburn (1921-2009), a copy boy at "The Advertiser" in 1938 who then worked in journalism for 45 years. He was press secretary to Sir Robert Menzies and wrote books about South Australian personalities.

Walter Desborough, dancer, who danced with Joseph Siebert's "Les Ballets Contemporains" and found his own ballet company in 1944 called the "Desborough Ballet Company". He was the dancer, dance director and choreographer and costume designer of this company. He died in 1951, aged 43.

Geoffrey Piers Henry Dutton (1922-98), a poet, who in 1940 was a close friend of Sam Kerr. They both loved poetry and encouraged each other's efforts. Geoffrey published a poem in the first edition of "Angry Penguins" and then other poems in subsequent editions. He and Sam were fellow debaters. After the War, Geoffrey Dutton became a writer of many genres. He was a biographer, literary critic, historian, travel writer, writer of books for children and translator of Russian poetry and a co-founder of Sun Books, an Australian paperback publishing venture promoting Australian themes.

Dr Sam Fitzpatrick (1892-1991), born in Victoria, Australia, became a world expert on hydatids. He settled in Hamilton in 1920, and from 1936 lived at The Gables, a beautiful example of a Federation Queen Anne-styled house.

Ronda Beryl Gehling, pianist, obtained a Degree of Bachelor of Music in 1943 from the Elder Conservatorium and was one of Australia's most renowned pianists in the 1950's.

David Lloyd George (1863-1945), was Prime Minister of the United Kingdom between 1916 and 1922, and Leader of the Liberal Party from 1926 to 1931. He was a Welshman and friends with Eirliw Harding

Browne's family in Harlech, North Wales. Her brother Louis was a solicitor in Lloyd George's law firm in Criccieth, and her father, Dr Richard Jones, encouraged Lloyd George in his early political career. Eirliw Harding Browne attended school with Lloyd George's daughter Olwen.

The Geschmays were one of the last of the Czechoslovakian refugees to reach England before the German occupation. They came to Adelaide in August 1939. Dr Zigmund Geschmay had a veterinary practice in Murray Bridge in 1940 and later at Hutt Street, Adelaide.

Madame Gregor Wood, died in 1951. She sang to Melbourne audiences for 50 years and was a contralto soloist for the Melbourne Philharmonic Society. She and her husband James Gregor Wood were popular Scottish singers.

Philip Hargrave, Adelaide child pianist, who from 1933 to 36 toured Australia, electrifying audiences with his playing. He then abandoned music as a career and in 1941 was studying law. He served during the War as a member of the R.A.A.F. Welfare and Entertainment section, where he played to servicemen, and gave concerts for the Red Cross and Comforts Fund. After the War he lived in France.

Max Harris (1921-95), poet, who established and co-edited with Donald Beviss Kerr the literary journal "Angry Penguins". Max gains the patronage of Melbourne lawyer John Reed in 1942, and they include visual art by professional artists in the journal. Later, two poets invent a hoax poet called Ern Malley, who writes in a modern free-wheeling way. Max publishes these poems and the Adelaide police charge him with obscenity. The trial increases the fame of the journal but also leads to its demise in 1946. Then Max becomes a partner with his friend Mary Martin in the Mary Martin Bookshop in Adelaide. He promotes Australian writers and becomes a co-founder of Sun Books. He later becomes a columnist for "The Australian" newspaper.

John Horner (1899-1973), an organist, born in Scotland, was on the staff of the Elder Conservatorium since 1928, and by March 1941 was serving in Australia with the R.A.A.F. After the War, towards the end of his career, he became President of the South Australian division of the Australian Arts Council.

Marjorie Horner (nee Marjorie Laura Ball) (1904-77), musician, born in Burma, received a Bachelor of Music from Edinburgh University and married John Horner in 1928. She then played a significant part in the musical life of Adelaide as a pianist, an accompanist, a composer, a conductor of choirs and a director of school orchestras.

Elliott Johnston (1918-2011), became a communist in 1941, and in 1983 was the only communist in Australia ever to become a Supreme Court judge, though he had to renounce his membership of the Communist Party to accept this position. He is remembered as a kind man who always had time for the underdog.

Charles Jury (1893-1958), poet, an Acting Lecturer in English Language and Literature in 1933, and encourager of the poetry of Max Harris, Sam Kerr and Paul Pfeiffer. He was a patron and contributor to the early editions of "Angry Penguins". From 1946-49 he was Professor of English Language and Literature at the University of Adelaide.

Spruhan Kennedy (1901-84), a pianist, teacher and composer who with John Horner musically notated songs collected by T. G. Strehlow from the Arrernte people of Central Australia. Spruhan's wife Vera Van Rij was a dancer with Anna Pavlova's company and a teacher of Joe Siebert.

Arthur (Art) Maskell, drummer with the Alf Holyoak's quintet. A feature artist on swing shows, and one of the best known exponents of rhythm in South Australia.

Dr Eugen Abraham Mitzenmacher (Matison), born in Russia in 1888, came to Australia in 1913 from America where he had graduated in medicine. An ear, nose and throat surgeon, he had rooms in the Liberal Club Building on North Terrace, Adelaide from 1926. He bought Springfield House on Elmgrade Road, Springfield in 1934. An English styled timbered gabled house, it was one of the largest and most historic homes in Adelaide. After the War, Dr Matison being a philanthropist and a keen music lover, had musical afternoons at Springfield House, to raise money for the Arts Council of South Australia.

Ernest Edward Mühlstein (Milston) (1893 -1968), born in Czecho-slovakia, was a lieutenant in the Austrian Army in World War I. He was a prestigious and modernist Prague architect for 19 years before the Germans occupied Prague in 1939. He escaped with the aid of some English architectural friends and came to Adelaide in April 1940, where he worked with the architects Lawson and Cheesman. He did the décor in 1941 for Joe Siebert's ballet company "Les Ballets Contemporains". In March 1942 he was a civilian draughtsman with the Department of the Army, and later that year he enlisted and served with the Royal Austra-lian Engineers. He was a painter known for his love of vivid and striking colour. He was an original member of an Adelaide group of artists called "Group 9" who began exhibiting in 1944. After the War he lived in Mel-bourne. He is remembered now as the designer of the 1939-45 Forecourt of Melbourne's Shrine of Remembrance.

The Orient Line (The Orient Steam Navigation Co) was originally a British shipping company which began in 1797. In 1877 it had its first direct steam connection between Australia and London. By November 1934 its steamships could accommodate 1800 passengers. In 1937 it also had cruises to the Pacific and New Zealand Islands but by the 1960's the P&O had taken it over.

The Oxford Group was a Christian, evangelical movement which was very popular throughout England, Europe and America in the 1930's. It later adopted a new name called "Moral Re-Armament". It was founded by Dr Frank Buchman. Carys was swept up by this movement in 1939 for a few months and she tried to convert some of her school. She writes in her diary 28/8/39: "We decided to play the Moral Re-Armament song for Assembly to the kids so they would know it. With jeers we stalked down to the courts with my gramophone and played a hymn to them. I felt like an early Christian. Everyone laughed but after a while they sang and before long crowds were listening."

Professor G.V. Portus (1883-1954), father of John Portus, was a priest, later a teacher and Professor of Political Science and History at the Univer-sity of Adelaide (1934-48). He wrote the first popular Australian history book for school students in 1932 called "Australia since 1606".

Geoffrey Sandford Reed LL.B., K.C. (1892-1970), was for some years a lecturer at Adelaide University in law; then Acting Judge, Supreme Court of S.A., 1935-37; and a King's Counsel from August 1937. In 1942 he was Chairman of the South Australian National Security Advisory Committee and was made a judge in 1943. In March 1949 he was the founding director-general of the Australian Security Intelligence Organization (A.S.I.O.).

William Ricketts (1898-1993), a violinist, later famous for his baked clay sculptures of aboriginal people, many of which are displayed today in the William Ricketts Sanctuary in Victoria's Dandenong Ranges.

Sydney Dattilo Rubbo (1911-69), was the son of Antonio Dattilo-Rubbo (1870-1955), an Italian born artist who came to Australia in 1897 and taught modernism to many well-known painters. Sydney Dattilo Rubbo was probably influenced in 1933 by the death of his brother Mark, aged 16, from meningitis, to pursue a career in bacteriology. He was appointed Professor of Bacteriology in 1945 and then in 1964 appointed Professor of Microbiology at the University of Melbourne. Known as an inspirational lecturer, he made innovations in the development of antiseptic drugs and co-discovered the anti-tuberculosis drug verazide. His department of microbiology became the best in Australia.

Ellen Rubbo (nee Gray) (1911-1977), an artist, born in Sydney, she studied at the Julian Ashton School and in London. A designer and painter, she also worked as a graphic artist. She trained as a dancer with the "School of the German Dance" in Sydney in the 1930's. She was renowned as a watercolourist and she regularly exhibited paintings in Melbourne, mainly in Georges Gallery and at the Victorian Artists' Society galleries. She has paintings in the National Gallery of Victoria and the Art Gallery of New South Wales.

Elizabeth Fulton Salter (1918-1981), who planned a soirée with Carys in January 1942, left Australia for England in 1952. She was secretary to Edith Sitwell from 1957-64 and published a biography of Sitwell in 1967 called "The Last Years of a Rebel: a Memoir of Edith Sitwell". She later wrote biographies of Daisy Bates (1971), John Peter Russell (1976) and Robert Helpmann (1978) and detective novels.

Sir James Wallace Sandford (1879-1958), businessman, was president of the Taxpayers' Association of South Australia when Carys's father was secretary there. His son A. W. "Mic" Sandford was at Balliol College, Oxford where he contributed his own poetry and edited the book "New Oxford Poetry, 1936". Mic was a private in the army at Keswick Barracks in 1940, and later took part in the evacuation of Crete and saw service in the North African campaign and in Syria. He became A.I.F. Commanding Officer at the Central Bureau in Brisbane, the top secret signals intelligence organization which intercepted and decoded Japanese radio communications. After the War he lived in Italy.

Schwabs (Ludvik Schwab) (1880-1948), Czechoslovakian pianist and viola player, living in Adelaide in 1942 and married to Adelaide pianist Merle Robertson.

Joseph (Joe) Siebert, dancer. For five months in 1939, Carys had dancing lessons with Joe Siebert at the Hut in the University of Adelaide. She describes it as "a dim, dim room with crickets singing through the open windows, Joe tall and fair and graceful in tights, and girls in ballet frocks, black tights and foppish white blouses. The chairs piled back in the dancing theatre; a little stage and a grey curtain." Joe also had the Studio Theatre in Tynte Place, North Adelaide which lasted until 1946, when it was sold. Joe's company, "Les Ballets Contemporains" existed from 1938 until 1950.

Lea Sonia, a variety artist known as "The Gay Deceiver" came from England in 1940 under contract to the Tivoli Theatres. He was regarded then as the best female impersonator to have acted in Australia. He was killed by a tram in the brownout in Oxford Street, Sydney on the 31/1/42, when running across the street for a taxi.

Sir Josiah Symon K.C. (1846-1934), was for many years South Australia's leading barrister who helped form the Australian Constitution. He bequeathed his collection of over 7,500 literary books to the State Library of South Australia in 1935.

Oscar Symon (1891-1950), son of Sir Josiah Symon, a brilliant student at Roseworthy Agricultural College, but because of ill health and failed business ventures, contested his father's will. He wrote many articles for the "S.A. Naturalist" and the "South Australian Ornithologist".

The Tuxedo Night Club (Tux) was on the corner of Hindley and Peel Streets. It opened in August 1939 and members could go there from 10pm to 3 am on weekdays, with an extension to 4am on Saturdays and holidays. Owing to the critical war situation, from January 1942, was opened only on Friday and Saturday nights. By June 1944 the Tuxedo Night Club was non-existent. It was replaced by a new service hostel for American servicemen on leave or in transit through Adelaide.

Max Worthley (1913-1999), tenor and choirmaster of the North Adelaide Baptist Church in 1940. After the War, he had success singing in England but returned to Adelaide in 1952 because of his wife's ill health. He became teacher of singing at the Elder Conservatorium and sang with The Deller Consort.

The Youth Movement: Elizabeth Carter who married Charles Price remembers the inaugural meeting of Charles's Youth Movement at Belair National Park. Elizabeth says the Youth Movement did not last long as the men were called up and the women went into war service. Youth Movements in Australia at this time were started to counter the German equivalent which had been such a driving force behind the rise of Nazism. A University of Adelaide arts student talks in "The Mail" 17/8/40 of this movement, where she says the purpose was for young men and women to improve themselves physically, mentally and intellectually, but also demand a place in national affairs.

ACKNOWLEDGEMENTS
AND THANKS

Cam Rungie for love and support.

My four brothers, Richard, Philip, Martin, Matthew and their partners Virginia, Martyn and Amanda for love and support.

Professor Margaret Allen for encouragement, and Kathy Byrne for suggestions and help with formatting of photographs.

Julia Beaven for suggestions and Heather Kerr for advice.

I am especially indebted to Susanna Lobez and Nynke van der Schaaf and my brother Martin Portus who have been so helpful with advice and corrections.

http://trove.nla.gov.au/ (Digitised newspapers and more) for information and verification of names and places and details mentioned in Carys's diaries.

Other information has been found from Australian biographies, 1940-1 Radio Call newspapers, old South Australian Directories, Passenger Arrival Lists, the Land Titles Office, old school magazines, University Archives, the National Archives of Australia and the Australian War Memorial records.

John Miles who first told the story of D. B. Kerr in his beautifully written book, "Lost Angry Penguins".

Stewart Cockburn who suggested to me that I edit my mother's diaries.

Many people have given me information and remembrances and special thanks go to Mollie Scobie, Graham Brookman, Bill Wills, Margaret Hodge, Stewart Cockburn, Jenny Cockburn, Bob Chappel, John

Chappel, Jim Bowen, Anne Dow, Colin McArthur, Wally Wickham, Elizabeth Price, Nicholas Tipping, Andrew Kerr, Richard Harvey, Christopher Good and Ian Pennack and Margaret Hone.

Archivists Samantha Cooper at Pulteney Grammar School, Monica Smith at St Mark's College, and Helen Bruce and Susan Coppin at the University of Adelaide for information.

Cheryl Hoskin, Special Collections Librarian at the Barr Smith Library for information and scanning of documents and photographs.

D. B. Kerr's poem "If You Should Go" published in "Angry Pen-guins, No. 1" and his poem "The Spring Is Quick" published in "Angry Penguins, No. 3".

Michael Mayo for allowing me to scan photos from his grandmother, Mrs Brookman's photo album, and lending me her memoirs to read.

INDEX

Tucker, David 172
Tuxedo Night Club (Tux) 17, 36, 38, 40,
43-5, 47, 50, 53, 55-6, 105-6, 127, 152, 163-4,
166, 181, 216
University of Adelaide 5-6, 11-5, 18-9, 31-2,
47, 51, 63, 86, 96, 99, 110, 112, 129-30, 176,
184, 188, 193, 195, 212-6, 218
Van Rij, Vera 187, 212
Veitch, Mr 40, 43
Verchinina, Nina 30
Victoria Square 146
Vignola Café 13, 15, 17, 30, 37, 41,
44, 47, 63
Voltaire 112, 116, 144
W.A.A.A.F. 134, 136, 162
Wallach, Mr 176
Wallach, Sheila 171, 174, 176, 184
Wallach, Stewart 176, 184, 189
Walters, David 8, 136
Walters, John 99, 130, 132, 136
Walters, Margaret (Margo) 99, 130, 136, 155
Ward, Miss, Training College 5, 8, 14, 16-7,
20-3, 25, 28, 31-3, 35, 38, 150, 194
Waterhouse, Diana 181
Waterhouse, Margaret (Margo) 69, 77, 119,
167
Waters, Frank 12, 25
Wavell, Sir Archibald 142, 168
Webb, Alvin 120-1, 126, 129, 136,150, 157,
169-70, 178
Webb, Mrs 153
Wesley-Smith, Harry 151
White, Jim 157
Wickes, Mr 140, 183
Wigg, Dr 20, 22, 59-60, 105, 158-9, 180,
Wilderness School 5, 12, 29, 56
Williams, Bruce 190
Wills, R. A. (Dick) 40, 55, 195
Winterbottom, Denis 103-4
Woodside Military Camp 5, 9, 63, 69, 75, 206
Woolf, Virginia 107, 109-13, 166
Workers' Educational Association (W.E.A.)
12-4, 16, 28, 34-5, 38, 40, 49, 54
Worthley, Max 23, 216
Yates, Mary 168
Yates, Tom 9
Yeatman, Sue 36, 81, 86, 140, 147
Young, Tony 153
Youth Movement 39, 216
Youth Theatre 99

www.ingramcontent.com/pod-product-compliance
Lightning Source LLC
Chambersburg PA
CBHW021224090426
42740CB00006B/368